SHAKESPEARE,
Man of the Theater

SHAKESPEARE,
Man of the Theater

Proceedings of the Second Congress
of the International Shakespeare Association, 1981

Edited by
Kenneth Muir

Jay L. Halio   D. J. Palmer

Newark
University of Delaware Press
London and Toronto: Associated University Presses

Associated University Presses, Inc.
4 Cornwall Drive
East Brunswick, NJ 08816

Associated University Presses Ltd
27 Chancery Lane
London WC2A 1NF, England

Associated University Presses
2133 Royal Windsor Drive
Unit 1
Mississauga, Ontario, L5J 1K5, Canada

Library of Congress Cataloging in Publication Data

International Shakespeare Association. Congress
(2nd : 1981 : Stratford-upon-Avon, Warwickshire)
Shakespeare, man of the theater.

Includes bibliographical references.
1. Shakespeare, William, 1564–1616—Congresses.
2. Shakespeare, William, 1564–1616—Dramatic production—
Congresses.   3. Shakespeare, William, 1564–1616—Stage
history—Congresses.   I. Muir, Kenneth.   II. Halio,
Jay L.   III. Palmer, D. J.   IV. Title.
PR2889.I57   1981   822.3′3   82-40346
ISBN 0-87413-217-7

Printed in the United States of America

IN MEMORIAM

C. L. Barber
G. Bullough

Contents

Preface

The second Congress of the International Shakespeare Association (ISA) was held at Stratford-upon-Avon in the first week of August 1981, under the auspices of the ISA, the Shakespeare Association of America, the Shakespeare Birthplace Trust, the Shakespeare Institute (of the University of Birmingham) and the Royal Shakespeare Theatre. It was attended by some 650 scholars from all over the world.

The Congress began with an open-air reception at the Hilton Hotel on Saturday, 1 August. On Sunday there was a service in Holy Trinity Church, based, like that in the Washington Cathedral in 1976, on the 1559 Prayer Book, with an eloquent sermon by the Reverend Professor W. Moelwyn Merchant. The first plenary session consisted of a lecture by John Mortimer. In the evening there was a recital in the theater, devised by Roger Pringle and delivered by John Gielgud, Barbara Leigh-Hunt, Richard Pasco, and Robert Spencer. It was a delight and a privilege to hear the president of the ISA in some of his famous roles, including Richard II, Hamlet, Lear, and Prospero.

For the rest of the week the Congress had a full program of lectures, papers, and seminars—a list of which is given in the Appendix. Two sessions consisted of forums with theater directors, and there were workshop sessions with members of the Royal Shakespeare Company. In the evenings there were performances of *The Winter's Tale, A Midsummer Night's Dream,* and *A Doll's House.* There were also opportunities to see the Coventry Mystery plays, televised versions of *Macbeth* and *Antony and Cleopatra,* as well as scenes from a film of *Richard III,* performed by the Rustaveli Company of Georgia, U.S.S.R.

In view of the theme of the Congress—Shakespeare, Man of the Theater—we were fortunate to meet in the town where Shakespeare was born, christened, schooled and married and died, and to have had the cooperation of the Royal Shakespeare Company.

The editors of these proceedings would have liked to include all the lectures and a generous selection of the papers presented at the twenty-four seminars, but this proved to be impossible. Some papers were already promised to other publications; others were delivered from notes and could not be written up in time. Those papers that have been crowded out will doubtless find a home elsewhere.

The Congress was also the ninth annual meeting of the Shakespeare Association of America (SAA), the final plenary session consisting of the annual lecture by G. E. Bentley; and the last event in the program was the annual luncheon of the SAA, to which all delegates were invited. We are grateful to the officers of the SAA for agreeing to hold a joint congress, and especially to Ann Jennalie Cook for organizing the seminars and providing the secretariat.

This volume, selected from some 250 papers, will remind those who attended the Congress of some of the sessions they enjoyed and of those they missed through schedule clashes; it will also, we hope, give some idea to those who were not there of the present state of Shakespeare studies.

> Kenneth Muir
> Chairman, International Shakespeare Association
>
> S. Schoenbaum
> President, Shakespeare Association of America (1980–81)

Contributors

Anne Barton, University of Oxford
Bernard Beckerman, Columbia University
A. R. Braunmuller, University of California, Los Angeles
H. Neville Davies, Shakespeare Institute ,
Mary Judith Dunbar, University of Santa Clara
Philip Edwards, University of Liverpool
Inga-Stina Ewbank, University of London
Jörg Hasler, University of Trier
Harriett Hawkins, Linacre College, Oxford
G. R. Hibbard, University of Waterloo
Emrys Jones, University of Oxford
M. T. Jones-Davies, University of Paris, Sorbonne
W. Moelwyn Merchant, Leamington Spa, Warwickshire
John Mortimer, Henley-on-Thames, Oxfordshire
Stephen Orgel, Johns Hopkins University
Jeanne Addison Roberts, American University
Adele Seeff, University of Maryland, College Park
Roger Warren, University of Leicester
Robert Weimann, Akademie der Wissenschaften, Berlin

SHAKESPEARE,
Man of the Theater

A Sermon Delivered at Holy Trinity Church, Stratford-upon-Avon, Sunday, August 2, 1981

by THE REVEREND PROFESSOR W. MOELWYN MERCHANT

It is fitting that this Shakespeare Congress should open in this Church of the Holy Trinity, Stratford-upon-Avon, where Shakespeare was baptized, where he worshipped, and where he lies buried. You have now experienced the majestic rhythms of the Elizabethan liturgy of Morning Prayer, Litany, and Ante-Communion, a rare opportunity to share an experience which was very familiar to Shakespeare. Before the Congress begins its scholarly exploration of the dramatic texts, we have a brief opportunity to examine one aspect of his work which must have been materially affected by the content and temper of the liturgy in which we are engaged.

Hamlet appears to offer the audience a familiar Elizabethan pattern of ghost and revenge plot. It opens with a brilliant exposition of the popular convention and then a remarkable shift of tone takes place which has all the excitement of a change of key and of rhythm in a symphony. The soldier, Marcellus, comments on the cock-crow in words which raise the convention to a wholly different plane:

> Some say that ever 'gainst that season comes
> Wherein our Saviour's birth is celebrated,
> This bird of dawning singeth all night long;
> And then they say no spirit dare stir abroad,
> The nights are wholesome, then no planets strike,

15

> No fairy takes nor witch hath power to charm
> So hallowed and so gracious is the time.

We are no longer in the world of revenge-drama, or rather, that world has been transfigured in the presence of the Incarnation.

Later in the play a similar "change of key" takes place: Claudius has become convinced of Hamlet's intuition of his guilt, and alone, in the posture of prayer, he is crushed by a new self-realization. But this is no temporal exploration of his guilt before the world; in the charged phrases, "the primal eldest curse, a brother's murder," the stage villain is transposed to the image of Cain, the instrument of fratricide and of the first invasion of the world by death. The symphonic pattern has been changed and enhanced in one brief soliloquy.

And comedy shares with tragedy in this power of transformation. *As You Like It*, that play which argues with the clarity of a syllogism the antithesis of court and country, of nature and sophistication, opens with the apparently conventional antagonism of two brothers; but sunk in the exchanges between Orlando and Oliver is a mosaic of phrases:

> Shall I keep your hogs and eat husks? . . . What prodigal portion have I spent? . . . Come, come, elder brother, you are too young in this. . . . Give me the poor allottery my father left me.

It would be difficult for anyone, even in the theater, to miss the reference here to the parable of the Prodigal Son; what is perhaps not so obvious is the virtuosity with which Shakespeare inverts, transposes, manipulates the substance of the parable, again raising a convention— this time of courtly pastoral—to a new and unexpected level.

The history plays tease us with a long-drawn image which performs a similar function and traverses four plays. John of Gaunt, in deploring the devastation Richard is bringing to his realm, speaks of "this England" not only in terms of almost priceless value but as a "demi-paradise" (a remarkable concession by an Englishman that it is no more than halfway back to Eden). We are then led through the long travail of Bolingbroke's penance and the slow maturity of Hal to the opening of *Henry the Fifth*. The Archbishop and the Bishop of Ely (easy prey for actors' vulgarity) discuss young Henry's transformation in terms of learning and statecraft. And then once more comes the change of key:

> Yea, at that very moment
> Consideration like an angel came
> And whipp'd the offending Adam out of him
> Leaving his body as a paradise.

No qualifying "demi" this time; the proper pitch has been reached and England (and her embodiment in Henry) has been restored to paradisal glory. Much in the next four acts will deny this grace but the assertion has been made and should remain as a reverberating overtone in the disquieting passages that follow.

The last word must inevitably be with *King Lear.* After the long agony, the reconciliation of Lear and Cordelia ("ask a blessing" . . . "ask forgiveness") transcends even the radiance of Leontes and Hermione. At the human level it is deeply moving but Shakespeare once more modulates and intensifies the tone. As they accept and move towards imprisonment to "sing like birds i'the cage," Lear and Cordelia take upon them

> the mystery of things
> As if we were God's spies.

The doings of great ones, "who's in, who's out," are not despised but seen with the compassionate irony of those whose perspective is from the bar of heaven, "God's spies." Tragically this is not the end of the play and events have to play themselves out to the death of Cordelia and the heartbreak of Lear. Again in human terms this is unendurable but Shakespeare retains for the full tragic close an altogether deeper tone; in three bewildered sentences:

> Is this the promised end?
> Or image of that horror?
> Fall and cease . . .

the shattering of lives with which the play ends is given a cosmic orchestration; the "horror" of "the promised end" is the *Dies Irae* itself, the dissolution of the universe in "the last things" and the final divine session of judgment.

And so we return to the last phase of this morning's liturgy, the tone and movement of which will certainly have given to Shakespeare the sureness of touch which transfigures his drama in all its moods and explorations.

Inaugural Lecture
Shakespeare and a Playwright of Today

by JOHN MORTIMER

I cannot think why there has fallen on me the honor of being the first to address this most learned and distinguished congress. My only claim to fame, my one proud boast, is that I am undoubtedly the best British playwright ever to have defended a murderer at the Old Bailey, our Central Criminal Court. However, whenever I tell that to the murderers I have defended they never look particularly encouraged.

With such limited qualifications I have, of course, been extremely doubtful as to what I could add to the deliberations of so many experts. I have decided that the only thoughts of interest I might have are as a British dramatist who started work in the theater, films, and television some 340 years after Shakespeare's death—a British dramatist, moreover, who was brought up on the plays of Shakespeare much as a later generation was brought up on Ministry of Health orange juice or the works of Dr. Spock.

> Is execution done on Cawdor? Are not
> Those in commission yet return'd?

From my earliest years my father would repeatedly ask me these questions that, at the age of six, I was at a loss to answer. At other moments he would look at me in a threatening manner and say, casting himself as Hubert the jailer and me as the youthful Prince Arthur, about to be blinded,

> Heat me these irons hot; and look thou stand
> Within the arras: when I strike my foot

18

Upon the bosom of the ground, rush forth,
And bind the boy. . . .

So the words of the plays became a sort of family code and the subject of our jokes. "Is execution done on Cawdor?" was a line of hilarious comedy and "Rush Forth and Bind the Boy" a firm of dubious lawyers.

From an early age I began to act the tragedies, in an abridged version, for the benefit of my mother and father, at the end of the dining room. Unfortunately I was an only child and so had to act all the parts. This gives me an additional qualification. I must be one of the few speakers here who has dueled with himself, played a bedroom scene with himself as his own mother, and forced himself to drink his own poisoned chalice. They were productions that must have been far more enjoyable to perform than to watch.

My father was not musical, and the words of the plays took the place of music for him. He would, in the middle of breakfast, or while taking geranium cuttings, suddenly intone, "Nymph in thy orisons be all my sins remembered," or "Of one whose subdued eyes / Albeit unused to the melting mood, / Dropt tears as fast as the Arabian trees / Their medicinable gum." He would repeat these words, as other men might hum a phrase from Puccini or a favorite tune from *Oklahoma*. I too have never ceased to be moved by the sheer music of Shakespeare, although today's actors, who race towards familiar quotations in a kind of embarrassed mutter, as though shying at some obscenity, have done their best to teach me otherwise.

When I was a child my father took me each year to see the plays in this theater, and he was able to help out the actors by reciting most of their lines quite loudly and a couple of beats before they did. As his eyes failed he would ask me to keep up a running commentary on the action. We became, I suppose, two of the most unpopular members of the audience. At night we stayed in the Shakespeare Hotel, where the rooms were named after Shakespeare's characters. I remember at an early age standing terrified in "Macbeth" and seeing, reflected in the wardrobe mirror, a terrible hooded figure with spindly legs and a body that seemed to be nothing but a whitish blur. It was surely some ghastly emanation from the cauldron, I thought, and stood paralyzed with fear until I realized that the reflection was me taking off my shirt. I was brought to my senses by a horrendous matrimonial quarrel going on in "Romeo and Juliet" next door.

The point of these random reminiscences is only that I cannot remember a time when my head was not full of pages of Shakespeare, any more than I can now remember not being able to swim. I cannot remember, for instance, not knowing how *The Merchant of Venice* ends, and I am sure it is hard for us all to appreciate the effect that twist in plotting must have had on its first audience. My feeling for Shakespeare was, perhaps, like a child's feeling towards a half-understood religion. I was impressed, indeed intoxicated, by the incantations, fascinated by the mysteries, terrified by the ghosts.

It was not until I grew up to be a writer that I was able to understand Shakespeare's extraordinary mastery of that most difficult of all literary crafts, the practice of dramatic writing.

When I started to write some television plays loosely based on the life of Shakespeare, I was told by the late, greatly lamented Professor Terence Spencer that you could write all that was known of Shakespeare's life on a postcard and leave room for the stamp.

I have since found that this is not altogether true, and that we know as much of Shakespeare as we would of any prosperous middle-class Elizabethan who was never an aristocrat or tried for treason.

I suppose any consideration of Shakespeare as a worker in the theater must start with him as a man. No one who writes anything about Shakespeare will have failed to receive communications from the Francis Bacon Society. I have, in my life, known many cold-blooded lawyers such as Francis Bacon was, and not one of them would have been capable of writing the plays of Shakespeare. Two facts are beyond dispute, the inscription in the church in this parish, erected in 1623, which likens William Shakespeare of Stratford to Socrates and Virgil, and the First Folio in the same year in which Ben Jonson calls him "The Sweet Swan of Avon." I therefore venture to suggest that we proceed on this basis. If the plays were not by Shakespeare they were written by someone who lived in the same time and at the same place, and happened to have exactly the same name.

All of you here today will have spent a great part of your time thinking of what sort of a man Shakespeare was. He was born an alderman's son, far from the London theater, just as Rudolf Nureyev was born a poor boy in a Siberian town, far from any ballet company, and Kiri te Kanawa in a Maori village across the world from Covent Garden. Yet the instinct of the artist, strange and incalculable as the instinct of the homing pigeon or the emigrating swallow, drove these artists inevitably to the place where they could practice their various arts. After an early marriage we lose track of Shakespeare for a number of years, a convenient period in which we can make him anything we want him to be, a lawyer's clerk, a soldier of fortune, or a schoolteacher.

It is clear, however, and beyond dispute that Shakespeare became an actor, and then a writer who enjoyed, from his early start with the three parts of *Henry VI*, an enormous popular and box-office success. He was singularly free from that nightmare of the contemporary dramatist, the self-advertising dramatic critic. He seems to have had only one bad notice, when the no doubt envious Robert Greene called him an "upstart crow, beautified with our feathers, [who] supposes he is as well able to bombast out a blank verse as the best of you and . . . is in his own conceit the only Shake Scene in a country." Despite this unfavorable review early in his career it is clear that Shakespeare went on to make a comfortable living in the theater and was able to buy property and retire early to his hometown, a way of life that the Commissioners of Inland Revenue have made impossible for a dramatist today.

The search for Shakespeare's character behind this bland chronicle of success has been, of course, neverending, and as Professor Schoenbaum has pointed out entertainingly in his *Shakespeare's Lives*, everyone finds his own Shakespeare. For nineteenth-century romantics he was a simple, handsome country lad who poached deer at Charlecote and grew up to write plays that were really too good for such a vulgar place as the theater. For Oscar Wilde and Lord Alfred Douglas he was a poet of the nineties, in love with a boy actor called Willy Hughes. He may suit us best as the tormented bisexual of the Sonnets or the disillusioned pessimist of *Troilus and Cressida* who saw no future after a pointless and all-destroying war. You can, to a large extent, look in the plays and find the Shakespeare you want. If you wish him to be egalitarian and antiestablishment, he will oblige with

> Take physic, pomp,
> Expose thyself to feel what wretches feel

and

> Handy dandy, which is the Justice, which is the thief?

If you want him to be an implacable conservative he will give you

> Oh, when degree is shak'd,
> Which is the ladder to all high designs,
> The enterprise is sick!

and

> Take but degree away, untune that string,
> And, hark, what discord follows!

He can sound a clarion call to free love:

> Therefore despite of fruitless chastity,
> Love-lacking vestals, and self-loving nuns

> That on the earth would breed a scarcity
> And barren dearth of daughters and of sons,
> Be prodigal:

and denounce the pleasures of the flesh with fierce contempt with

> The expense of spirit in a waste of shame
> Is lust in action.

Is he a humanist, on the side of man against the indifferent gods?

> As flies to wanton boys are we to the gods.
> They kill us for their sport.

Or is he deeply religious?

> Why, all the souls that were were forfeit once,
> And He who might the vantage best have took,
> Found out the remedy.

So to a large extent Shakespeare will think what you want him to think. But with some exceptions. He will not be mean and he will not be pompous, or pretentious, or falsely sentimental, and he will not be a hypocrite.

It is generally supposed that Shakespeare suffered some secret trauma, some period when fate or his fellows treated him mercilessly, leaving him filled with bitterness and thoughts of man's ingratitude. This may be so; and yet it is often misleading to study a playwright's characters in the hope of finding the playwright's character. The dramatist must perform incessantly and take on a variety of roles beyond the range of even an Alec Guinness or a Peter Sellers.

Shakespeare could turn himself, without effort, into Falstaff and Juliet, Cleopatra and Shallow, Hamlet and Doll Tearsheet. No doubt he had something of all these persons in him, perhaps we all have; and yet there is a danger in identifying a writer too closely with his creations. From a study of John Osborne's excellent plays, works that out-Timon Timon in angry railing against almost everything, you might suppose that he was an embittered, angry, and cynical man. Those who have had the pleasure of meeting Mr. Osborne have been surprised to find him a gentle, kindly, humorous fellow who often goes to Evensong and entertains his local vicar. Although Timon railed against the world, it may be a mistake to suppose that Shakespeare was more of a Timon than a Horatio.

There are other contradictions in this character. Like the great majority of English writers, Shakespeare came from the middle class, and yet he wrote almost exclusively of princes or peasants. The middle-class burgher, depicted in much Elizabethan drama, hardly appears in his plays. Was Shakespeare, after being pressed into a teenage marriage with an older woman, revolting against the narrow, provincial bourgeois world that was his inheritance? He clearly loved the Warwickshire countryside passionately, and yet he wrote better than anyone of a London tavern and the low life of a city.

The voyage behind that pale, domelike forehead, into the secret thoughts behind those dark eyes, is of endless fascination and must always be attempted. It may be that he even deserved the reputation for sweetness that Ben Jonson gave him, but perhaps his wife would not have agreed.

We think of him now, down the corridor of years, and try to get to know him, but I wonder if even his contemporaries really knew Shakespeare, although they clearly loved him. No doubt he was witty, charming, capable of deep friendship and sudden bitterness, particularly to those he loved. I think we should have liked Shakespeare, surrendered to his charm, listened to his stories of the theater and Warwickshire legends. But he would have left us, even then, with his mysteries intact.

We are on such ground when we join him in his great obsession, mastering what is, as I have said, by far the hardest task a writer faces, the creation of drama.

The extraordinary thing about the Elizabethan theater, the great medium through which Shakespeare exercised his art, is the shortness of its existence. It was an instrument available to writers with a life, in terms of history, as short as that of the mayfly that dies in a day. Not much over sixty years from the building of the first regular theater in Shoreditch, the Puritans were in power and passed the laws closing theaters and forbidding public stage plays as suitable for "seasons of humiliation." The great Elizabethan theaters stood derelict, many of them to be used again only as stables and sheep pens, and actors drifted off to become unsuitable recruits in the armed services or starve. Those who tried to avoid the ban were fined or imprisoned, or whipped as strolling vagabonds.

So, by some miracle for us, Shakespeare managed to be born in the short life of the Elizabethan playhouse, before the Puritans took over and destroyed the drama. There are, it seems, two strands in the British national character; and the playwrights and creators always have to contend with those who regard the theater as a place of sin. From the battle still being waged between the National Theatre and Mrs. Whitehouse it seems that the war is in no way over.

What the Elizabethan theater offered was a freedom in dramatic writing that the playwright did not regain until this century, with the invention of the movies and television, and the return of serious theater to the open, uncluttered stages of Tudor times. Shakespeare had the freedom of the cine camera to travel the world, the speed of film or videotape to cut from short scene to short scene without long intervals for changing scenery when the audience has to be plunged into boring, coughing, sweet-paper rustling darkness. He had the radio writer's wonderful opportunity to paint scenery with the two finest materials available, words and the audience's imagination. In fact the Elizabethan theater gave the dramatic writer all the advantages that he was to lose and not recover for another 300 years.

So I think of Shakespeare at the start of his career, faced with a blank stage and a blank piece of paper, equipped with a snatch or two of old history, and perhaps some fragments of old plays that his task was to cobble into the three parts of *Henry VI*.

He had, of course, no idea that he would manage to survive to write a total of thirty-six or thirty-seven deathless plays: no writer believes he will ever get beyond the work he is engaged on and each has grave doubts if he is going to finish that. He had no way of knowing that he was to enter into the period of the Supreme Tragedies, or the plays of bitterness, ending up with the Great Comedies of Reconciliation. He probably never dreamed that he would end up rich and respected with a coat of arms, home in Stratford, and perhaps being invited to give a lecture. He had no thoughts of having university chairs and hotel bedrooms dedicated to him. He felt, I am sure, like any contemporary playwright that any day he might fall a victim to the pox, or the police, or that the theaters might be closed by the Plague, or war, or, what was worse, by the Puritans. Any play he wrote might have been his last, and before death or the Privy Council or the little Children of Saint Paul's spoiled everything, his concern was to get together, for that yawningly empty platform, some sort of an entertainment.

A stage is an empty space. Put one thing on it, a throne, say, or a bed, and it looks important; add another and its importance is halved. The emptiness of Shakespeare's stage meant that props, even costumes, I suspect, were of minor importance. The power in the theater was the word, and the word was Shakespeare's. I believe the word to be the most important thing in the theater and in television and even in the cinema, but today's dramatist has to fight for his words against the competition of scenic effects, visual excitement, and beautiful pictures. Shakespeare was in a better position because the beautiful pictures could only be provided by his words.

Every working dramatist has learned that the most enjoyable performances of his plays come at the end of the rehearsal period, when the actors know the words, but before the set has been built, before the costumes have arrived, before the lighting man has got to work and before the makeup (and before, let it be said, the audience is let in). The play always seems to speak, in such final rehearsals, with a particular intensity and conviction, with actors wearing their own clothes and a few props to stimulate but not take over from the imagination. In such final rehearsals we get closer, I am sure, to the theater Shakespeare knew. The word is all.

It is obvious, and has often been said, that Shakespeare was the master stage designer. He could do it with one sentence:

This is Illyria, lady.

And the bare boards of the stage become a sun-drenched sea coast. He could write

> Light thickens, and the crow
> Makes wing to the rooky wood:
> Good things of day begin to droop and drowse,
> Whiles night's black agents to their preys do rouse.

And Shakespeare's stage, in the middle of a sunny afternoon, became filled with terrifying and entirely verbal darkness. Today, of course, the director, the designer, and the lighting man would all lend a hand. The stage would actually go dark and the absence of light, as everyone knows, makes words inaudible. Things were better for Shakespeare in this respect: his words were given their due and were the only decor.

Do you want a war?

> This battle fares like to the morning's war
> When dying clouds contend with growing light,
> What time the shepherd, blowing of his nails,
> Can neither call it perfect day nor night.
> Now sways it this way, like a mighty sea
> Forced by the tide to combat with the wind;
> Now sways it that way, like the self same sea
> Forced to retire by fury of the wind. . . .

In the movies that would require a location in Yugoslavia, a thousand extras, a couple of hundred technicians, and an army of assistants to call out, "Ready when you are, Mr. De Mille." In the theater it would still call, perhaps, for strobe lighting, the reverberation of clashing swords, and that health hazard to present-day stalls customers, dense clouds of dry ice to send them coughing out at the intervals. All Shakespeare needed for a battle were words and one man, alone on a daylit platform, sitting on something he pretended was a molehill.

So the ability to change scenery with a word gave Shakespeare and his contemporaries a great freedom in time and place that the dramatist has only recently recovered. As with the modern scriptwriter, the world was Shakespeare's oyster: he could cut from Egypt to Rome, from Eastcheap to Harfleur, with the speed of a pair of scissors cutting into film. And the use of voice-over in films and television has made it possible for a dramatist to communicate a character's unspoken thoughts and has restored the soliloquy that the theater lost during the long interregnum of naturalistic drama that followed the Puritan ban on all public plays.

So when the Puritans forbade the theater in the streets they eventually drove it into the drawing room. The picture stage, the box set, gradually led the theater away from poetry and towards naturalism. The three-act play no longer flashed from Rome to Egypt, the curtain fell, and after a lengthy interval allowing time for a fight for a small warm drink wrenched from a sullen lady in black bombazine in the theater bar, the curtain rose again on "The same, three months later." Fairies and monsters, battles and executions were driven off stage and took refuge in the wings. It is true that in Ibsen's plays the trolls and water spirits are haunting the fjord, and that in Chekhov the great tide of history is gradually washing away the past, but these events are only dimly heard in their drawing rooms. The fairies and revolutions are anywhere but on the stage.

Perhaps the great theatrical events, during the nineteenth century, took refuge in the opera house. There music took over from poetry by allowing the theater to burst the bounds of naturalism, and characters could sing out their secret thoughts at the tops of their magnificent voices and the audience had no difficulty in accepting that no one else on the stage could possibly hear them.

It is above all, I believe, in his freedom from the literal demands of naturalism that the playwright of today can feel closest to Shakespeare and learn most from him.

Shakespeare was also, of course, a master scriptwriter. The author of a three-act play has to find two good curtain lines to send the audience out happy. A play split up into a multitude of short scenes depends, like a good film script, on finding the correct way of ending one scene and starting another, either by linking them with a similar image, or by a ferocious contrast. This is the technique the film writer, whose story proceeds in short bursts, has to learn, and Shakespeare knew it perfectly. *Macbeth* is full of instances.

The most obvious, perhaps, is the scene of Duncan's arrival and greeting by Lady Macbeth. At the end of the scene the king says:

> Give me your hand:
> Conduct me to mine host: we love him highly,
> And shall continue our graces towards him.
> By your leave, hostess.

And the very next scene starts with Macbeth alone:

> If it were done when 'tis done then 'twere well
> It were done quickly. . . .

Macbeth, whom Duncan spoke of so lovingly, is plotting Duncan's murder.

Earlier Shakespeare achieved a similar effect by a cut within a scene. Duncan speaks of the treacherous Cawdor, on whom execution has been done:

> There is no art
> To find the mind's construction in the face.
> He was a gentleman on whom I built
> An absolute trust.

And then

CUT TO
CLOSE SHOT   Macbeth entering, full of smiles.

The examples, of course, could be multiplied endlessly. But it was the timelessness, the simplicity of the Elizabethan stage that allowed Shakespeare to cut like a film writer, with savage irony that keeps his audience continually attentive.

Not only the links between, but the juxtaposition of scenes shows what a consummate master Shakespeare would have been of film or television, just as he is of the open stage. And the supreme art of such immediate contrast would have been impossible on the nineteenth-century picture stage.

A scene on the cold, windy, dark battlements, on which walks the restless ghost of a king who cannot sleep in peace, is followed by a huge, glittering court occasion in a room of state. The placing of these two scenes one after the other at the start of the play almost tells us the whole story of *Hamlet,* and it is incredible to me that in a recent production, where the ghost was reduced to a kind of fit of the collywobbles going on inside Hamlet, the first scene was cut, as though there is anyone alive today who could teach his stage technique to Shakespeare.

The essential trick of such juxtapositions is continual surprise. Everyone has pointed out the way in which the terrible knocking on the gate in *Macbeth* is followed, unexpectedly, by a monologue from a drunken porter. The porter is not very funny; he does not need to be. He is both a marvelous dramatic device, a way of keeping us waiting when it is unbearable to wait, and a true echo of the way life suddenly changes its mood at the most unexpected and inappropriate moments.

Such are the matters of technique. But what can a writer say of Shakespeare's characters that could possibly be of interest to those who have made a lifetime's study of his plays? What new thoughts could I possibly have?

The walls of libraries are lined with studies of the characters. The words written about them, if laid end to end, would no doubt stretch from here to the moon. And yet, reading so much that has been beautifully and intelligently written, it has often seemed to me that something of great importance has been forgotten when the characters in Shakespeare's plays are discussed. Characters in *plays* are what they are. They exist to make the plays work. They are an essential part of the artefact, the work of art. They are there to create the conflict, the tension, the drama, the pathos, the tragedy, or the jokes. Their business, their justification is on the stage. Take them off the stage, into the psychiatrist's consulting room, for instance, for a long session on the couch, or put them into the witness box and question their motives, and they become tongue-tied and self-contradictory, lapsing finally, perhaps, into an embarrassed and protective silence. This, I believe, is the reason for the dissatisfaction many academics, particularly former academics, feel about Shakespeare. And it is also the reason why audiences love his plays and writers must learn from them. *Hamlet* is a play that invariably works, even if done by a cast of nervous schoolgirls in a drafty drill hall in Wigan. Whenever or wherever it is produced it is a box-office success. And yet Hamlet as a man puzzles most of the academic writers who have discussed him. He appears, when closely examined as a human being, contradictory, inexplicable, unsatisfactory even: almost every fault can be found with him as a creation except his ability to produce great drama.

Every writer has had an actor come to him at some stage of a production to say, "Can you tell me *why* I say this, exactly. What's the motivation?" Every writer has been tempted to reply with the truth: "Your motivation is to get on with the play."

Why *does* Hamlet hesitate and procrastinate before he swoops to his revenge? A thousand times more words have been written on this subject than Shakespeare needed to write the play itself. Ingenious theories have been advanced, including the idea that Hamlet was a woman in disguise in love with Horatio, or had faked the ghost story as a political manoeuvre to get rid of Claudius. The late Andrew C. Bradley devoted many pages to all the possible explanations—that Hamlet was afraid no one would believe him if he denounced Claudius, or that he was deterred by moral scruple from murdering his uncle, or that he was too sensitive to act as an executioner, or that he, perhaps, was too much of an intellectual and thought so carefully that all physical activity became impossible. Professor Bradley discussed all these possibilities and plumped for the solution that Hamlet was afflicted with a profound melancholy, an "accidie" that paralyzed his will and accounted for four long acts of inactivity.

At which point it is tempting to imagine a conversation between Burbage and Shakespeare around the tea urn during the mid-morning break in the rehearsal room at the Globe Theatre.

"What's the matter with me, Will?" Burbage said. "Am I suffering from natural caution or am I too intellectual and profound or have I got melancholia? I mean, for God's sake, why don't I kill Claudius immediately after I've met the ghost in Act I, Scene IV?"

"Because if you did that, dear boy," Shakespeare might well have answered, warming his hands on his plastic mug of Nesquick, "we shouldn't have any blooming play!"

Now this may sound an extremely philistine remark and its attribution to Shakespeare, the Divine Poet, almost sacrilege. Such a thought, I dare swear, never entered the mind of Professor Bradley when he set out the various reasons for Hamlet's prevarication under carefully numbered paragraphs. But before I am dismissed entirely as a hack with a forehead villainous low, unfit to address this distinguished gathering, may I say something about the way in which I think the examination of the characters in Shakespeare's plays, and indeed in any drama, may have been given a wrong emphasis.

In the last century Shakespeare's characters were regarded as *heroes*, and they seemed to become heroes irrespective of, and perhaps in spite of, the slightly disagreeable fact that they were involved in stage plays. A hero, so the Victorians thought, is more fitted for the library than the stage and he exists, in his heroic fashion, in a world greater and more prolonged than a temporary evening in the theater. Now a hero is not a hero unless his greatness can be explained. It is true that if he is a tragic Shakespearian hero he has a "fatal flaw," but the flaw itself is of heroic dimensions and must also be attributable to some understandable and heroic quality. Thus melancholy explained Hamlet, ambition Macbeth, jealousy Othello, and so on.

With the passage of time, and the arrival of Dr. Freud in Vienna, men and women began to lose their heroic characters. But they still have to be explicable in other terms, by their relations with their mothers, or their jealousy of their fathers, by insufficient weaning, or an infant glimpse of their parents making love. These explanations suit very well realistic or totally naturalistic drama. They come to their logical conclusion in American plays of the fifties, when every character arrived on the stage fitted with a series of complexes derived from some textbook on psychology. Actors even prepared to take part in such plays by long sessions of talk in the Actors Studio about the early life of the characters they were playing, how much they loved their mothers or were jealous of their fathers or whether they were dropped when young.

The late Noel Coward, when actors asked him what their motivation was, would answer, "Your paycheck at the end of the week," and would counsel them to concentrate on remembering the lines and on trying not to bump into the furniture. I do not suppose Shakespeare ever said anything as rude as that to Burbage and it is not necessary, of course, to dismiss all such questions on motivation quite so brusquely. Such questions may be relevant to the characters in the plays of Tennessee Williams or Arthur Miller. They are quite irrelevant when you happen to be dealing with Lady Macbeth.

No doubt in the Actors Studio a long discussion could take place about Lady Macbeth's relationship with the child to whom she had given suck, or of her exact feelings about her father whom, as we know, the sleeping Duncan resembled. Such discussion could take place, but it would be futile. Lady Macbeth does not come as a subject for an essay or a clinical study. She came out of the tiring room onto a platform one afternoon and there she was—bang!—a character of blazing intensity who needs no explanation, no excuse, except for her huge effect on the drama that she will help to produce.

Or let us take Iago. Iago presented Professor Bradley with enormous problems. Was he possessed, as Coleridge had suggested, of "motiveless malignity"? Critics, like lawyers, are anxious to find a motive for everything, and dislike nothing more than an effect without a discernible cause. So Iago is "motivated" by his enjoyment of power. He can be explained. Iago the character has an explanation and so, curiously enough, the play becomes less disturbing and the drama as a whole, may I suggest, is diminished by becoming more rational.

Another question authors are frequently asked by actors is what such and such a line "means." The author who knows his business, as to be sure Shakespeare did, is tempted to answer, "It means what it says. If there were another way of saying it I should have used it." And again, if the line is learned, and said so it is audible, and the furniture avoided, and the author knows his business, the line will work in the theater, although it may look quite puzzling when taken out and analyzed.

So may I humbly submit, as we say down at the Old Bailey, that in the days to come you discover, you experience, above all you enjoy the work of Shakespeare . . . but perhaps, just perhaps, you do not spend too much time in trying to explain. Perhaps this is because any explanation has to be given in words other than Shakespeare's and his words are, invariably and after all, the best.

May we take a moment to consider how Shakespeare, how any good serious dramatist from 1580 or 1980, went to work. He had a theme, no doubt, that he wanted for the moment to express about pride, about ambition, about man's ingratitude, about kingship and the unity of a nation, about mistaken identity, or about the magic of a wood. Such themes can produce either comedy or tragedy. Handled differently, Othello's handkerchief might have been the stuff of farce, and Malvolio's downfall has the whiff of tragedy in it. Given a theme, the playwright needs a plot. This is the most difficult part, so Shakespeare often solved the problem by pinching someone else's. When he had thought of his main character, he had to provide other characters who would produce conflict, which, either in comedy or tragedy, is the stuff of drama. When a playwright is working well, his characters assume an existence of their own, take things into their own hands, and surprise him by what they do. Of one thing there can be no doubt. Shakespeare was usually working well.

And one thing also. Just as the scenery for his plays depended on an act of the imagination and was in no way naturalistic, just as his language used everyday speech and played with it, rearranged it, and fired the imagination so that it was in no way naturalistic, just as Burbage's acting no doubt started with life in the court or on the streets, but magnified the gestures, colored the emotions, and raised it at least two feet above the ground, so the people in Shakespeare's plays exist at that level which is best called theatrical. They are not all explained. A great deal of space is left for us to fill in. They are not painted photographically like realistic scenery. They call for us all, and that is one of their great virtues, to exercise the imagination and leave us free to a large extent—you and me and Coleridge and Professor Bradley—to see in them what we want to see, which is perhaps why audiences have never tired of the plays and why, since he got over his first bad notice from Greene, Shakespeare has been such an astonishingly popular success.

Because with Shakespeare it is not the philosophy or the psychology or the realistic study of character that is important. It is The Play that's the thing. And whatever else happens, the play can be seen to work. And it is the working of the play in theatrical terms that is the element former critics missed. Professor Bradley, whom I have knocked quite enough and may now after so much critical fervor be allowed to sleep well, thought that if he could not explain the characters, if he found them inconsistent, or mysterious, or surprising, Shakespeare had fallen down on his job. But Shakespeare's job was not to explain human nature to Professor Bradley, but to excite and enthrall and intoxicate with drama whoever would be kind enough to pay for a ticket next Wednesday afternoon.

So what should we learn from this marvelous collection of plays, those of us who have the honor of carrying on, so imperfectly, the theatrical traditions Shakespeare left us, and work to produce drama either on stage like this, or on films or television? I would say that we should learn that naturalism is not the last or the only word. That an empty platform and a call to the imagination are worth more than all the elaborate machinery that has never been made to work in the National Theatre. That stage characters, rooted in real life, can take off and grow and gesture with the greatest theatricality. If their feet start firmly on the ground they can be made to rise ten feet above it. They exist in a world in which psychological realism is only part of the equation. And we can learn that at the heart of every great play, as at the heart of life itself, is a mystery that each of us must interpret as best we can. And finally we can learn that any character who behaves consistently, according to a logical and reasonable plan laid down by his implacable creator, is very likely to be a crashing bore.

When I undertook the task of writing some television plays about Shakespeare I found the most difficult thing to do was to prevent him coming out like St. Francis of Assisi. Perhaps it was in fact the last revenge of a rival poet, but Ben Jonson's "sweet" Shakespeare has stuck down the ages with a somewhat cloying effect. Yet this was the man who could also leave his family for many years to pursue, with ruthless ambition, his career in London, who could be torn between a dark mistress and a fair friend, the one producing in him tormented lust, the other some particularly fulsome flattery. He could end up no doubt as a level-but not hard-headed landlord and man of property.

And yet he appeared, I am sure, as "sweet Shakespeare" among his friends in the Mermaid Tavern. His obsession, I am convinced, was with his work, his ambition was to survive, to keep out of trouble so that he might continue with it for as long as he had the strength and, when he was not writing, to notice, to watch, and to listen to everything. His is a character that, like those of Falstaff and Hamlet and Iago, defies, in the last instance, analysis.

However, we do not go to playwrights to seek answers to questions about politics or philosophy or religion. If a continuously exciting sense of theater and an infallible ear for dialogue and stage poetry equipped men to answer us about such matters we should, no doubt, elect Mr. Pinter prime minister and Mr. Osborne Archbishop of Canterbury. We go to playwrights for their art, and when that art is as great as Shakespeare's, it expresses, in terms of theater, the splendors and miseries, the cruelty and mercy, the huge seriousness and enormous absurdity of life itself.

No doubt in the days to come you will learn much, much more than I could ever know of the life of that great playmaker who was born and married here and who came back here to die. Many will have ideas about who the dark lady was, and who the fair friend, and some of such ideas may well be correct. Many will be able to analyze the plays and their characters with a deeper learning and a greater ingenuity than I could ever command. But you will not, even a body as learned and distinguished as this will not, quite, be able to pluck the heart out of his mystery. I sincerely hope.

Shakespeare Imagines a Theater

by STEPHEN ORGEL

This essay makes some very speculative observations about the Renaissance's way of conceiving theater, and puts together for comparison and analysis examples that are rarely considered relevant to each other: architectural models, an emblematic frontispiece, eyewitness sketches, Shakespearean scenes. In all these cases, I am interested both in how the stage is imagined to represent its action and in how that action is to be perceived—that is, its relation to an audience.

Consider first three Renaissance artists imagining theaters. In 1545 the Italian architect Sebastiano Serlio devised prototype stage sets for the three traditional kinds of drama—the tragic, the comic, and the satiric or pastoral (figs. 1–3). These are architectural models designed to be employed in the theater of a noble house in the neoclassic style. Serlio is adapting Vitruvius to the uses of the Italian Renaissance; Vitruvius has a chapter on public theaters, but Serlio assumes that a great house will include a theater of its own. The tragic setting consists of palaces and temples, aristocratic and public buildings, and monuments. Its perspective is open, with a triumphal arch at its apex, and beyond the arch a forum of architectural hieroglyphs: pyramid, obelisk, the mysterious embodiments of ancient wisdom. The comic setting, in contrast, consists of middle-class architecture: Serlio says these are merchants' houses, and they clearly belong to a Renaissance Italian cityscape. A shop is visible halfway back on the left, and the perspective is closed by the façade of a Renaissance church with its medieval tower, partly decayed, the only visible link with a monumental past. In the right foreground Serlio has placed a brothel, inscribed with the name Rufia, presumably the madam. No such character figures in any play of Plautus or Terence; Rufia is in fact not a proper name at all, but the Italian comedy's generic term for a loose woman—Serlio's comedy, if he has one in mind, is a modern one. The satiric or pastoral scene consists of rustic buildings, trees, and a mass

Fig. 1. The Tragic Scene, from Sebastiano Serlio, *Architettura*, 1545.

Fig. 2. Serlio, the Comic Scene.

Fig. 3. Serlio, the Satiric or Pastoral Scene.

of birds filling what is visible of the sky. Its huts are strictly utilitarian, in no recognizable architectural style, and are visibly overwhelmed by the surrounding nature. This setting makes no temporal assumptions at all: it is a world that has always been with us. But also, its action takes place somewhere altogether different, in the woods, in nature, without the comforting order imposed by architectural façades, and barely controlled by symmetry.

For Serlio, then, the tragic is urban, noble, ancient, open, and mysterious; the comic urban, middle-class, modern, closed, and rational; the pastoral rustic, humble, timeless, and natural or wild. The kinds of drama are, for Serlio, internally consistent and mutually exclusive, both topographically and chronologically.

Let us turn now to another Renaissance artist, this time imagining a real play on stage (fig. 4). In 1595 Henry Peacham (or more probably somebody else) drew this scene from *Titus Andronicus*. In the center Queen Tamora pleads with Titus for the lives of her sons, who kneel on

Enter Tamora pleadinge for her sonnes going to execution

Fig. 4. Henry Peacham (?), a scene from *Titus Andronicus*, 1595. (Harley Papers, Longleat. Reproduced with permission.)

the right, guarded by Aaron the Moor. On the left, two soldiers stand armed with pikes. The stage itself is represented quite schematically— there is simply a line for the front and no indication of a back façade— but the costumes and properties have been vividly rendered, though of course there is no way of knowing whether they are being imagined by Peacham or remembered from a performance. Titus is in Roman dress and the queen is in some sort of generalized royal dress, certainly not either Roman or Elizabethan. The Moor and his prisoners are in simple costumes that might be either Roman or contemporary: the shorts could be either classical bases (military skirts) or Elizabethan puff-pants, the shirtsleeves of the Moor and the son on the right look Elizabethan, but the son on the left wears the same sort of sash as Titus, and that is clearly intended to be Roman. There is, however, no ambiguity about the two soldiers: they are in full Elizabethan military outfits. Obviously, what is important here is not any sense of historical accuracy, or even of consistency, but that the costume be an index to every character's role. Roman general, medieval queen, Elizabethan guardsmen are grouped together in an integral though anachronistic stage picture. If we recall the temporal exclusiveness of Serlio's prototype stages, we shall see that Peacham is expressing a significantly different idea of what and how the theater *represents*.

Now let us look at a Jacobean example, the frontispiece to what is arguably the most far-reaching conception of theater the English Ren-

Fig. 5. William Hole, title page to *The Workes of Benjamin Jonson*, 1616.

aissance produced. Figure 5 is the title page to the Jonson folio of 1616, engraved by William Hole, clearly to Jonson's specifications. It has the form of a triumphal arch. On either side of a central cartouche stand the figures of Tragedy and Comedy; below them are two scenes illustrating the ancient sources of drama. On the left is the *plaustrum,* or cart of Thespis, with the sacrificial goat, the tragedian's prize, tethered to it, and on the right is a small amphitheater, labeled in Latin *visorium,* with a choric dance in progress. Above Tragedy and Comedy the third of the ancient genres, the satiric or pastoral, is anatomized: on the left a satyr plays a Pan's pipe of seven reeds, on the right a shepherd plays a shaum. Between them is a Roman theater, and above that, at the very top of the arch, stands Tragicomedy, flanked by the tiny figures of Bacchus on the left and Apollo on the right, the two patrons of ancient theater. Jonson's title page, with characteristic gravity, presents nothing so transient and particular as a scene from a play. It defines the drama in relation to its history and its kinds, and offers a set of generic possibilities.

What these very different conceptions of theater appear to have in common is their failure to include an audience. And yet, if we look deeper, their sense of an audience may in fact be taken as a crucial, and indeed a defining feature, and the element that makes them enlightening in relation to Shakespeare.

Near the beginning of his career, Shakespeare wrote a play with the problematic of theater at its center, *The Taming of the Shrew.* The drunken Christopher Sly is deceived by a mischievous lord into believing he is an amnesiac aristocrat. He is entertained, in the fashion appropriate to noble houses, with an Italian play, *The Taming of the Shrew.* But the play soon bores him, and he sums up his reaction with what turn out to be his final words: " 'Tis a very excellent piece of work . . . would 'twere done."

By dismissing the comedy, however, Sly has annihilated himself: *The Taming of the Shrew* becomes the play, its world expands and fills the stage, and neither Sly nor the mischievous lord is heard of again. It is the play that has dismissed its audience, declaring its autonomy not only of Sly but of its patron, the trifling lord, as well; and Shakespeare's drama is called not *The Gulling of Christopher Sly,* but *The Taming of the Shrew.* And where is the audience in all this? Clearly not in agreement with Sly, or else the play would not continue. Shakespeare has imagined an ideal audience, and then, by a piece of theatrical sleight of hand, turned us into it.

" 'Tis a very excellent piece of work . . . would 'twere done." Plays within Shakespeare plays generally displease their audiences, and always end badly. Hamlet's mousetrap is designed to be offensive, *Pyramus and*

Thisbe constitutes a running battle between play and spectators, Cleopatra proleptically disdains her own drama—"Antony / Shall be brought drunken forth, and I shall see / Some squeaking Cleopatra boy my greatness / I' th'posture of a whore"—and its audience as well, "Mechanic slaves / With greasy aprons, rules and hammers"; and Hamlet the playwright and critic scorns the groundlings to their faces, half the Globe's paying customers In all these instances, an audience is invented that is conceived to be invidious to the success of the play, and then the uncomprehending or hostile spectators are banished, or the inept or threatening performance is canceled. This is more than a parodic exorcism or an expression of the playwright's anxieties. It is a way of imagining and defining the *real* audience, on whose deep complicity the success of the drama depends.

Where is the audience in the theater Shakespeare imagines? Serlio and Peacham seem to imagine no audience at all: their visions of theater are confined to the stage. Jonson imagines an audience, but it seems to be one of readers for the new classic that his *Works* comprise. Figure 6, Johannes de Witt's drawing of the Swan, provides a striking embodiment of the theater of Shakespeare's *Shrew:* the play takes place in an empty playhouse before an imaginary audience; the only visible spectators appear in the gallery of the stage.

I want to focus on a scene in which Shakespeare's conception of his audience is particularly problematical, the Dover Cliff scene in *King Lear*. Edgar invents a setting and an imaginary *agon* for Gloucester to perform. It is a scene bewildering in its confusion of false and true, in which the real and the imaginary are indistinguishable. There is nothing in what Edgar says as the scene opens to indicate that his account of the ascent to the cliff and the prospect from it are not the scene's realities; we know about setting and action in this theater by what we are told, and if what Edgar describes were the truth, his lines would read no differently. This perception has led recent criticism to argue that the audience is deceived, just as Gloucester is, into believing that he is in fact being brought to the edge of Dover Cliff, and that we are enlightened only through Edgar's revelation, in an aside, that the setting is all his invention. This theory was first proposed by Harry Levin in 1958; it has recently been repeated by James Black in the last *Shakespeare Survey,* and before it becomes doctrine I want to object to it.

The thesis takes into account only what Edgar says; it ignores Gloucester's words and the action, and it is simplistic about the audience. Gloucester and Edgar give contradictory accounts of what is happening onstage, but it is perfectly obvious from the moment of their entrance whether they are struggling to walk uphill or not: any director who tried to deceive the audience on this point would find the scene unstageable.

The following labels appear within the drawing:

- tectum
- porticus
- sedilia
- orchestra
- ingressus
- mimorum ædes
- proscænium
- planties sive arena

quintum f(?)... et ...ura, bestiarum ro...cta...
...ni d...inatum, in quo multi orsi taur..., et ...udin...
mag...itudinis canes, ...tis cant...... septis alintur; qui
                                                    ...d

Fig. 6. Arend von Buchel after Johannes de Witt, the Swan Theatre, London, c. 1595. (University of Utrecht Library. Reproduced with permission.)

Gloucester's is a precisely accurate version of what the spectator sees: "Methinks the ground is even"—"Horrible steep," says Edgar. "Hark, do you hear the sea?"—"No, truly," says Gloucester. I would think that the point here is that we do not know what's going on, but Gloucester is obviously telling the truth—we can see that he is—and it is a truth reinforced by the fact that what he describes are the palpable facts of the Elizabethan theater: the stage *is* a flat platform and there are no sound effects, no audible wind and sea. But the bare facts, we also know, are in this theater subject to an infinite range of interpretation, and there is no way of interpreting Gloucester's truth. As for Edgar, it is clear at the outset from the action that he is lying to Gloucester, but the question is why. Thirty-five lines into the episode, when Edgar finally takes us into his confidence, it is not to confess the falsehood but to explain it, which he does with a piece of odd double syntax: "Why I do trifle thus with his despair / Is done to cure it." But (as James Black correctly observes in the same *Shakespeare Survey* article) it is the revelation that is ineffective here; we remain sufficiently convinced of the presence of heights and distances for Gloucester's otherwise baffling fall to work. That is, for the rest of the scene to make any sense, we must be able to imagine Gloucester on the edge of *something*, not simply on the flat platform of the stage. "He kneels . . . he falls," says the quarto's laconic stage direction. The modern stage convention goes the quarto one better and has him kneeling on a little step. What that stage convention says is that surely he *does* fall.

We take the fall seriously but substitute a little one for a great one. We experience the emotional force of the scene from Gloucester's point of view; we stage the scene effectively and *want* it to work precisely because of the extraordinary effectiveness of Edgar's lies, which are some of the best poetry in the play. We accept it all, ignoring the evidence of our eyes (or of the text), just as we accept Edgar's rationale for his lies, to cure Gloucester's despair. And then, as Gloucester wakes from his swoon, we watch Edgar produce an even more elaborate set of lies: "Ten masts at each make not the altitude / Which thou hast perpendicularly fell"; he saw Gloucester accompanied, he says, by a fiend, "his eyes / Were two full moons; he had a thousand noses, / Horns whelked and waved like the enridgèd sea." Gloucester's cure, it seems, requires not the hard truths one might expect, but outright and even outrageous lies.

They are quintessentially theatrical lies: the Dover Cliff scene is a paradigm not simply for Shakespeare's stage, but for all theater. It is a linguistic fact of every western language that the word for the imitation of an action—the classic definition of drama—is the same as the word for the action: both are *act*. In *all* theater the imaginary is taken for, is indistinguishable from, the real. And Edgar's curative theatrical lies have their roots in Aristotelian catharsis: a medical metaphor described the operation of theater—it purged and thereby healed, through pity and terror. By the same token Gower, the storyteller of *Pericles*, describes the fantastic legend he is recounting as a restorative, and the old tales of *The Winter's Tale*, through the protagonist/audience's willingness to believe in them, heal the afflictions of his mind and disordered state.

And, to go a logical step further, there are many places where Shakespeare puts the audience in Leontes' or Gloucester's position, lying to us about things we know to be true, misrepresenting action we have seen taking place. There is, for example, for an audience, no question about whether Hermione is really dead at the end of the trial scene: Leontes himself demands to see the bodies of his wife and son and orders them buried in a single grave: if Mamilius is dead, so is Hermione. Or again, at the end of *Cymbeline*, when the play is finally clearing up all its confusions, both Iachimo and Pisanio, claiming to confess all, produce egregiously (and pointlessly) inaccurate accounts of their roles in the tragic events of the play. The most blatant instance is surely the famous double-time scheme of *Othello*, in which our willingness to believe, like Othello, in the plausibility of a whole sequence of events for which there is literally no time in the play's structure, makes the play a serious tragedy rather than a preposterous farce.

What do such examples in which we accept what we know to be untrue imply about audiences? Obviously not that they are inattentive, but that the drama's reality is infinitely adjustable: that drama for Shakespeare does not create a world. The text itself is unstable: think for a moment about the Elizabethan theatrical companies' unwillingness to see their plays in print. We try to explain this by saying that they are simply protecting their interests, which are dependent on the paying spectator, not on the reader; but why is it assumed that if one can read a play one will not go to see it? Italian and French acting companies believed just the opposite—that publication constituted the best advertising, that a good way to arouse interest in a new play was to make the text available. This seems, on the face of it, more likely to be the truth—truer, that is, to the psychology of audiences. I would think that the English resistance to print goes deeper, to characteristic assumptions about the nature of theater itself: that the script is *essentially* unstable and changes as the performers decide to change it; that it is the property of the performers, not of playwrights, audiences, or readers; that the *real* play is the performance, not the text; that to fix the text, transform it into a book, is to defeat it. I would think that the textual history of *Hamlet* or *Lear*, or that palimpsest *Macbeth*, bears this out. And Jonson the playwright, asserting his control over his drama, can only do so by publishing it.

If the drama's reality is infinitely adjustable, if drama for Shakespeare

Fig. 7. Inigo Jones, setting for *Artenice* (Racan), 1626. (Devonshire Collection, Chatsworth. Reproduced by permission of the Trustees of the Chatsworth Settlement.)

does not create a world, what, then, does it create? What it creates, I would like to suggest, is something the Renaissance would have recognized as an *argument*. This is what critics from Horace to Castelvetro and Sidney mean when they say that mimesis is only the means of drama, not its end. Its end, they assume, is the same as the end of poetry and the other verbal arts—to persuade.

Let us now return to our images of the Renaissance theater. I suggest that when they offer an architectural model for the action of a play, as Serlio's stage settings do, that model in fact belies something essential to the Renaissance theater and in certain ways to the Renaissance notion of art generally: first, a basic fluidity or disjunctiveness, and second, the extent to which it depends for its truth upon its audience. The parts of a Renaissance play do not fit together like architectural structures, but like rhetorical ones; that is, they fit together only in the mind, through the assent—the complicity, really—of the spectator, listener, reader. Peacham's sketch of *Titus Andronicus* is disjunctive in this way: it persuades the viewer of the significance, position, status of its figures. It does not mime a consistent world but expresses an action. Its elements fit together only insofar as a viewer interprets and understands them.

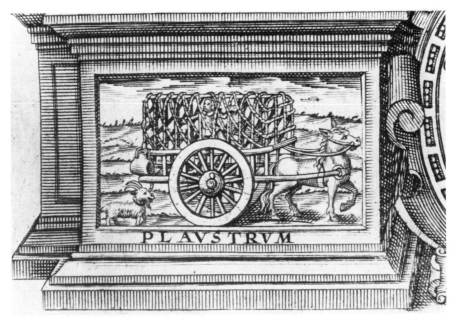

Fig. 8. The cart of Thespis, from the title page of Jonson's *Workes*, 1616.

Fig. 9. A classical ampitheatre, from the title page of Jonson's *Workes*, 1616.

The same sort of disjunctiveness will be apparent in any play in a mixed genre that uses for its stage the Serlian model. Serlio's sets look very solid and consistent, and their genres are, as we have observed, mutually exclusive. But note in figure 7 the Serlian setting by Inigo Jones for a court play called *Artenice* in 1626. This elegant drawing has more relevance to the Peacham sketch than is apparent at first glance. In this play the queen is to perform, therefore Jones includes the noble classical architecture and the open perspective of the Tragic Scene; but it is also a comedy, so the set includes a merchant's house with its Italian Renaissance loggia; but the queen and her ladies play shepherdesses, so it includes the rustic huts and woods of the Pastoral scene (it is a heroical-comical-pastoral). What this means is not that Serlio was conceiving of a drama that was generically pure, but that Serlio's constructs were taken to be analytic, not descriptive. Even the purest of Renaissance tragedies would have appeared *to an audience* to belong to a mixed genre because in performance it would have included *intermezzi* between the acts, or in England, jigs at the end. As Serlio conceived them, the genres constituted not an idea about the necessary structure of plays, but an idea about the potentialities of theaters to realize the classic forms. And what the models then offered to someone like Inigo Jones was just the opposite of that rigid consistency we find in them: a very fluid set of possibilities.

Finally, consider again the statement made by Jonson's title page to the folio of his *Workes*. The architectural model is especially powerful, and we might expect this doctrinaire classicist to be making a programmatic assertion about the sources of his art and its relation to a classic ideal. To a certain extent the title page does this, and the viewer participates in the enterprise in an essentially passive way: the parts of the structure and the figures are all labeled, the effort of interpretation is minimal, and we look on as outsiders—that is, until we look closely. Notice particularly the two plinths. Figure 8 shows Thespis in his cart with the sacrificial goat, the tragedian's prize. Thespis is the founder of tragedy, a figure lost in antiquity and legend. But in fact if we look carefully, we see that he is in Jacobean dress, a modern playwright—Jonson himself—and clearly one of us. Figure 9 depicts the amphitheater, labeled *visorium*. To begin with, *visorium* is not the Roman word for amphitheater. It is not a Roman word at all; it exists in no classical or medieval source, but is a pure Renaissance coinage. And the chorus that dances within this *visorium* is, like Thespis, Jacobean. Jonson's ambivalence toward, and indeed open hostility to, his theatrical audience is notorious. The audience imagined in the folio is that learned group of understanders, the ideal spectators, who are one with him and who here both observe and enact his drama.

Historic and Iconic Time in Late Tudor Drama

by BERNARD BECKERMAN

In one of his early plays, *Sapho and Phao,* John Lyly has an arresting passage on time. It is part of a conversation between Trachinus and his fellow philosopher Pandion. To Pandion, newly come to the court of Sapho from the world of learning, Trachinus observes

> There [at the university] times paste are read of in old bookes, times present set downe by new devises, times to come conjectured at by aime, by prophesie, or chaunce: here [at court] are times in perfection, not by devise, as fables, but in execution, as trueths. [1. 2. 14–17][1]

Seldom has anyone in so brief a space so aptly contrasted the two central modes of conceiving time. On one side—at the university, according to Trachinus—time is seen as full of change. While it is true Trachinus seems to scorn the academics for vainly trying to understand and master time, his scorn aside, he does describe neatly their preoccupation with what is indeed *historic* time. That preoccupation is characterized by acute awareness of past, present, and future. By shedding the past and grasping the present, a human being can influence the future. But influencing the future requires extraordinary willpower. One must overcome obstacles. One must accept the fact that people and events change, and change irreversibly. Nothing is perfect, yet everything aspires to ultimate perfection. It is such an image of time, historic time, that we most commonly associate with the drama.

To this management of time Lyly opposes another notion of duration: "times in perfection." At court, time is not subject to the changeability of events. It exists fully realized, immutable. Nor is its immutability merely metaphorical, as fables, but is continually being verified by demonstration, and thus verified, confirms truths in absoluteness. We can call this image of perfected time *iconic*. "The icon," in Muriel Bradbrook's phrase, "inhabits an eternal present."[2] In the world where iconic time holds sway, change can only produce corruption, for where there is perfection, the ideal, whatever its nature, can only endure; it can never improve. Lyly celebrates the ideal by vesting it in the queen Sapho, who can be weakened in her endurance but never overcome, or the demigoddess Cynthia, whose perfection can never be tainted.

These alternate images of time do not originate with Lyly, of course. They go back to concepts in Greek and Judaeo-Christian thought. Plato for one anticipates Lyly's ideal of the court when he has Socrates speak of the unchanging perfection of the Gods in the second book of *The Republic*.[3] It is this aspiration to timeless purity that leads historians to identify the notion of cyclical time with Plato while they trace the general idea of linear time to Biblical tradition. Yet the division is not neat. Though Saint Augustine, the most important Christian influence on sixteenth-century temporal attitudes, stressed the irresistible passage of earthly time, he also recognized, as G. F. Waller notes, a "transcendental realm of eternity which is unaffected by the mutability of the universe and of men's lives."[4] It was this realm that was undermined by "the Renaissance discovery of time," to use Ricardo Quinones's words.[5] That discovery, however, was a discovery only in part. The medieval Christians were aware of both images of time, as mutability and as eternity. But whereas they chose to fix their eyes on the latter, the men of the Renaissance shifted their gaze to the ebb and flow of daily existence. It is this change of attitude toward time that Florence experienced in the fourteenth century and England in the sixteenth. And whether by cause or chance, it is this change that coincides with the emergence of the great age of Elizabethan drama.

Iconic time, which radiated through the plays and entertainments of the sixteenth century, is not natural to drama, however. Drama normally relies on constantly changing circumstances, on characters moving purposefully toward conclusions. As we watch a situation unfold, we expect one moment to be different from another, we anticipate successive moments building to a crisis of some sort. But iconic time implies stasis, a steady state of being, an undifferentiated timelessness that demonstrates an abiding truth. The truth need not be the truth of virtue, as long as it is a perfected state of being, even of evil. Yet stasis is antithetical to the dynamic quality of drama. That is why the dramatist who creates an action in iconic time fights his medium. He fights it in the same way that a painter who creates a three-dimensional view on a two-dimensional surface fights the graphic medium. In both cases, the artist challenges the very nature of his discipline, and, if successful, triumphs through the challenge.

Working in iconic time, a dramatist tends to create an image of an idea rather than an image of time passing. We can see this emphasis vividly illustrated in the direct address of the moral interludes. In *Like Will to Like,* Virtuous Living delivers an exposition on Saint Augustine. He commences impersonally but then gradually concentrates his message upon the audience present.[6] The Virtues in *The Trial of Treasure* move from teaching of God to singing about Him.[7] In these ways both plays affirm timeless truths through spatial movement rather than temporal progression. Even the Vice by his varieties of disruption works in iconic time in order to destroy it. Iconic time, then, as we find it in sixteenth-century drama, stresses the repetitive and cyclical features of life, the eternal battle of the psychomachia, and the subjection of experience to idea.

As long as audiences and artists of Elizabethan England saw events as moving through iconic time, they continued to celebrate virtue with a persistence we can hardly appreciate. The perfect chastity of Thomas Garter's Susanna and the perfect friendship of Richard Edwardes's Damon and Pythias inhabit iconic time. But as Elizabethans became less fixed in their assumptions about religion, science, and social process, they came to see time as increasingly historical. The change was gradual, of course. For decades the sense of time iconic and time historic existed as alternative contexts of action in the minds of audiences. Even so, a steady turn toward a more historical perspective was taking place.

Lyly, who so brilliantly expounds the difference between the two types of time, is writing in the twilight of the iconic. He obviously yearns for the cocoon of the iconic, for the timeless world of the court. But to celebrate that court without ignoring the prevailing code of social hierarchy produces the dramatic tension suitable to historic times, not "times in perfection." In *Sapho and Phao* he brings the titular characters to the edge of historic time by introducing a cryptic, interfering Venus. She disturbs Phao's residence in iconic time. This residence is reflected in Lyly's extensive use of soliloquy in the play. In the first soliloquy (1. 1. 1–16) Phao assures himself of the sweetness of his lowly lot, and in this way weaves an image of a continuing happy state of being. How fitting it is that he is a ferryman. He need not flow with time but can oscillate between its banks. Into that motionless reverie Venus causes Cupid to discharge an arrow of love. This leads Phao to accuse himself of pride, blame Venus directly for having cursed him with passion, and then attack himself and his beauty. Partly a lament, this second soliloquy (2. 1. 1–12) portrays the initial disruption of iconic time. The succeeding two soliloquies show Phao's struggle against love and his final yielding to it (2. 4. 1–27; 129–30).

The counteraction of the play begins with Sapho's soliloquy abusing

Venus for arousing love (3. 3. 83–113). Realizing she is possessed, Sapho urges herself to resist love, to die rather than be dishonored by loving one beneath her. Her second soliloquy is in song, through which she curses love's cruelty (3. 3. 135–50); in the end though she confesses her love of Phao. Song, through its recurrent melody and closed form, offers Lyly the means to create the sustained tone of iconic timelessness.

The conflict Lyly raises within and between Sapho and Phao can hardly be resolved in soliloquy, however. He has to bring his lowly lover and tormented queen together. But their meeting is abortive. Sapho and Phao have a glancing confrontation (3. 4), full of sighs and tremors. They engage in word-play on "you" and "y-e-w," but their exchange is inconclusive since Venus dismisses Phao and relieves Sapho's anguish. Thus, the potentially rich encounter of the reluctant lovers is defused and diffused. Lyly cannot permit them to enter the historic realm of social misalliance.

In *Endimion* Lyly once again treats the love of an inferior male for a superior female.[8] This time, however, his lover Endimion is devoted to the divine Cynthia from the very beginning of the play. This play has fewer soliloquies than *Sapho and Phao*, but what there are is equally revealing. In the first of his two soliloquies (2.1), Endimion utters a double invocation: "O Fayre Cynthia! O Unfortunate Endimion," thus immediately announcing the theme of their separation. Much of his speech is addressed to the absent Cynthia. He asks how she might be won, telling her how faithful he has been to her. In the course of this rather long speech of about forty-six lines, Endimion testifies to his constancy and thus endeavors to erect an iconic state between them. In his second soliloquy (2. 3. 1–23), Endimion unhappily recognizes that "thy Majestie Cynthia al the world knoweth and wondereth at, but not one in the world that can immitate it, or comprehend it" (16–18). Hopeless, Endimion urges himself to escape into sleep or death. Tellus makes this sleep an endless one. As he sleeps he ages, thus suffering but not knowing the passage of time. He is ultimately awakened by Cynthia's power and by her power again restored to youth—that is, he is returned to iconic time. The mutability of time is thus overcome not by a character acting to overcome an obstacle, but by means of a magic kiss given in grace. The final image of the play, the eternal adoration of Cynthia by Endimion, is a wan admission by Lyly that iconic time is no more than a fantasy. Yet it is a fantasy he continues to pursue, for in 1600 through another song, he delivers an Ode to Cynthia in which he celebrates the way "time which all doth mowe [down],/ Her alone doth cherish."[9]

That Shakespeare contributed to the erosion of iconic time is evident in a curious example embedded in the much-disputed connection of *The Taming of the Shrew* to *The Taming of a Shrew*. The exact nature of that connection remains to be convincingly explicated. Perhaps the comparison I draw here will add another perspective to the view of their relationship.

Many parts of the two plays are tantalizingly alike, yet they are different, too. Among these curiously similar-dissimilar sections are the final speeches on obedience spoken by the two Kates. Each Kate, prompted respectively by husband Petruchio in one case and Ferando in the other, lectures her two fellow brides on the proper behavior of wife to mate. Both begin their lectures at the behest of their husbands, who tell them, in almost identical words, to inform "these headstrong women / What duty they do owe their lords and husbands."[10] Both women confirm their submission by symbolically or actually placing their hands below their husbands' feet. Thus, in circumstance, attitude, and outcome, the two scenes are much alike.

If, however, one looks not at the general situation but at the substance of each Kate's lesson, one discovers significant disparities. Shakespeare has his Kate first admonish the brides for their unfriendly glances at their husbands. She then expounds on woman's nature. When moved—that is, impassioned—that nature loses its clarity and brilliance. Accordingly, woman must restrain herself. Man's authority is certified not only by the natural order of things but by his commitment to hard labor for the woman. Man's superior right is thus founded partly on an economic contract and partly on the biological distinction between his strength and her frailty.

The Kate of *A Shrew* speaks in another voice. Her opening statement, instead of being specifically directed at the "headstrong women," has a more declamatory tone.

> Then you that live thus by your pompered wills,
> Now list to me and marke what I shall say. . . .
>
> [18.15–16]

This injunction could very well be aimed at women in the audience as readily as at the female characters on stage. In this respect the opening is a throwback to the direct address of the 1560s and 1570s, rather than an expression of the more indirect forms of the late 1580s and 1590s.

Kate then goes on to speak of God's power and to describe the creation of the world out of chaos.

> The first world was, a forme, without a forme,
> A heape confusd a mixture all deformd. . . .
>
> [18.23–24]

God in heaven brought order and

> made all things to stand in perfit course,
> Then to his image he did make a man,
> Olde *Adam* and from his side asleepe,
> A rib was taken. . . .

[18.30–33]

Thus, woman's origin stems from the establishment of order in the universe and so God's example must be taken as a precedent. Kate asserts that

> As *Sara* to her husband, so should we,
> Obey them, love them, keepe, and nourish them.

[18.37–38]

The conclusion is hurried and may reflect textual corruption. It ends where Shakespeare concludes, with Kate laying her hand beneath her husband's foot.

Immediately it is apparent that Kate's speech in *A Shrew* is cosmic and moral rather than contractual and biological. Its argument is eternal, unchanging. It assumes the pervasiveness of iconic time. By comparison, the argument of Shakespeare's Kate unfolds in historic time. Her words are subject to challenge. Once time has reduced the importance of man's hardiness and rebutted the charge of woman's weakness, as now it has, the lesson loses its force.

The author of *A Shrew*—if it was not Shakespeare—must have assumed the existence of iconic time. Early in Kate's speech he is at pains to have Kate evoke a special order of time. Before going on to describe how God created form out of void, she invokes his eternal power

> that with his only breath,
> Shall cause this end and this beginning frame.

[18.17–18]

That power of his, moreover, shall operate

> Not in time, nor before time, but with time.

[18.19]

How better to express God's moving, timeless presence! The line places Kate's instruction to her sisters in the frame of iconic time. The rhetorical and declamatory manner of her utterance is the necessary instrument for manifesting this temporal state, and so calls for some form of hieratic performance.

The comparison of the two speeches tends to support the hypothesis that Shakespeare's *Shrew* follows the anonymous *Shrew*. It suggests a Shakespeare sharing a prevailing trend in Elizabethan dramaturgy. His far superior version of Kate's speech is not merely an improvement in quality, however, but a difference in kind. The two versions appear as a crossroads in the shift from one type of perception to another.

Yet if *The Shrew* reveals Shakespeare moving toward historic time, *King Lear* shows him wrestling with its oppressive power. Whatever else it is, the tragedy is also a battleground for the iconic and historic conceptions of time, a battleground laid out from the very start. Puzzling though it often seems, the first scene is unquestionably a demonstration of sorts. Lear thinks he can display the unshakeable state of familial devotion because he assumes that he inhabits iconic time. His injunctions to Apollo and the Olympian pantheon reflect this conviction. But the clarity and steadiness of iconic time is yielding to another temporal scheme, one full of discord and treasons, one where son is "against father . . . father against child," one full of confusion for many of the characters—Lear, Gloucester, Edgar, Albany.[11] "We have seen the best of our time," says Gloucester (1. 2. 109).[12] And there lies the tragedy: it is in the triumph of historic time with all its uncertainties, changes, and conflicts. Edgar thinks that by resorting to the courtly action of iconic time, trial by combat, he can restore virtue to the world. But there is no restoration, no reconciliation. Time is irreversible. As the final speaker says (is it Albany? is it Edgar?), "The weight of this sad time we must obey . . ." (5. 3. 324).

But the shift from iconic to historic was not absolute. Although the affirmation of iconic time went out of fashion, it did not disappear entirely. It resurfaces again and again in a wide variety of plays by Shakespeare and other writers such as Jonson, Heywood, and even Webster. It helps to relieve and vary the relentless march of historic time. Its occasional reappearance in the later plays reminds the new age of the timeless universe that once existed. Nor are these traces of iconic time merely a memory of another day. The theater of the present is actively engaged in trying to recreate illusions of absoluteness. In the work of Peter Brook, Jerzy Grotowski, and Joseph Chaikin, in the experiments of Robert Wilson, and in the writing of the African Wole Soyinka, the theater seems to reverse the ravages of history and discover new dimensions of iconic time.[13]

Notes

1. John Lyly, *Sapho and Phao*, in *The Complete Works of John Lyly*, ed. R. W. Bond (Oxford: Clarendon Press, 1902), 2. All quotations from *Sapho and Phao* are from this text.

2. Muriel C. Bradbrook, *English Dramatic Form* (New York: Barnes & Noble, 1965), p. 14.

3. Plato, *The Republic*, Book 2, trans. Paul Shorey, in Loeb Classical Library (London: Heinemann, 1930), 1:189–93.

4. G. F. Waller, *The Strong Necessity of Time* (The Hague: Mouton, 1976), p. 18.

5. Ricardo J. Quinones, *The Renaissance Discovery of Time* (Cambridge, Mass.: Harvard University Press, 1972).

6. *Like Will to Like* as printed in *Tudor Interludes*, ed. P. Happe (Baltimore, Md.: Penguin Books, 1972), p. 348.

7. *The Trial of Treasure* (1567) C 4ʳ19–D 2ʳ22, in Students' Facsimile Edition (J. S. Farmer, 1914?).

8. John Lyly, *Endimion*, in *Complete Works*, ed. Bond, 3. All quotations from *Endimion* are from this text.

9. John Lyly, *Ode on Cynthia*, in *Complete Works*, ed. Bond, 1:414–15.

10. *The Taming of The Shrew*, 5. 2. 135–36 (Pelican edition of William Shakespeare, *The Complete Works*, ed. Alfred Harbage [Baltimore, Md.: Penguin Books, 1969]). The equivalent lines by Ferando are "tell unto these hedstrong women/What dutie wives doo owe unto their husbands," *The Taming of A Shrew*, sc. 18. 13–14, as printed in *Narrative and Dramatic Sources of Shakespeare*, ed. G. Bullough (London and New York: Routledge and Kegan Paul/Columbia University Press, 1966), vol. 1.

11. The iconic enactment of son against father, father against child is prefigured in Shakespeare's *Henry VI, part 3*, 2. 5. 55–93.

12. All quotations from *King Lear* come from the Pelican edition of the play.

13. I have in mind Peter Brook's "mythic" productions of *The Ik* and *Ubu Roi* as well as the general style of Robert Wilson's work. For Wole Soyinka, see *Death and the King's Horseman* (London: Eyre Methuen, 1975).

The Word in the Theater

by INGA-STINA EWBANK

When Othello claims that "it is not words that shakes me thus,"[1] he is
both terribly wrong and terribly right; and in that apparent paradox lies
my subject. He is wrong, insofar as *words* are what has brought him to
this pass: the power of one man to affect by words alone ("the ocular
proof," such as it is, is yet to come) the will and mind and whole vision of
reality in another. What is more, *words* are at this moment in the theater
shaking the audience. His line is part and pivot of a speech peculiarly
designed to do this: it begins with some grimly uncomic puns on the
words "lie" and "belie" and continues into a verbal demonstration that
"Othello's occupation's gone." Chaos—the words show—has come again,
into Othello's logic ("First, to be hanged, and then to confess") and into
his syntax, which dissolves into a repetition of keywords ("Confess?—
Handkerchief?—O devil!"). But Othello is also right, insofar as words
are just the means Iago has used, and what shakes him "thus" is the
reality (i.e., what he takes to be the reality) forced upon him, as signified
by his vision of adulterous "noses, ears and lips." And to us, the audience, the words of the speech are of course not the only signs, or signals,
sent out from the stage to shake us and, in so doing, to convey the
"thus"-ness of this moment. In the theater this will also be contained in
the actor's expression, in gestures—such as those made explicit in the
stage direction: *He fals downe*, Q1; *Falls in a Traunce*, F—and in the stage
grouping implicit in the text as Iago gloats over the insensible body
("Work on, My medicine, work").

If, then, Othello can be at the same time both right and wrong about
the place of words—cause? effect? neither? both?—in his passion, no
wonder that students of Shakespeare have found it difficult to determine precisely what is the relationship between the word and the other
elements that go to make up the theatrical experience. I take it that this
relationship is one of the concerns of this Congress, and I propose in this

paper not to presume to offer an answer but to ask some further, simple, and basic questions about it.

Of course the difficulty can be exaggerated, and barriers of distinction between "literary" and "theatrical" approaches can be erected where none need exist. It is to an exploration of Shakespeare's verbal poetry (and prose) that we owe much of the valuable criticism of the last fifty or so years, but such criticism has also usually been written by theatergoers and theater-lovers, indeed even practitioners: without mentioning anyone at this Congress, one might refer to G. Wilson Knight, Una Ellis-Fermor, and Wolfgang Clemen. In theory, at least, recent approaches agree both on the importance of the theater and on the primacy of the text. Madeleine Doran's fine book, *Shakespeare's Dramatic Language*, published in 1976, states in its opening pages that "of course language is the primary means of the theater," much as Michael Goldman, speaking in the same year to the First International Shakespeare Congress on Shakespeare's text as "a design for performance," declared that "there can be no question that Shakespeare's text must be primary for us."[2] Perhaps the problem is that, in practice, primariness has tended to turn to preoccupation: it is easier to teach students to count images and to recognize and name rhetorical patterns than it is to convey to them the language of today's subject, "The Living Theater." Not ten years ago, and in a university not a hundred miles from here, a group of undergraduates in a seminar on *The Spanish Tragedy* told me that Horatio and Belimperia go into the arbor for the purpose of having *stichomythia*. It is against such "textual imperialism" that students of semiotics of the theater wish to see the text "restored to its place of one system among the systems of the whole of the performance."[3] The aim is laudable, and yet it might precipitate—and sometimes has done so—a rush into the arms of another form of imperialism. Many who listened to Maynard Mack's Shakespeare Association Lecture in 1978 were grateful to be "rescued" from the tyranny of "the School of Performance," which holds that "Shakespeare's plays are only to be known aright in actual productions,"[4] for, as Professor Mack pointed out, that way to "knowledge" lies a dangerous relativism: which production, of which period in theater history? or even; which performance of which production? Many more fight shy of theater semiotics for fear or suspicion of the mixture of practical commonsense with an outlandish vocabulary that seems to characterize this discipline. Not everyone is prepared to read to the end of a sentence like this:

> By disambiguating (or by rendering still more ambiguous) the illocutionary mode of the utterances through such "illocutionary force indicators" as stress, intonation, kinesic markers and facial expressions

. . . the actor is able to suggest the intentions, purposes and motivations involved.[5]

And yet the point made—and made more lucidly, if with a dubious conclusion, in the next sentence: "If dramatic discourse were illocutionarily self-sufficient on the page, the performance would be all but superfluous"—is crucial. It reminds us that Shakespeare's was the spoken and acted, as against written, word.

We should not need reminding that by an inflection of voice and a facial expression—to simplify the list of "indicators" above—the actress (or boy) taking the part of Olivia can determine whether the text's "Most wonderful!" (*Twelfth Night*, 5. 1. 217) signifies joy or horror at seeing two husbands instead of one, or awe before a miracle; whether she, and the play, is to be laughed *at*, or *with*, or whether the emotion is altogether too deep for laughter. We may not like a terminology that seems to turn the art of the theater into a set of "codes"—linguistic, spatial, gestural, scenographic, illuminational, and so on—but it may be preferable as an alternative to a morass of imprecision in writing about Shakespeare—and in thinking about his art, if and when not to be able to name elements also means not to be able to recognize them. Happily it is not the only alternative. Whether we call it semiotics or not, the investigation of stage "signals" can be as judicious and revealing as, to take a recent example, G. K. Hunter's essay entitled "Flatcaps and Bluecoats: Visual Signals on the Elizabethan Stage." Professor Hunter discusses costume as "a visual expression of social reality" and demonstrates that the Elizabethan stage depended on a visual "language of movement" in a "landscape of persons," and so challenges any easy assumption that the "bare stage" turned spectators into auditors.[6]

All the same, I take from this Congress a sense that Shakespeareans are at present feeling the lack of, and are searching for, a critical language that can encompass both literary and theatrical observations and value judgments. For myself, I can only hope that we shall never arrive at a set methodology or vocabulary for describing the literary *and* theatrical art of Shakespeare—a sort of Interglossa that might well freeze his plays, for us, into something less than living theater. My own experience has been that theater people and Shakespeare scholars hold each other in almost exaggerated awe and that, like Scandinavians, they communicate best when each uses his or her own language—derived, after all, from a common root. Perhaps we should each go on doing our own thing, that which we are best at, while always learning from each other.

I say this because a dichotomy has also been voiced in discussions at this Congress: as if there were an unbridgeable gap between a sophisticated literary criticism on the one hand, and a simple, emotional response to human realities in the theater on the other—a gap, for example, between *King Lear* as a structure of verbal images, allusions, and meanings, and the same play as a sequence of theatrical moments in which we are shaken by the sufferings of an old man. The latter is clearly the real thing. Or is it? Is it possible that Shakespeare scholars and critics are suffering from a guilt complex, castigating themselves for being "purely literary" (a common phrase of disapproval in the journals), and compensating by adopting would-be "theatrical" approaches that at worst belie insights otherwise arrived at? If so, rather than bending over backwards to apologize, perhaps we should stand still and realize that, even in the theater, and whatever our profession or level of education, some of our keenest responses have to be literary—or why bother to put on *King Lear,* when the audience could be directed to the nearest old folks' home? When we are moved by Shakespeare in the theater, I do not for a moment believe that the word speaks only to the scholars and literary critics, and that the rest of the audience responds to other signals. Of course there will be verbal intricacies, echoes, and so on, not available to anyone but the scholar. R. A. Foakes, in a serious and important encounter with the problem of how we respond to Shakespeare's language in the theater, has recently warned us not to "have the meaning and miss the experience."[7] I very much doubt, however, that we can separate the two, and my point in this paper is simply that, in the end, it is the word that stimulates and structures our experience.

It is Shakespeare's words I want to speak about, but this is an occasion when many of us have also been to The Other Place and in two consecutive nights seen *The Winter's Tale* and *A Doll's House,* and so a comparison may be useful. In the maps of the world we shall find not only Stratford but Skien: there is a river in both, and for all I know "there is salmons in both."[8] Certainly both *The Winter's Tale* and *A Doll's House* are about a man and his wife (and children); in both the man misunderstands his wife; both end with the wife beginning a new life: in the resolution of one, a statue comes alive, in the other a doll comes alive.

Obviously it is dangerous to find, with Fluellen, "figures in all things." The two plays spring from two very different social and dramatic traditions. *A Doll's House,* written and first staged in 1879, was conceived for a fully furnished set, to be played behind a proscenium arch.[9] *The Winter's Tale,* some 270 years earlier, was conceived for a Jacobean stage (Blackfriars and possibly also the Globe) where the visual language would consist mainly of costumes, groupings, and gestures, and where the ear would be appealed to by music as well as words. In these terms, the last— and climactic—scene of each play would seem to put comparison beyond the reach of even Fluellen. As "dear life," through music and Paulina's solemn ritual, "redeems" Hermione, the reunion of husband and wife is itself presented as a wordless miracle. In *A Doll's House* husband and wife sit down and argue out—or, she argues and he remonstrates, with less and less assurance—what has been wrong. Are we to conclude, from this, that the word is less important in Shakespeare's theater than in Ibsen's?

Clearly not. But the prima facie absurdity of such a conclusion is also an invitation to look more closely at the functions of the words in each theater. As this has to be done, initially, in minute particulars, I would turn now to two passages dramatizing the return of someone from being thought dead or from intended death, to a new life; and to have the advantage of a semantic link between the two passages, I would draw Shakespeare's from the play that most anticipates *The Winter's Tale,* namely *Pericles.*

In his attempt to put into words what he, as well as the audience, feels to be the turning point of his life (and of *A Doll's House*), Torvald Helmer reaches for a metaphor which is curiously like that in which Pericles expresses his recognition of his lost daughter:

Thou that beget'st him that did thee beget.

Pericles says that Marina has given new birth to him, Helmer that he has given new birth to Nora:

> O Helicanus, strike me, honour'd sir!
> Give me a gash, put me to present pain,
> Lest this great sea of joys rushing upon me
> O'erbear the shores of my mortality,
> And drown me with their sweetness. O, come hither,
> Thou that beget'st him that did thee beget;
> Thou that wast born at sea, buried at Tharsus,
> And found at sea again.
>
> [*Pericles,* 5. 1. 190–97]

> Oh, you don't know how a real man feels, Nora. To a man, there is something so unspeakably sweet and satisfying in the consciousness that he has forgiven his wife,—that he has forgiven her from a full and sincere heart. For then, you know, she has, as it were, become his property in a double sense; he has, as it were, given her new birth; she has, in a way, become both his wife and his child, as well. That's how you shall be to me, here, from now on, you confused little, helpless little creature. [*A Doll's House,* act 3][10]

In both passages, extreme situations beget extreme imagery. The language offers us a perspective in which Marina becomes both daughter and mother, Nora both wife and daughter. Initially, however, the differences are likely to be more apparent than the verbal similarities.

First of all, Ibsen is using a not particularly distinguished prose, Shakespeare a haunting verse. Ibsen's language is apparently governed by the principle of verisimilitude; Shakespeare's is, in its rhythm, diction and imagery, part of the poetic whole of the play, as well as expressing character. But this does not get us very far; nor is it even wholly true. For Torvald Helmer is speaking a language that is *not* such as men do use but such as Ibsen characters do speak when the playwright wants to lay bare their motives. Helmer's speech does what we have been taught to rebuke writers, and particularly playwrights, for doing: describe emotion ("so unspeakably sweet and satisfying") rather than suggest it. But of course this is exactly the point. In Pericles' speech the strength lies in the specific realization of experience, first of the speaker's reaction to the breaking wonder ("O Helicanus, strike me . . . Lest this great sea of joys . . .") and second of his sense of what his interlocutor is and means ("Thou that . . . Thou that . . ."). In Helmer's speech the whole affair is conducted at a hazy remove from the specific, in the third person ("a real man," "a man," "he," "she") and with a generalized vision of forgiving and creating "man" making do as an insight into his own experience. He therefore also closes the door on that experience ("That's how you shall be to me, here, from now on"), whereas in *Pericles*, as C. L. Barber has so well put it, "individual experience is not lost but transformed into something more important."[11] Whether in the theater or on the page, the vocabulary, rhythm, and syntactical pattern of Helmer's speech are all part of Ibsen's dialogue with his audience: he is showing us Helmer fumbling to build a fiction to square with his assumptions about life, to create a wife—and a relationship—that we know does not exist. The ineptitude is Helmer's, not Ibsen's. The very inelegance of the character's language points to an underlying uncertainty:[12] the repeated qualifying phrase ("as it were"), the tautology of "both" and "as well" in one clause. The gentleman doth protest too much. Torvald Helmer is giving himself *away;* the play's action has moved out of his reach. Pericles is *giving* himself, to an experience so beyond even "points that seem impossible" that the only way to render it is literally to put into the simplest words the plot and his daughter's curriculum vitae (the two at this point being one): "Thou that wast born at sea, buried at Tharsus, / And found at sea again." Pericles' definition of Marina becomes a *credo*, Helmer's of Nora ("you confused little, helpless little creature") a travesty. Each in his way shakes us with his words: Helmer's prose with its desperate, self-enclosed lack of understanding, and Pericles' verse with its opening out of understanding into knowledge, suggesting dimensions that we can only call religious.

The language of these characters, then, not only conveys to the audience their respective experiences, but it also stirs and guides our imaginative apprehension of the meaning of those experiences. Again the gulf between the passages looms large, as Ibsen is aiming at ironic detachment in the audience, Shakespeare at an unquestioning wonder. Ibsen's art here is the exposing of illusion, Shakespeare's a revelation of truth. Yet, even as we pursue this distinction, it begins to dissolve itself into a similarity, a shared function of language in the theater: that of forming a "grammar" of relationships. Incidentally, too, it begins at the same time to become clear that there are larger issues at stake in *A Doll's House* than simply female emancipation (not that this is, in itself, a simple issue).

Shortly before he speaks the lines quoted, Helmer has learned of Nora's forgery, and his only thought has been for himself, his own "ruined happiness" and his "future, laid waste." Nora had been expecting this revelation to produce a "miracle" of mutual love, and she had been intending to sacrifice her life in order to prevent Helmer from sacrificing his honor for her. What actually happens is almost exactly the opposite. Nora goes, leaving husband and children, but not the way, or for the reasons, she had expected to go. The dialogue immediately after the revelation in which Nora offers her love, only to have it rejected as "play-acting," brings her to a sudden "understanding." The letter from Krogstad arrives, removing all danger of public exposure; Helmer has to be prodded by Nora to modify his instinctive reaction, "I am saved!", to a half-grudging "You, too, of course; we are saved, both of us"; and by tearing and burning the IOU he thinks to have transformed the past agony into a mere "dream." Nora's attitude is unintelligible to him, and as we move into the moment held by the quoted lines, all he can (or dare) think is that she is unable to grasp the fact that he has forgiven her. By now he is alone on stage, speaking to Nora, who is packing to leave (though he does not know it) on the other side of the door. That door and Ibsen's stage direction for waiting for Nora—"*walks about near the door*"—are the visual images of a loneliness and separateness, tragicomically self-inflicted, which Helmer's monologue translates into words. One could hardly think of a greater contrast to this theatrical image than the *Pericles* reunion, with its supreme togetherness. Pericles' self-imposed isolation shattered, father and daughter form a grouping that is ineluctably moving, and the participation of Helicanus, the bystander, no doubt contributes to the effect. As so often, Shakespeare's words contain stage directions; they imply a pattern of movement and vision ("O, come hither," "O Helicanus, Down on thy knees," "Rise; thou art my child."). In both situations, the words of the text are indeed only an element of the communication in the theater, and in both the visual image has an emblematic clarity that conveys in an instant something of the essence of, respectively, a broken relationship and a reunion. But only something: for a full realization of this particular breach or reunion we need the words spoken. For, in both situations, it is the language—its rhythm and diction, its tenses and moods—that provides what I would call the grammar of the situation: that establishes the present moment in relation to what has been and what will be, to what could have been and what might be. And in so doing, it renders the specificness of this moment as well as its connection with wider issues.

This is where the Shakespearean comparison helps us to be aware of the magnitude of what Helmer is so trivially saying, in lines like "he has, as it were, given her new birth; she has, in a way, become both his wife and his child, as well." One might imagine a different *Doll's House*[13] in which a new Helmer and a new Nora—their relations transformed— were reunited. Such a "miracle of miracles" is hinted at in Nora's closing speeches, but surely only with the effect of a tantalizing impossibility, as there is no sign of the "*forvandling*" ("transformation") that would have to take place for them to get together again. In *Pericles* and *The Winter's Tale,* as C. L. Barber pointed out, "those recovered become ikons for a pious love which finds in them the mysterious powers which create and renew life."[14] *A Doll's House* sets up a deliberate antitype to that kind of resolution. Helmer's rather perversely comic image of himself as both husband and father (or mother? or God?) is different in kind and not just in degree from the male chauvinism of regarding Nora as his "property in a double sense." Its celebration of his own generative powers, denying those powers in Nora, is a culpable infringement of nature. Helmer denies not only Nora's independence (as he has been doing throughout the play) but also her femininity and so closes himself off from the regenerative power in life. Pericles recovers not only Marina but, in his apprehension of her, that very power: "Thou that beget'st him that did thee beget."

There are no recovered relations in *A Doll's House,* only Nora's recovery—or, rather, discovery—of herself. In itself, this is of course a quintessential Ibsenism. It is as true for Nora as for Helmer, and for all of Ibsen's heroes and heroines, that they are and remain largely unaware of the identities, needs, and potentials of anyone outside their own supreme selves. They do not on the whole listen, as Pericles listens to Marina, or Leontes to Paulina—or as Lear learns to listen to Cordelia— and they are more likely to die gazing up to a mountaintop (literal or metaphorical) than into someone else's face, hoping to see a sign of life there. Even the *Liebestod* at the end of *Rosmersholm* comes about to prove to Rosmer that his calling—to ennoble others—has borne fruit, and not in order to die upon a kiss. In Ibsen's plays, the quest leads away from the family; it is the lonely individual's search for himself, usually at the expense of others—all those women who never became wives and those children who never grew up.[15] The stark geography that is part of the greatness of an Ibsen play—whether its stage setting is a realistic parlor or a symbolical mountain—is made up of such individuals, whose trajectories may meet (indeed collide) but never merge, except as in the burned-out resignation of the visual and verbal image that closes *John Gabriel Borkman:*

> *Mrs. Borkman.* We two—twin sisters—over the man we both loved.
> *Ella.* We two shadows—over the dead man.

Shakespeare's "bare" stage, on the other hand, is from the beginning to the end of his career in the fullest sense a landscape of people—one in which individuals are utterly involved in their relationships with others and where their words trace that involvement, whether in the conventional diction of an early comedy—

> Silvia is myself; banish'd from her
> Is self from self. A deadly banishment—
> [*Two Gentlemen of Verona*, 3.1.72–73]

or in the poignancy of an ordinary phrase, such as Cleopatra's "Husband, I come." But the point is that, however different their landscapes, both Ibsen and Shakespeare—like most other dramatists—rely on the word not only to probe the minds of their characters but also to measure the space between them.

Where, finally, the *Pericles* passage is greater theater language than that from *A Doll's House* is not in the poetry as such, or in the meaning as such, but in the power of these particular lines of poetry to contract experience and meaning into one theatrical moment. If we probe the line "Thou that beget'st him that did thee beget" in a "literary" fashion, we find that its peculiar strength lies in the conjunction of vocabulary and pattern. "Beget" is in itself an emotionally charged word,[16] and the *polyptoton* is an effective rhetorical device of repetition;[17] but, joined by the grammar of the line, they come together to complete a circle, to enact that meeting of past and future in the present and that fulfilment of the family, which are what shakes us thus in the theater.

There are of course related moments in the canon. When the Abbess at the end of *The Comedy of Errors* sums up past sufferings and present joy in an image of birth,

Thirty-three years have I but gone in travail
Of you, my sons; and till this present hour
My heavy burden ne'er delivered,
                    [*The Comedy of Errors*, 5. 1. 399–401]

and when Cymbeline sees himself (like Helmer, in supreme disregard of his sex) as "a mother to the birth of three" (*Cymbeline*, 5. 5. 370), then every Shakespeare scholar and student in the audience recognizes the theme of rebirth and knows that a typical Shakespearean romance structure has been completed. Such knowledge may well enhance and enrich our experience of the *Pericles* reunion, as may the recognition of an allusion to the Mother of God in "Thou that beget'st. . . ." But my concern is equally with the nontypical aspects of this moment: with the way, in the immediacy of the theater, we have a unique experience proved on our pulses. We are moved exactly because this is not just an emblem of rebirth; because in this particular piece of dramatic fiction this miracle is happening to this particular man; and because he speaks out his understanding of the miracle. We see and hear and feel the general *through* the particular. Pericles' words bridge the gap (if there is one) between the scholar and the nonscholar; they are as literary as they are theatrical, for the simple reason that here the language *is* the dramatic situation. If I am short of a vocabulary at this point, it may at least partly be because in this case the whole miraculous experience is beyond words.

It is time to be more general, but I hope this exegesis of the *Pericles* passage, and in the end of a single line, has shown what I mean by speaking of the language in the theater as providing the "grammar" of the situation and the experience. Pericles and the audience feel both the past and the future in an instant. A related point that needs to be made is very simple, but we sometimes forget it in our analytical labors: a Shakespeare play is not a series of emblems or separate tableaux-like moments (however much it may contain such moments). A dramatic situation is not a static sum of visual, verbal, and other signs but a dynamic meeting and interaction of people, and therefore of present, past, and future, and of the indicative and the subjunctive. The art of the dramatist is indeed to show as well as to speak; but how, except by words, do you show what does not meet the eye: not only "that within which passeth show" but also that which has been, will be, may be, or might have been, or could be if . . .? What other theatrical "code" could render Hamlet's last stance before the duel—

If it be now, 'tis not to come; if it be not to come, it will
be now; if it be not now, yet it will come—the readiness is all—
                    [*Hamlet*, 5. 2. 212–14]

or convey Macbeth's attitude to the thought of murdering Duncan (in itself a "deed without a name"): "If it were done . . ."? These are, of course, extreme examples, and ones where the grammar of the verbs very literally carries much of the burden of communication.[18] Perhaps, too, they simply take us back to the eternal *Laocoon* question of how to suggest a time dimension in the visual arts. If so, they remind us that it is in the nature of drama to be particularly dependent on that dimension, and in the nature of Shakespearean drama to build its most poignant moments on an interaction of moods and tenses.[19] Sebastian, on the verge of recognition, enriches the situation far beyond the conventional by appealing to a past that was not:

> Do I stand there? I never had a brother;
> . . . .
> . . . . I had a sister
> Whom the blind waves and surges have devour'd.
>
> [*Twelfth Night*, 5. 1. 218–21]

And Gertrude brings in a future that was not to be:

> I hop'd thou shouldst have been my Hamlet's wife;
> I thought thy bride-bed to have deck'd, sweet maid,
> And not have strew'd thy grave.
>
> [*Hamlet*, 5. 1. 238–40]

In these examples—and legions of others—the verbs come bringing images that analyze and modify the character's experience as it is transmitted to us. We are reminded that we oversimplify Shakespeare's theatrical art if we speak of it merely as visual and verbal—i.e., as if those two categories exclusively defined the means by which he works on us—and, even more, if we speak as if his visual and verbal languages merely duplicated each other—i.e., as if the words, like the text of an emblem, merely performed a literal translation of the visual statement.

To exemplify this last point, I would turn to Coriolanus's description of the procession of those who, "*in mourning habits,*" come to plead with him for Rome (*Coriolanus*, 5. 3. 22–37). It is a scene popular with Shakespeare illustrators[20] and strong in visual impact in the theater. Expressions, gestures, and groupings give the situation in sharp outline. But the drama lies not just in the fact that Coriolanus yields but in why and how he does so (and at first does not). Shakespeare has given the actor images and rhythms that suggest and verbs that define. Even the opening, apparently descriptive, lines move from a simple stage direction— "My wife comes foremost"—to show that reality lies in the eyes of the beholder:

                    then the honour'd mould
          Wherein this trunk was fram'd, and in her hand
          The grandchild to her blood.

Coriolanus is translating what he sees into what it means to him; and this provokes, but also undermines, a defiance (voiced in imperatives) of blood and emotional ties—

                    But out, affection!
          All bond and privilege of Nature break!
          Let it be virtuous to be obstinate—

which then colors his vision even as it is reported:

          What is that curtsy worth? or those dove's eyes,
          Which can make gods forsworn?

The traditional lover's diction contradicts the ostensible purpose of his rhetorical question and prepares us for the turn-about:

                              I melt, and am not
          Of stronger earth than others;

and the "melting" is then enacted in the way his vision is now both reported and interpreted in explicit or implicit "as if's":

                              My mother bows,
          As if Olympus to a molehill should
          In supplication nod; and my young boy
          Hath an aspect of intercession which
          Great Nature cries, "Deny not."

But then, in a fashion that at this stage of the play we know to be characteristic of the hero, the caesura gives space to a complete reaction and a swing to the opposite standpoint:

                              Let the Volsces
          Plough Rome and harrow Italy; I'll never
          Be such a gosling to obey instinct, but stand
          As if a man were author of himself
          And knew no other kin.

All the signs in the theater show how erroneous a premise this "as if" is, and the speech acts on the audience with an irony similar to that of the words in which Torvald Helmer, with similarly—though less heroic- ally—faulty self-knowledge, claims that it is "as if" he had given birth to his wife.

If this scene is a tableau, it is also one which makes the point that the gift of language is to communicate the complex, to convey particular and unique states of mind and relationships, and to mediate between the specific and the general. The scene in *3 Henry VI* where enter a son who has killed his father and a father who has killed his son is a harrowing emblem of civil war, but it is in the patterning of words that meaning and experience meet—words like the Son's

> And I, who at his hands receiv'd my life,
> Have by my hands of life bereaved him.
>
> [*3 Henry VI*, 2. 5. 67–68]

If this is true in a case where the characters have no other life in the play, and where their speech is very much the standard tragic idiom of the late 1580s and early 1590s (in itself a splendid idiom, capable of shaking an audience with paradoxes and antitheses, as here), then it is all the more true in the case of *King Lear*, where the entry of Lear with Cordelia dead in his arms will move us as words could not, but where the direction and the depth of the theatrical experience will depend, ultimately, on the words of Lear and of those around him. It is through Lear's repeated "Howl!", his imprecations and his vain hopes, as well as through the bystanders' speeches, revealing their absorption in Lear's experience, that the pieta of Lear and his daughter reaches inwards, to the individual agony, and outwards, to doomsday dimensions.

Thanks to such scholars as Muriel Bradbrook and Glynne Wickham we are now aware of how deeply rooted Shakespeare's drama is in pageantry and other emblematic arts of the period. We owe it to these scholars not to confuse the root that they have laid bare with the tree that is the living theater. It is important to remember that drama becomes drama exactly where it fuses its pageant and emblem origin with the specific and dynamic realization of human life that can only be communicated by words—and by words that do not simply illustrate a picture. Where they do so in Shakespeare, as in the procession of *imprese* in *Pericles*, 2. 2 (which may not be Shakespeare's, in any case), some character is likely to crop up to warn of the limits of visual signs, as does Simonides after interpreting Pericles' emblem and "motto":

> Opinion's but a fool, that makes us scan
> The outward habit by the inward man.
>
> [*Pericles*, 2. 2 55–56]

Hamlet makes much the same point in his list of "codes" for conveying grief (*Hamlet*, 5. 2. 76–86). The spectacular shows of the Last Plays are also often highly verbal: Jupiter descends to Posthumus in a dream but leaves a "book" behind for his waking thoughts; Diana appears to Pericles in order to give him a specific set of instructions; and the spectacle in *The Tempest* tends to become a kind of shock therapy—preparing for Ariel's speech to the "three men of sin" or Prospero's meditation on evanescence. Characters in Shakespeare often describe what is not seen—like Duncan and Banquo on Macbeth's castle (*Macbeth*, 1. 6. 1–9), or Horatio on "the morn, in russet mantle clad" (*Hamlet*, 1. 1. 166–67)— and when they describe what is seen on stage, they are not just translating visual signs but creating out of them a mood that tells more of the speaker than of what he sees (as with Iachimo in Imogen's bedchamber, *Cymbeline*, 2. 1. 11–51) or is even quite at variance with what we see (as in Marcus's encounter with the newly ravished Lavinia (*Titus Andronicus*, 2. 4. 11–57). His emblematic imagery is often clearly *not* meant to be visualized: Paulina, described as having had (off-stage) "one eye declin'd for the loss of her husband, another elevated that the oracle was fulfill'd" (*The Winter's Tale*, 5. 2. 72–73), is no more of a squinter than Claudius "With an auspicious and a dropping eye" (*Hamlet*, 1. 2. 11). If this sounds frivolous, it may be because simply to describe what is seen tends to invite platitude. We can surely tell Shakespeare's awareness of this from the following speech by Constance. She is talking to Salisbury who, off-stage, has told her of the marriage of the Dauphin to Blanch; and, as she runs through all the codes of the theater with more heat than intelligence, her unwillingness to believe his news makes her sound like a very bad semiologist:

> What dost thou mean by shaking of thy head?
> Why dost thou look so sadly on my son?
> What means that hand upon that breast of thine?
> Why holds thine eye that lamentable rheum,
> Like a proud river peering o'er his bounds?
> Be these sad signs confirmers of thy words?
>
> [*King John*, 2. 2. 19–24]

In regard to speaking pictures, one feels, Shakespeare would have agreed with Blake's sneer at "Moral Painting": "That which can be made Explicit to the Idiot is not worth my care."[21] Of course Shakespeare draws on emblems, but for his own, dramatic purposes. When Pericles addresses Marina thus:

> Yet thou dost look
> Like Patience gazing on kings' graves, and smiling
> Extremity out of act,
>
> [*Pericles*, 5. 1. 136–38]

what moves us is not the funereal emblem as such but the fact that it is spoken by a prince who has suffered to a girl who has suffered equally but who is about to give him new life, rather than gaze on his grave. The interplay between what we see and what we hear takes us into regions where the categories of "visual" and "verbal" cannot satisfactorily describe the total impact.

I do not wish to appear to be underestimating the visual element in Shakespeare's plays, and particularly not in the Last Plays—where, after all, a whole scene in *The Winter's Tale* is devoted to gentlemen describing "a sight which was to be seen, cannot be spoken of" (5. 2). In the reunion of Leontes and Polixenes, "there was speech in their dumbness, language in their very gesture" (ll. 13–14), much as there will be in the reunion of Hermione and Leontes, their gestures described in the stage directions spoken by Polixenes and Camillo: "She embraces him!" "She hangs about his neck!" (5. 3. 111–12). I merely wish to emphasize Shakespeare's awareness, and his use, of the complexity of the interaction of word and vision. For act 5, scene 2, in *The Winter's Tale* is after all not a dumb-show; the vision (and how much of it do we visualize?) is created in words, and some of these point to the imprecision or ambiguity of a purely visual scene:

> A notable passion of wonder appeared in them; but the wisest behold-
> er that knew no more but seeing could not say if the importance was
> joy or sorrow.
>
> [Ll. 16–18]

Imogen, brought in disguise to Milford Haven, questions Pisanio's expression and gestures in a speech that at first may seem much like that by Constance which I just quoted:

> What is in thy mind
> That makes thee stare thus? Wherefore breaks that sigh
> From th'inward of thee? . . .
> . . . .
> Why tender'st thou that paper to me, with
> A look untender?
>
> [*Cymbeline*, 3. 4. 4–12]

But here the questioning is real and fearful of the unspeakable ("One but painted thus," Imogen says, "Would be interpreted a thing perplex'd / Beyond self-explication," ll. 6–8). It is also part of an issue that pervades the whole theatrical art of *Cymbeline:* the discrepancy between what is seen and what is. This dominates the scene where Imogen misreads the signs of the headless corpse she finds (4. 2). Here, as in the scene in *The Tempest* (2. 1) where the grass is green to Gonzalo but "tawny" to Antonio, or as in Leontes's descriptions of the "nothings" that he sees (*The Winter's Tale*, 1. 2. 284–95), Shakespeare is pursuing his interest in the imagination that makes us create what we see.

In his own art, of course, he relies on this aspect of the imagination all the time, making us accept as "real" characters, for the duration of the play, the actors we see move about on the stage, and telling us—as extreme examples—to swallow such blatant visual absurdities as the supposed identity of appearance in Sebastian and Cesario/Viola, or in the two pairs of twins in *The Comedy of Errors*. Within the plays, characters are variously concerned with reading what they see as they want to, or with seeing what they want to see. King John, thinking that Hubert has murdered young Arthur, ironically turns on him for having been party to an act of communication that did not pass through speech:

> But thou didst understand me by my signs
> And didst in signs again parley with sin;
> Yea, without stop, didst let thy heart consent
> And consequently thy rude hand to act
> The deed which both our tongues held vild to name.
> [*King John*, 4. 2. 237–41]

There are anticipations here of *Macbeth*, which is perhaps the play where Shakespeare most fully explores the power of ambiguity of "signs," not only in speech but also in visual imagery, from the "fatal vision" of the dagger to the coming of Birnam wood to Dunsinane. In the show that the witches put on for him in act 4, scene 1, Macbeth reacts much as Dr. Faustus does when he thinks that the show of the Seven Deadly Sins is a sight "as pleasant to me as paradise was to Adam the first day of his creation."[22] Allowed only to "listen, but speak not," he becomes a wishful iconographer, completing the Third Apparition's "motto,"

> Macbeth shall never vanquish'd be, until
> Great Birnam Wood to high Dunsinane Hill
> Shall come against him,

with an unhesitating

> That will never be.
> [*Macbeth*, 4. 1. 92–94]

Macbeth makes his own reality out of words, until the tongue and sword of Macduff (5. 8. 7 and 16) slice through it. The irony, to the audience, is that it backfires: when Macbeth names "our dear friend Banquo, whom we miss. / Would he were here!", the Ghost of Banquo appears. Both he and Lady Macbeth call for a world where name and deed (the "it" of "If it were done"), and deed and vision, are separated ("yet let that be / Which the eye fears, when it is done, to see," 1. 4. 52–53); and they produce unspeakable horrors and deeds that "Tongue nor heart cannot conceive nor name" (2. 3. 63). Truly "nothing is but what is not."

There are, of course, moments in Shakespeare when a character will tell us that what we see is truer than any fiction, beyond words: Edgar's comment on the meeting of mad Lear and blind Gloucester—

> I would not take this from report. It is,
> And my heart breaks at it—
>
> > [*King Lear*, 4. 6. 141–42]

or Paulina's on the "statue" of Hermione,

> That she is living,
> Were it but told you, should be hooted at
> Like an old tale: but it appears she lives
> Though yet she speak not.
>
> > [*The Winter's Tale*, 5. 3. 115–18]

But far more often he builds his drama on characters who use words to invent a reality at variance with the visual signs we perceive. Thus the conscious deceivers—Iago making Othello see Desdemona as a whore, Richard Gloucester getting his way with Lady Anne—as well as the more or less deliberately self-deceived, from Proteus ("I will forget that Julia is alive, / Rememb'ring that my love to her is dead," *Two Gentlemen of Verona*, 2. 6. 27–28) to Leontes ("Ha' not you seen, Camillo. . . . My wife is slippery?" *The Winter's Tale*, 1. 2. 267–74). All of them, in words, make their own version of reality. In one sense they all repeat in small what Shakespeare and the actors do at large. In another sense they remind us—thus bringing me back to my point that language is the grammar of the dramatic situation—that all language (whether or not we agree with the theory that language originated with the need to deceive) has the power to create that which is not seen, and to suggest that which is not. It may be only the momentary glimpse of a possibility contained in an "if":

> Lend me a looking glass;
> If that her breath will mist or stain the stone,
> Why, then she lives.
>
> > [*King Lear*, 5. 3. 261–63]

If Lear's words enrich our experience of the ending of the play by a thought, however fleeting, of the tragicomedy that might have been; and if the king at the end of *All's Well* forces a passing glance at the tragedy that could (and some think should) have come about—

> All yet seems well, and if it end so meet,
> The bitter past, more welcome is the sweet—

then it is probably time that we devoted more attention to the dramatic and theatrical function of Shakespeare's grammar, a subject surprisingly unexplored, despite Dolores Burton's pioneering book.[23] There is a whole book to be written on Shakespeare's use of the word *if* alone: on the glorious disappearance of conditionality from Rosalind's *if*'s that resolves *As You Like It*;[24] on the gaping horror of the *if*'s by which Troilus tries to refuse to accept the reality of what he has seen ("If beauty have a soul, this is not she. . . ," *Troilus and Cressida*, 5. 2. 136–40); or on the troubled effect of the speech in which Isabella kneels to ask the Duke to look upon Angelo "as if my brother liv'd" (*Measure for Measure*, 5. 1. 443). An *if* can justify the ways of God to men and hold, as in Lear's lines, all happiness or unhappiness:

> This feather stirs; she lives! if it be so,
> It is a chance which does redeem all sorrows
> That ever I have felt.
>
> [*King Lear*, 5. 3. 265–67]

Lear is in a situation—like Edgar's "It is, / And my heart breaks at it"— where what he says cannot create a reality against what he sees, and we see. Or can it?

> Do you see this? Look on her, look, her lips,
> Look there, look there!
>
> [Ll. 310–11]

Is this seeing or saying; is the image that the audience receives mainly visual or verbal? Is it words that shake us thus?

Perhaps, finally, this can best be answered by a return to the statue scene in *The Winter's Tale*. If this is an emblematic or masquelike moment, it also has a grammar and syntax that convey the past of the sixteen years compressed into the play's structure, and the future that might grow out of it. The statue dominates, visually, but after an initial silence, as it is "discovered" to him, Leontes weaves a web of tenses and moods round the visual object:

Leontes.	Her natural posture!
	Chide me, dear stone, that I may say indeed
	Thou art Hermione; or rather, thou art she
	In thy not chiding; for she was as tender
	As infancy and grace. But yet, Paulina,
	Hermione was not so much wrinkled, nothing
	So aged as this seems.
Polixenes.	O, not by much.
Paulina.	So much the more our carver's excellence,
	Which lets go by some sixteen years and makes her
	As she liv'd now.

Leontes.   As now she might have done,
So much to my good comfort as it is
Now piercing to my soul. O, thus she stood,
Even with such life of majesty, warm life,
As now it coldly stands, when first I woo'd her!
                                        [*The Winter's Tale*, 5. 3. 23–36]

It is a natural human reaction that the statue should have "my evils conjur'd to remembrance" (as Leontes goes on to say). It is also natural to Leontes—a sign of the same lively imagination as once found Hermione's "entertainment" of Polixenes "Too hot, too hot!"—to make up a kind of dialogue with the statue ("Chide me . . ."). As he moves from a present "thou" to the "she" of a remembered past and back to the present and "this," he is unwittingly performing a dress-rehearsal of the moment to come, when all those pronouns will merge—and be swallowed up in silence. The alleged carver's realism—"As [if] she liv'd now"—stings Leontes into a sense of what "might have" been, the immediacy of the "piercing" performed by the "it" (the vagueness of the antecedent making "it" refer both to the "comfort" that might have been and the regret that it is not) suggested by the way he completes the rhythmic unit begun by Paulina. This stance, in turn, blurs into an indicative past, as the image of the statue "As now it coldly stands" is overlaid with that, of "such life of majesty, warm life," of the Hermione he once wooed. When, a few moments later, the "statue" is discovered to be alive—"O, she's warm!"—and the "as if" becomes a "thus," he is silent, but to the audience the very silence of Leontes is structured by the words we have heard.

In the systems of signs that go to make up Shakespearean drama, it is impossible to say that one has priority over all the others. A playwright's imagination creates the character and the action in which he finds himself—be he Leontes, or Othello, or Torvald Helmer—and suggests to the actor what response to elicit from the audience. But if we have to say through what it creates, we could find worse answers than the Gospel's: "In the beginning was the Word."

Notes

1. *Othello*, 4. 1. 41. M. R. Ridley, in the New Arden edition of the play, follows the Old Arden in silently "correcting" the main verb to the plural—"shake"—thus missing the effect surely suggested by the folio's "shakes": that the real antecedent of the verb is not "words" but the terrible, unspeakable discovery—that which has caused the "shadowing passion" of the previous sentence. The usage—singular verb in a relative clause where the antecedent is plural—is not unique either in the period or in Shakespeare (see Variorum ed. note on *Othello*, 1. 3. 12), but in this line Shakespeare would seem to be putting

grammatical license to a unique use. The line (like the surrounding ones, from "To confess" to "devil") is in F and Q2 but not in Q1; and I cannot agree with Ridley when he is "not clear that F's lines add much," or when he thinks that they are justified only because "Othello's raving passion needed for verisimilitude longer to develop before he 'falls in a trance.'"

2. Madeleine Doran, *Shakespeare's Dramatic Language* (Madison: University of Wisconsin Press, 1976), p. 4; Michael Goldman, "Acting Values and Shakespearean Meaning: Some Suggestions," in David Bevington and Jay L. Halio, eds., *Shakespeare: Pattern of Excelling Nature* (Newark: University of Delaware Press, 1978), p. 190.

3. Susan Bassnett-McGuire, in "An Introduction to Theatre Semiotics," *Theatre Quarterly* (Winter 1980): 50, quoting Patrice Pavis.

4. Maynard Mack, *Rescuing Shakespeare* (Oxford: International Shakespeare Assn., 1979).

5. Keir Elam, *The Semiotics of Theatre and Drama* (London: Methuen, 1980), p. 166.

6. In *Essays and Studies 1980* (London: English Association), 1980, pp. 16–47.

7. R. A. Foakes, "Poetic Language and Dramatic Significance in Shakespeare," in P. Edwards, I-S. Ewbank, and G. K. Hunter, eds., *Shakespeare's Styles: Essays in Honour of Kenneth Muir* (London: Cambridge University Press, 1980), p. 92.

8. *Henry V*, 4. 7. 15ff.

9. Adrian Noble's superb production of the play at The Other Place, Stratford-upon-Avon, in the summer of 1981, made it clear that Ibsen's "realism" is a matter not so much of verisimilitude as of his making real what he wants us to see. Set "in the round," the production gave us a box (or doll's house) with all four walls removed—a world both enclosed and exposed, realized through intense theatrical moments.

10. The Ibsen passage is my own literal translation.

11. C. L. Barber, "'Thou that beget'st him that did thee beget': Transformation in *Pericles* and *The Winter's Tale*," in *Shakespeare Survey 22* (New York: Cambridge University Press, 1969), p. 67.

12. In the Criterion Theatre production of the play in 1973, Colin Blakeley as Helmer made much of this uncertainty: he seemed utterly lost, repeating words he did not believe in, and so managed to draw the audience's sympathy towards Helmer at this point.

13. Obviously I am not thinking of the happy-ending version of *A Doll's House* that Ibsen had to agree to for German consumption, nor of the English one called *Breaking a Butterfly*.

14. C. L. Barber, "'Thou that beget'st him . . . ,'" p. 61.

15. For women, see, e.g., Lona Hessel in *Pillars of the Community*, Ella Rentheim in *John Gabriel Borkman*, and Irene in *When We Dead Awaken*; for children drowned, lost by fire, or simply wasted for lack of sunshine, see *Little Eyolf*, *The Master Builder* and *Brand*.

16. Apart from its biblical associations, reference to other Shakespeare plays shows that there is much literal begetting in the Histories, and much metaphorical begetting—of opinion, falsehood, villainy, remedy, temperance, friends, love, etc.—in other plays; and that in the late plays the word tends to be associated with a sense of wonder. The arrival of Florizel and Perdita reminds Leontes that he "lost a couple that 'twixt heaven and earth/ Might thus have stood begetting wonder as/You, gracious couple, do" (*The Winter's Tale*, 5. 1. 131–33); and in *Two Noble Kinsmen* Arcite tells Palamon: "We are one another's wife, ever begetting/New births of love" (2. 1. 134–35: Penguin ed.).

17. For the *polyptoton*, see Warren Taylor, *Tudor Figures of Rhetoric* (Whitewater, Wis.: Language Press, 1972), p. 119. There is a pattern very similar to that in *Pericles* in *King John*, 3. 1. 315, where Constance urges the French to resume arms against the English, and Blanch, newly married to the Dauphin, asks him "What motive may/Be stronger with thee than the name of wife?" to which Constance replies: "That which upholdeth him that thee upholds,/His honour." But the effect here is of cruel irony, rather than affirmed mutuality; nor is there a time element built into the verb as in Pericles' two *begets*.

18. Cf. Francis Berry, *Poet's Grammar: Person, Time and Mood in Poetry* (London: Routledge, 1958), especially the section entitled "Macbeth: Tense and Mood," pp. 48–57.

19. Just as Ibsen builds the past into his plays by visual signs—the family portraits on the wall in *Rosmersholm*, e.g., or Osvald's kissing of Regina—so Shakespeare of course relies on nonverbal patterns to relate the present to the past: the two severed heads in *Macbeth*, e.g., or the repeated kneelings in *King Lear*. Modern producers have tended to underscore such continuities and contrasts: one remembers, to take a glaring example, the reappearances of the council table in the Peter Hall/John Barton *Wars of the Roses*. The future—let alone the subjunctive mood—is rather less amenable to visual representation, however.

20. Cf. Moelwyn Merchant, *Shakespeare and the Artist* (London: Oxford University Press, 1959), chap. 11, pp. 178–89.

21. Letter to the Rev. Dr. Trusler, August 23, 1799, in *The Complete Writings of William Blake*, ed. Geoffrey Keynes (London: Oxford University Press, 1966), p. 793.

22. *Dr. Faustus*, ed. John D. Jump (Revels ed., Cambridge, Mass.: Harvard University Press, 1962), sc. 6, ll. 108–9.

23. Dolores Burton, *Shakespeare's Grammatical Style* (Austin: University of Texas Press, 1973).

24. Maura Slattery Kuhn has a discussion of *if*'s at the end of *As You Like It* in "Much Virtue in *If*," *Shakespeare Quarterly* 28 (Winter 1977): 40–50. Madeleine Doran, in *Shakespeare's Dramatic Language*, devotes her Othello chapter to "Iago's *If*: Conditional and Subjunctive in *Othello*."

"The Players . . . Will Tell All," or the Actor's Role in Renaissance Drama

by M. T. JONES-DAVIES

With *Hamlet* as a starting point, I shall refer to what is sometimes called Renaissance metadrama—i.e., plays in which the dramatists are preoccupied with the nature of playing—and more particularly to *The Knight of the Burning Pestle* and Philip Massinger's tragedy, *The Roman Actor,* where the process of production is approached critically. These plays are a sort of Defense and Illustration of the actor's role, like Pierre Corneille's later theater manifesto, *L'Illusion Comique,* of which Hamlet's questionable words "The players . . . will tell all" could be the epitome. A recent production of *L'Illusion Comique* in Paris stressed its relevance to the present topic: a magician—the poet—conjures up a game of appearances to help a wretched father—Pridament—find again his lost son, Clindor. The game of appearances turns out to be a journey of initiation into knowledge, the knowledge of others and the knowledge of self in which all is told. Pridament is made to watch a representation of his son's

Quotations are from the following editions of the plays:

Shakespeare, *The Complete Works,* ed. Peter Alexander (London: Collins, 1961).

Francis Beaumont and John Fletcher, *The Knight of the Burning Pestle,* Q1, 1613.

Philip Massinger, *The Roman Actor,* ed. Arthur Symons, the Mermaid Series (London: T. Fisher Unwin), vol. 2.

All quotations of Plato are from *The Dialogues of Plato,* trans. Benjamin Jowett, vol. 7 in *Great Books of the Western World,* ed. R. Maynard Hutchins (London: Encyclopedia Britannica, 1977). I am also indebted to Professor J. P. Dumont of the University of Lille III for directing my attention to some of Plato's texts that have been quoted.

past and present life, enacted by "speaking shadows," the actors. Clindor's latest adventures merge into a play-within-the-play, as Clindor has actually become an actor: he is seen dying an actor's death, which Pridament confuses with reality. Yet the only reality that is left materializes in the takings that the players—the false dead—are shown to share at the end of the illusion.

The Elizabethan audience, as all Renaissance audiences, is like Pridament engaged in a passionate quest of knowledge. The play's secret should be kept as long as possible, as Lope de Vega insists in his *Arte Nuevo*, since the public will turn its back on the stage when it has nothing more to learn.[1] The players are instruments of knowledge insofar as the dramatic fable is concerned, but do they really tell all about the actor's function? What can an actor really tell? Hamlet's phrase can be understood on different levels.

Quince, the clumsy Prologue to "Pyramus and Thisby" (*A Midsummer Night's Dream*, 5. 1. 116), is ready to promise

> The actors are at hand; and by their show
> You shall know all.

When in *Love's Labour's Lost* (4. 3. 74–76)—in a scene quoted in another context by Anne Barton in her book *Shakespeare and the Idea of the Play*,[2] on the evolution of the play metaphor—Berowne, who has climbed into a tree, sits like a demigod in the sky, "heedfully o'ereying . . . wretched fools' secrets," he is at once actor and spectator: he views what looks like "an old infant play"—"all hid, all hid." The playworld's secrets, their discovery or nondiscovery, and the sharing of secrets by actor and spectator are at the heart of the theater game. The spectator's privileged situation as demigod is contrasted with the fools'—the actors'—helpless condition on the theater stage and on the world stage. But this situation is apt to be reversed.

Because their role is not clearly defined, the actors are not always the mediators between poet and spectators. Plato alludes to the poet who quarreled with the actor that spoiled his poems in repeating them (*Charmides*, 162 d); and Hamlet is not the only one to complain of "the fellow that tears a passion to tatters. . . ." As Dekker writes, it sometimes "fares with [the poet and the player] as it does with good stuff and a bad taylor: it is not mard in the wearing but in the cutting out"; or "The labours of writers are as unhappie as the children of a beautiful woman, being spoiled by ill nurses, within a month after they come into the world" (*The Whore of Babylon*, Preface). Elsewhere, however, the same Dekker sums up the ideal dynamics of the theater: the actor is the link in the golden chain uniting poet and audience:

> Give me that man [the poet]
> Can give an actor Sorrow, Rage, Joy, Passion
> Whilst he again [the actor] (by self-same agitation)
> Commands the hearers, sometimes drawing out teares
> Then smiles, and fills them both with hopes and feares.
> [*If it be not good, the Devil is in it,* Prologue]

The actor's magic consists in maintaining the flow of life and feeling that passes in the dialectic established between the stage and the public.

Hamlet's statement, "The players cannot keep counsel, they'll tell all," evokes the etymological definition of the Greek word *Aletheia:* "that which does not hide"; accordingly, the players would be the spokesmen for truth, which contradicts the received idea that the actors appearing disguised on the stage are wholly committed to counterfeiting. The expression "counterfeiting players" is found in *3 Henry VI*, 2. 3. 282; and Theseus voices the common opinion about plays *and* actors when he says (*A Midsummer Night's Dream,* 5. 1. 209–11): "the best in this kind are but shadows." To Hamlet, the First Player's "function," his action together with his gestures and facial expression, act out a fiction, "and all for nothing" (2. 2. 549–50). Although in his delusive semblance he is a fraud, his artifice can move the Prince, which is not the case for the players mentioned in act 3, who "imitate humanity abominably," meaning "inhumanly," if we accept the wrong spelling of Q2 and F, "abhominably" supposedly derived from the Latin *ab homine.*

In *The Republic,* Plato had disparagingly classed the actor (*hupokritès*), together with the poet among imitators (373 b), "those whose callings are not required by any natural want," which implied the notion of imposture. The Renaissance theory of verisimilitude rescued the imitator from this stigma, and Minturno's words on the poet would apply to the actor: "Great praise is owing the poet [we could say the actor] who wins for things feigned a wondrous faith," even though the ethical view that the verisimilar should be morally useful was not forgotten.[3] Here mimetic inadequacy, rather than the actual nature of the actor's role, is underlined.

In *The Roman Actor,* Paris observes that in a tragedy "acted to the life" a guilty hearer was forced to make discovery of his murder. "Acted to the life" echoes "the very cunning of the scene"—that is, "the skilful acting" in the parallel passage of *Hamlet:* "guilty creatures sitting at a play/Have by the very cunning of the scene/Been struck so to the soul . . ." (2. 2. 585–87). Massinger's Paris (2. 1. p. 26) speaks of the stage as of a mirror where Philargus shall see himself so "Truly described, that I much hope the object/Will work compunction in him." The fiction actually performed is thought to be a practical means to communicate with the audience, and the imaginary construction is a stimulus that produces intellectual and moral, but also physical or affective reactions in the spectator. In the *Hamlet* lines on Hecuba, the hearer is called upon to identify with the actor and Hamlet wonders "What would *he* do/Had *he* the motive . . . for passion/That *I* have." The spectator is enticed into the game—which is the meaning of *in-lusio (illusio)*[4]—to share in the deliberate deception of the stage, and that because everyman is a potential actor, as Shakespeare and his fellow dramatists show: Hamlet's histrionics are a good example, as also Christopher Sly, who forgets his former self to assume the part of a lord, or Malvolio, who is only too ready to enact the playlet invented by Maria. The most striking case is that of Ralph in *The Knight of the Burning Pestle,* who accompanies his master and mistress to the Blackfriars theater, and on the spur of the moment speaks "a huffing part," successively imitates Palmerin of England, delivers the Mayday speech upon a conduit, or lords it over as captain of the militia. The reactions of George and Nell, who have launched their apprentice on this theatrical venture, enlighten the relationship of actor and audience. To the grocer and his wife, Ralph is *now* the awesome personage who can kill a lion with a pestle and relieve distressed damsels, and *now* the boy whose health they are responsible for. Wife confides to George: "I'm afraid of my boy . . . say they shall put him into a straight paire of Gaskins, 'twere worse than knot-grass, he would never grow after it . . ." (2. 2. 33–35). But their trust is infinite in the competence of their actor-apprentice because he is a "discoverer": when some "abomination knavery" is "a-brewing" in the major plot, "Rafe will find all out, I warrant you" (1. 1. 67), as Nell says.

Ralph metamorphosed into an actor is for his spectators an equivocal figure pertaining to a double world, at once true and false. When he relates the last moments of his life, how "Death caught a pound of pepper in his hand/And sprinkled all my face and body ore" (5. 3. 142–43), the citizen coolly rejects the snare of illusion and declares, "a pretty fiction, i'faith." At this point, for all his naïveté, George remains conscious that the play is a play. In the end his credulity is more or less consciously cultivated. We recall Mannoni's study on comic illusion,[5] which he explains is different from other illusions: it is not so much a question of belief or unbelief in a false reality as the acceptance of a theatrical convention making of the spectator an accomplice with the actors. George would exemplify this kind of illusion, whereas Nell somehow represents the childish fantasies that survive in each of us. They illustrate between them the complex illusion of the theater game. It is as if George, much more than Nell, were able to separate in his mind the concrete truth of the theater from the rest of reality. To him the play-world becomes autonomous; it is not like a waking dream that would be governed by the dreamer, but similar to a true dream that the dreamer, although present, cannot govern. The action is given as true, but the spectator is made to deny it in the performance: thus a constant exchange can exist between the perception of the fictional and its performance. The measure of the spectator's delight in Mimesis, Sidney's "speaking picture,"[6] in which he does not actually believe, is in proportion to his understanding. It is the pleasure of knowing that the secret of the theater is artificial. The intelligentsia, for instance the Inns of Court men, the young lawyers who would form a large part of Beaumont's audience, would most of all experience this pleasure, but a Boeotian, a fool like Nell, cannot share in it. As for George, he is slowly and gradually being educated by the theater. Education—a word related to *educere*, to lead forth—is the awareness of the *in-lusio* I have mentioned.

In *Timaeus* (72 b), Plato compares "those that some persons call prophets" to actors—*hupokritai*—because they propose the reflection of a message they do not *completely* comprehend; ". . . they are only the expositors of dark sayings and visions, and are not to be called prophets at all, but only interpreters of prophecy." But these interpreters are "honest hypocrites," as William Hazlitt describes the actors.[7] They carry the spectators with them, initiating the process of knowing, thereby apparently contradicting Plato. Like the actors in Corneille's play, by their living presence and their movement they recreate the spectator's past, appealing to the act of memory. This *anamnesis* is creative. The actors put the spectators in "remembrance of things past" in the words of Shakespeare's *Sonnet 30*. In this sense, they can tell all, setting men—thanks to reminiscence—on their way to knowledge and self-knowledge. This is an obvious allusion to Plato's *Meno* (85), which shows that recollection *is* knowledge. George recognizes in Ralph's performance his own youthful exploits with the militia. Anne Ubersfeld would here discern some sort of Proustian delight in the pleasure offered by the actor.[8] The actor also flatters the spectator's utopian wish to become *other* than he is and explore his own "Mundus Imaginalis." Ben Jonson stressed this when he wrote, "Life is like a play wherein every man, forgetful of himself, is in travail with expression of another."[9] Sly or Malvolio, George and Nell resemble mythomaniacs, attracted by what Bacon calls "vaine opinions, flattering hopes, false valuations, imaginations as one would . . ." (Of Truth). Through the mediation of Ralph, George gets his share of the inaccessible. He follows Ralph in his heroic visions of honor and is emancipated from the narrow limits of his body, just like Malvolio, who narcissistically imagines he can possess Olivia. He would be "king of infinite space" and enters what is for Gilbert Durand in his *Exploration de l'Imaginarie* "the gigantic net of dreams and desires of mankind, which also catches the small everyday realities."[10] In this sense, George is the willing dupe of the "honest hypocrite." No wonder then that the actor should have the "arrogance" to educate—that is, to lead the spectator away from everyday life to the confines of a country from where no traveler returns.

Two examples bring out the importance of the theme of death in the context of the Renaissance attempt at understanding the function of the actor. In *The Knight of the Burning Pestle* and in *The Roman Actor,* the actor is seen to die *and* not to die. The problem of the actor's death is used to question the reality of the most undeniable truth of all: death. It is as if Hamlet's alternative "to be *or* not to be" became, in the case of the actor, "to be *and* not to be."

When in *The Knight of the Burning Pestle* George insists that his actor—Ralph—must die, even in a comedy, he wants to exorcise the most widespread fear of all—the fear of death; and when the grocer commands, "Rafe, come away quickly and die, boy," he knows that Ralph will rise again after such a death—as if he were dreaming that "there could be a death that would not be true death," to quote Anne Ubersfeld once more.[11] The Elizabethan spectator is even encouraged to rediscover another reality through appearances, that of Ralph appearing as a celebrant in a rite of renewal, which the whole truly ritual comedy tends to prove, with the Mayday speech symbolizing the myth of constant rebirth and, in the major plot, with Jasper also rising from his coffin.[12]

Thus by indirections will the actor help find directions out. Thus could we define the metaphorical role of the actor, which announces the stress laid on rhetoric in the Renaissance.

As for the second example in Massinger's tragedy, the Roman actor also suffers death, but death in earnest, at the conclusion of the play within the play, *The False Servant,* put on at the request of the emperor Domitian. The emperor becomes an actor: he will act the part of the injured lord, and to revenge himself for Domitia's infatuation with Paris, kills the actor. The "true" act replaces the usual vicarious experience of tragedy. Domitian would kill in honor: like Brutus, he would be sacrificer, not butcher, "and offer a dish fit for the gods":

> 'Twas my study
> To make thy end more glorious, to distinguish
> My Paris from all others . . .
> . . . 'twas my plot that thou
> Shouldst die in action . . .
> By our imperial hand.

Like Othello he claims he has committed "an honourable murder." In contrast with the truly ritual comic ending of *The Knight of the Burning Pestle,* this would-be ritual is deceit on both levels of action and words. Domitian, originally the spectator of the play, has judged Paris by ap-

pearances only: he is Domitia's and his own dupe. And in his farewell to
Paris—"His soul is freed/From the prison of his flesh; let it mount
upward" (4. 2. pp. 70–71)—we sense mere verbal manipulation. Tragic
irony imparts added meaning to the reality of Paris's death. The false
ritual is also enhanced in the last act, when the emperor, no longer an
actor, himself falls a despicable victim to the gods' revenge. In this he
differs from Othello, who avoids the reality of social justice by becoming
an actor, histrionically reenacting one of his glorious deeds, and in his
passing vision of the "circumcised dog," deliberately smiting himself (5.
2. 358–59).

Domitian, who stands for the world of reality as opposed to the fiction
on the stage, illustrates what Yvon Belaval defines as "la duperie des
signes," such as we witness it in everyday life.[13] But he is also an actor in
the major play, and, as an "honest hypocrite," his revelation of the process of knowing is complex. As Cassius and Brutus transform Caesar's
murder into an act of liberation by imagining "the lofty scene" acted
over in sport, "in accents yet unknown" (3. 1. 113–14), Domitian would
transmute Paris's sudden death into a stage event forever to be mourned
in "ravishing sorrows" by "glad spectators" (4. 2. p. 71)—one more hint of
the actor's power to impart to a human action new metaphorical dimensions, liable to be indefinitely reinterpreted.

Plato in *The Sophist* (252 c8) speaks of Eurykles, the wonderful ventriloquist (mentioned by Aristophanes in *The Wasps*), the man with two
voices, who carries his own contradiction in himself. He is a good figure
of the actor as he appears in Massinger's play: such is the paradox that
Paris would explain to the empress. The Roman actor is one of those
actors, who, in Brutus's words, was remarkable for his "formal constancy" (*Julius Caesar*, 2. 1. 227). The actor's paradox is stated in clear
terms by Empress Domitia (4. 2. pp. 61–62):

> Thou whom oft I have seen
> To personate a gentleman, noble, wise,
> . . . .
> Thou must be really, in some degree,
> The thing thou dost present.

In his answer, Paris, with "formal constancy," sums up the actor's condition:

> The argument
> Is the same . . . that I, acting
> A fool, a coward, a traitor, or cold cynic . . .
> Of force I must be such. . . .

Then

> How glorious soever, or deformed,
> I do appear in the scene, my part being ended,
> And all my borrowed ornaments put off,
> I am no more, nor less, than what I was
> Before I entered. . . .

Diderot, in his *Paradoxe sur le Comédien,* will not say anything else when, speaking of the great actor's qualities, he observes "son égale aptitude à toutes sortes de caractères et de rôles."[14] The actor's mastery of his multiple roles implies strict control over his emotions. It is this power that paradoxically transforms reality for the spectator. He knows he is not the character he represents, but the illusion is only for the spectator. Paris hints that the dialogue between his real body and the imaginary figure he impersonates is his own secret. Domitia's conflict between her naïve credulity, which gets wholly involved in Paris's acting, and her semiconsciousness that it is more than play, is an example of what Belaval describes as the paradox of the spectator, which follows from the paradox of the actor, the two being reciprocal.[15]

Massinger's play stresses this connection between the actor's and the spectator's secret. Both actor and spectator are caught in the riddle of ambiguity; from beginning to end in *The Roman Actor,* the contrast is underlined between acting in jest and acting in earnest—not only in the playworld, but also in reality. The tone is set from the first scene, when the players have been summoned to appear in Senate "for their jesting" and must, in Paris's words, act themselves (1. 1. p. 7). Paris says:

> What'er our sentence, think 'tis in sport;
> And though condemned, let's hear it without sorrow
> As if we were to live again to-morrow.

This can be opposed to the moment in act 4 when Paris is killed "in earnest." The two occasions throw light on the actor's double existence, and when at last Paris for one instant becomes the spectator of his own death, his two voices merge into one. There remains on the stage the body of a man that is but the shadow of an actor—only a mannequin, for, as Jean Vilar wrote, "Death does not ennoble the comedian."[16]

Whether he revives as Ralph, who, however, has met with death in the Moorfields of the comedy, or whether he dies in earnest, the actor is, in Hazlitt's words, "a hieroglyphic of humanity."[17] When Paris in his defense (1. 3) explains that actors, who deserve as much "as all the sects of the philosophers," do not "search into the secrets of the time" (l. 16) in order "to traduce and condemn" others for their crimes, he holds that what they present on the stage may help change men. Yet, as the emperor cynically states, it may happen that the fiction which looks impossible in the scene is weaker than the substance—the reality of life—and that the actor's play fails to convince. Genet's remark at the end of *The Balcony* would serve as good warning to an Elizabethan audience: "You must now go home, where everything—you can be quite sure—will be falser than here."[18] Genet thus points to the specificity of the actor's role: the transformation of reality into fiction and vice versa, and hence the difficulty for the spectator in hearing the actor's message. Jean Vilar's perceptive page on Hamlet's self-deception also comes to mind: "No, Prince . . . the guilty man will not confess his crime because he is made to see its parody. . . . It is the honest man and the honest woman, whose sense of guilt has not been blunted, who share in the fates of our heroes . . . for, in the work of art, they perceive faint echoes . . . of their secret lives."[19]

We remember how Vives, in his *Fabula de Homine*, relates that once man, the archmime, had been accepted to sit as spectator of the world among the gods, the gods themselves started examining "the many hidden secrets of man and derived more pleasure from this than from the spectacle of all the plays."[20] And yet, like a hieroglyphic of mankind, the actor keeps "the heart of his own mystery," which, no more than Hamlet's, can be "plucked out" (3. 2. 356–57). Renaissance metadrama seems to hint at a specific role for the actor that is denied him by Plato, a specific place for Eurykles, "the wonderful ventriloquist, who always carries about him an adversary"; it points to a positive reading of the actor's power to embody a secret that is due to the art of metaphor enabling him to challenge the logic of verisimilitude, as was noted in the representation of death. I would therefore suggest that in spite of Hamlet's opinion, the players in the Renaissance can never be expected to tell all. One remembers Berowne's words: "All hid, all hid."

Notes

1. *L'Arte Nuevo de Hacer Comedias*, 1609. Cf. also F. L.Lucas, *Tragedy* (London: Hogarth Press, 1966), p. 104.

2. Anne Barton, *Shakespeare and the Idea of the Play* (1962; reprint ed. Westport, Conn.: Greenwood Press, 1977), p. 151.

3. Madeleine Doran, *Endeavors of Art. A Study of Form in Elizabethan Drama* (Madison: University of Wisconsin Press, 1954), p. 75. Minturno, *L'Arte Poetica*, is quoted on p. 77.

4. J. Huizinga, *Homo Ludens. Essai sur la Fonction Sociale du Jeu*, NRF (Paris: Gallimard, 1951), p. 32.

5. O. Mannoni, *Clefs pour l'Imaginaire ou l'Autre Scène* (Paris: Le Seuil, 1969): "L'Illusion Comique ou le Théâtre du point de vue de l'Imaginaire," pp. 161–81.

6. Sir Philip Sidney, *The Defence of Poesie*, 1595 ed. in *Works*, A. Feuillerat, ed., vol. 3 (Cambridge: At the University Press, 1912).

7. William Hazlitt, "On Actors and Acting," *The Examiner*, 15 January 1817, reprinted in *Drama Criticism: Developments Since Ibsen*, Casebook Series, ed. Arnold P. Hinchliffe (London: Macmillan, 1979).

8. *L'Ecole du Spectateur. Lire le Théâtre 2* (Paris: Editions Sociales, 1981), p. 315.

9. Ben Jonson, *Discoveries*, in *Works*, ed. C. H. Herford and P. Simpson (Oxford: At the University Press, 1925), 8:597.

10. Gilbert Durand, "L'Exploration de l'Imaginaire" in *Circé* I. *Etudes et Recherches sur l'Imaginaire* (Paris: Jean Burgos, 1969).

11. Ubersfeld, *L'Ecole du Spectateur*, p. 340.

12. Cf. Jackson I. Cope, *The Theatre and the Dream: From Metaphor to Form in Renaissance Drama* (Baltimore, Md.: Johns Hopkins Press, 1973), p. 209.

13. Yvon Belaval, *L'Esthétique sans Paradoxe de Diderot*, NRF (Paris: Gallimard, 1950), p. 258.

14. Denis Diderot, *Le Paradoxe sur le Comédien* (Paris: Garnier-Flammarion, 1967), pp. 128, 157.

15. Belaval, *L'Esthétique sans Paradoxe de Diderot*, p. 258.

16. Jean Vilar, *De la Tradition Théâtrale*, Idées NRF (Paris: Gallimard, 1955), p. 152.

17. Hazlitt, "On Actors and Acting," pp. 42–43.

18. Jean Genet, *Le Balcon, Oeuvres complete*, vol. 4 (Paris: Gallimard, 1968), p. 135. See trans. Bernard Frechtman, rev. ed. (New York, 1966), p. 96, mentioned by R. Egan in *Drama within Drama* (New York: Columbia University Press, 1975), p. 3.

19. Vilar, *De la Tradition Théâtrale*, p. 154.

20. Juan Luis Vives, *Fabula de Homine*, trans. Nancy Lankeith, in *The Renaissance Philosophy of Man* (Chicago: University of Chicago Press, 1948), p. 391.

"To the Judgement of Your Eye": Iconography and the Theatrical Art of Pericles

by MARY JUDITH DUNBAR

Pericles' quest involves a fresh exploration of a problem central to classical, medieval, and Renaissance thought: what is the relation of fortune to the gods and to human virtue? This problem, as ancient as the *Odyssey* to which *Pericles* is related in the literary tradition, is richly depicted in Renaissance visual arts which deepen our understanding of verbal and visual images in the play.[1] Iconographical analysis, including awareness of the context of dramatic language and situation, suggests that *Pericles* is not, as some critics have thought, "purely spectacular," or "pictures more than drama."[2] Visual presentation in *Pericles* is integral both to the intellectual design of the play and to its theatrical art.

In *Pericles* images with analogues in the visual arts are part of the verbal and conceptual design of the play; some become fully developed visual stage images.[3] In Shakespeare's images analogous to those in non-dramatic visual traditions, we see his theatrical art. In his drama, visual images are modified by their intricate relation to fluid, temporal dramatic moments as well as to language; words and dramatic situations are not only the context for stage images but help to create their meaning.[4] Thus what, especially in emblem books, is sometimes static and simplified, becomes kinetic and complex; what is often designed to be recondite, Shakespeare is careful to clarify for the audience; what are

I am grateful for grants from the President's Fund, University of Santa Clara, which made possible the preparation and presentation of this paper.

often simply visual commonplaces become subtly changed and charged, in dramatic context, with fresh force.

Even when the dramatist gives verbal life to images with analogies in the visual arts without making them a full part of the visual art of the play, he adapts traditional images creatively to specific dramatic contexts. The shipwrecked Pericles uses a metaphor that occurs, for example, in Renaissance emblems: human beings are tennis balls in the hands of the gods or of fortune.[5] But instead of the familiar comparison of the earth to the court for fortune's tennis, the court is the sea. Pericles, his garments wet, presents himself as

> A man whom both the waters and the wind,
> In that vast tennis court, hath made the ball
> For them to play upon.[6]

More important to an understanding of Shakespeare's theatrical art are those images that are not only verbal but are very closely related to visual presentation on stage. The simplest of these are stage properties; the most remarkable, which reveal Shakespeare's stagecraft in the late plays, are complex stage images composed not only of properties, but of costumes, groupings of actors, gestures, and moments of action.

Death's Heads at Antioch

The opening scene at Antioch is a striking example of the use of symbolic stage properties: death's heads are presented to our eyes. They form the central image that defines Antiochus' court; the language suggests that these skulls of suitors for Antiochus' daughter are visible throughout the scene (probably affixed to part of the stage or to a stage property).[7] These properties are a theatrical use of the *memento mori* tradition and of allegorical traditions that link lust and death.

The viewer is given an ironic perspective that Pericles lacks, since Gower has told the audience of the incest between Antiochus and his daughter before Pericles enters. The daughter is unnamed; she is important as stage image. When we see her juxtaposed to the death's heads we already know what Pericles sees only later, that she is a "glorious casket stor'd with ill" (1. 1. 78). Even viewers who have little familiarity with iconography can sense a connection between lust and moral death because of the stage picture. Awareness of the common tradition of moral allegory linking lust and death would enrich their perception. Antiochus warns Pericles

> Before thee stands this fair Hesperides,
> With golden fruit, but dangerous to be touch'd;
> For death-like dragons here affright thee hard.
>
> [1. 1. 28–30]

With the aid of a dragon, the Hesperides, daughters of evening, guarded the garden containing the golden apples Hercules plucked. Shakespeare uses the classical story in the manner of Renaissance moral allegory, and connects the story to the theme of Hercules at the Crossroads, which was widely used in the Renaissance to symbolize the choice between the way of lust and the way of virtue. There is a woodcut, for example, of Hercules' choice in Sebastian Brant's *The Ship of Fooles* (1570?).[8] A young knight lies at the fork of a road which divides two ways: the broad path leads to a figure of a woman with death behind her, his skull by her head.

Ironically, Antiochus himself, for his own ends, suggests that Pericles should see the death's heads as symbolic images, which "with dead cheeks advise thee to desist" (l. 40). Pericles' reply shows his desire to understand the image:

> For death remember'd should be like a mirror,
> Who tells us life's but breath, to trust it error.
>
> [1. 1. 46–47]

Pericles sees the death's heads as a *memento mori*, and his couplet sounds like a quotation, as if he is a young man remembering his emblem book. Though he has the words, he misapplies their meaning. For the point of the *memento mori* tradition as represented by Peacham's emblem of a death's head in *Minerva Britanna*, for example, is that faced with one's mortality, one should steer a course toward heavenly joys, and attempt to live wisely.[9] Pericles draws a witty but wrong conclusion: he places heaven in the lady (1. 1. 48–54). The courtly parody of religious language is our clue. It is only when he solves the incest riddle and learns that Antiochus' "courtesy" covers "sin" (1. 1. 122) that Pericles chooses rightly.

The scene at Antioch uses symbolic properties for specific dramatic ends. Such properties establish Antioch as a court of death: a place where spectacle is used to conceal truth, where natural love is p rodied by its opposite, incest, where the heroic and chivalric code is misapplied. Pentapolis is its exact opposite.

Fortuna and Ars

The stage image confronting the viewer near the beginning of act 2 is of the storm-beaten Pericles.[10] Pericles himself is a figure of the suffering caused by storms of fortune. He cries to the "stars of heaven," which he feels are "angry" (2. 1. 1). But at the same time, the audience has the perspective given them by Gower the moment before Pericles' entrance: fortune "threw him ashore, to give him glad" (2. Ch. 38). This dramatic juxtaposition suggests the ambiguity of fortune in a fresh use of an iconographical commonplace: a ship in a storm is used to explore the problem of fortune, including mutability and the relation of chance to virtue and to the gods. In Whitney's *A Choice of Emblems,* for example, a ship in a storm is the picture to the motto *Res humanae in summo declinant* (p. 11); Whitney cites Ovid: *"Passibus ambiguis fortuna volubilis errat."* Shakespeare's use of this tradition is complex: the scene not only portrays the destructive instability of fortune, but hints that we are about to see its benign aspect.

To the figure of the shipwrecked Pericles is quickly juxtaposed a brief but moving stage image: a fisherman gives his gown to the cold, nearly naked Pericles. The stage picture speaks of charity. Its resonance would be richer for an audience familiar with the representation in visual art of charity: a person giving a garment to clothe another.[11] By stage gesture, the viewer sees one of the ways bad fortune can become benign: through a specific human virtue in action.

The dramatist suddenly presents a third stage image relevant to the problem of fortune and human action: *"Enter Second and Third Fishermen, drawing up a net"* (first quarto). In their net they recover part of Pericles' heritage: the armor of his father. The action makes clear that this gift of "Fortune" (2. 1. 120) could not have happened without the skill of the persistent men who fish despite the storm. The dramatist gives concrete theatrical form to a traditional visual representation of hope and of the skill that can overcome ill fortune.[12]

Pericles, to "rise" (2. 1. 165), seizes the occasion of the tournament at Pentapolis about which he now hears. The dramatic timing suggests the ancient antithesis of τύχη and τέχνη, sometimes stated in the Renaissance as *fortuna* and *ars*.[13] Pericles shows courageous virtue in choosing this occasion as the right moment to act and to try his skill, or art, of arms.

Imprese on the shields of the knights who sue for Simonides' daughter at Pentapolis are designed to show the moral purpose of each.[14] The important thing is not to claim sources for these *imprese* but to see how they are used in the dramatic context: the playwright creates a telling contrast of "outward show" (2. 2. 47) and inward worth. Motto and picture on the shields of the first four knights play upon the Renaissance love of what Mario Praz calls "that new-fangled wonder which was the perfect device": they are framed as ornate courtly conceits.[15] The fifth device is framed with serious wit: the "gold that's by the touchstone tried." It may be significant that Thaisa's reading of the motto *"Sic spec-*

tanda fides" is timed to occur just before the moment Pericles enters; but
the fundamental point is the contrast between richly costumed knights
and the ill-furnished Pericles in rough garb with a piece of rusty armor.
Having no shield he has had to make his own device, probably from a
natural branch; having no page, he would present his device himself
directly to Thaisa. Her description assists the audience in perceiving the
image:

> A wither'd branch, that's only green at top;
> The motto, *In hac spe vivo.*
>
> [2. 2. 42–43]

Even a viewer who has no familiarity with iconography can see the
fundamental meaning of the image: despite his "wither'd" state and
fortune, Pericles hopes for renewal. The dramatist is careful to clarify
the *impresa* further by Simonides' interpretative comment:[16]

> A pretty moral;
> From the dejected state wherein he is,
> He hopes by you his fortunes yet may flourish.
>
> [2. 2. 44–46]

It is perhaps fitting that no exact parallel to Pericles' device has yet
been found in books of devices, *imprese,* and emblems, because the very
purpose of the scene is to contrast fashionable and elaborate courtly
devices to a simpler one that Pericles must invent. The invention, however, is drawn from a widespread tradition. The dry and verdant tree or
branch recur in classical and Christian iconography to relate natural
(vegetative) reflowering and human renewal; in some instances, the image indicates the renascence of a noble family, despite death and time,
through the growth of children.[17] In the motto he gives Pericles, the
dramatist fuses these concepts with another that is crucial in the play at
this point: hope. Hope in his renascence counters the longing for death
Pericles experiences after shipwreck and impels him to continue the
quest that he began at Antioch, to renew his lines of life by marriage.

Grief and Patience

Pericles' quest seems to him to have ended in total loss when, believing
his wife dead, he is confronted with his daughter's tomb (4. 4); his
lineage now seems forever eradicated. A dramatic function of the dumb
show of Pericles at the tomb is that its visual heightening helps us hold a
sharp image in our minds: Pericles himself as a figure of grief.[18] The

stage picture is clear in the directions of the first quarto: ". . . *Pericles makes lamentation, puts on sackcloth, and in a mighty passion departs."* The ancient image of sackcloth is often used in the context of lamentation and mourning, as when Jacob thinks Joseph is dead (Gen. 37:34), or where Job expresses his extreme suffering (Job 16:15). Gower gives the verse to the picture of the dumb show: "See how belief may suffer by foul show!" (4. 4. 23).

Pericles becomes a symbolic figure also because of the language Gower uses to describe him. In a striking change from the two main sources of the play, which emphasize the literal storm Pericles meets as he sails from Tharsus,[19] the play stresses a highly metaphoric one.

> He bears
> A tempest, which his mortal vessel tears,
> And yet he rides it out.
>
> [4. 4. 29–31]

It is primarily a tempest of the mind and soul; it tears his body—which is identified in the compressed language with his ship.

When we next see Pericles, we are presented with the most powerful stage image of his suffering in the play: Pericles, on shipboard and in sackcloth, dumb with grief. The probable blocking (Pericles seated or reclining up stage and all on stage looking toward him), Pericles' silence, the pauses, and Helicanus' word *mortal*—all make the figure Pericles presents when discovered to the audience on stage and to us symbolic in force:

> *Hel.* Behold him. This was a goodly person,
> Till the disaster that, one mortal night,
> Drove him to this.
>
> [5. 1. 35–37]

Helicanus' language is not only finer than most emblem verses but is in the context of Pericles' particular grief; his words thus give the audience a vivid experiential awareness. At the same time, his language gains in symbolic force by functioning, in part, like verse to a pictorial emblem: he makes an explicit comment on the stage picture. There is thus the suggestion, with no overly emphatic moralizing, that Pericles' particular experience of the suffering caused by the radical contigencies of fortune, so striking when it happens to a "goodly person," could be the lot of anyone.

Pericles' "distemperature" (5. 1. 27) is a paralyzing "melancholy" (5. 1. 219) that makes him unable to act in adversity as the moralistic verse of emblem makers often advised—as a skillful pilot, or one who has hope as

his anchor.[20] Helicanus stresses the need for recovery (5. 1. 53). Gower
has made us aware of the ripe occasion of Pericles' meeting with Marina;
his ship has been "driven before the winds" to Mytilene at the very time
the "city striv'd/God Neptune's annual feast to keep" (5. Ch. 16–17).

The setting of Pericles' encounter with Marina is one Gower asks us to
hold in our imagination: "Of heavy Pericles, think this his bark" (5. Ch.
22). Not all visual images in *Pericles* are—or can be—represented to the
viewer's eye on stage; indeed it is part of Gower's role to play upon the
problem of representation in drama. But Gower's language can make
the stage itself symbolic. That Marina and Pericles are on shipboard
reinforces the awareness that each has lost a place in the world and has
been "toss'd from wrong to injury" (5. 1. 130), subject to that mutability
of fortune that emblems and other visual arts often symbolize by a ship
in a storm. Marina has earlier reflected, in emblematic terms, "This
world to me is as a lasting storm" (4. 1. 19); she now tells Pericles that she
is bound by "wayward fortune" and "awkward casualties" (5. 1. 89–94).

After Marina comes on shipboard, the inner state of separation from
others and from each other Pericles and Marina both experience is
suggested visually in the physical positioning on stage: Pericles, seated,
in sackcloth, apart; Marina, standing away from him after he has pushed
her back (1. 83). This blocking helps to create a stage image closely
related to Pericles' words at the next moment. He is amazed at what he
sees:

> thou dost look
> Like Patience gazing on kings' graves, and smiling
> Extremity out of act.
>
> [5. 1. 137–39]

The conceptual patterns of the play and its visual design are united here
in a moment when a verbal image is strongly intimated by what we see on
stage. This dramatic moment is not built on a simple one-to-one equiva-
lence of verbal and visual images. Greater complexity occurs in part
because of the dynamic, fluid situation in which Pericles is still testing the
truth of what he sees and hears. His moving declaration of the qualities
Marina seems to figure forth is filled with wonder, yet he is not fully
certain she is, as she says, "No other than I appear" (5. 1. 105). His
declarations are surrounded by questions—until he at last hears her say
her name, Marina (5. 1. 142).[21] There is symbolic intimation[22] here
rather than a simple equation of verbal and visual also because of the
metaphorical richness of the phrase "king's graves," when applied to
Pericles' state, and because the simile "Like Patience" is used suggestively
in the moment of Pericles' quickened perception, not as a mere label for
Marina. In this dramatic context, personification heightens, rather than

reduces, Marina's character. It gives her added symbolic force, while the stage image is rooted in the particularities of the situation: Pericles' own severe melancholy (especially as shown by his initial stony silence) has been deathlike; Marina has endured in the face of her own grief, and has undertaken the task of restoration for Pericles in his.

The stage image Shakespeare creates at this moment of action has many analogues in the visual arts. W. S. Heckscher thinks the image of patience in *Pericles* may be more closely related to monumental tomb sculpture than to two-dimensional representation.[23] Whether or not there are specific types of "inspiration" for Shakespeare's images, it is important, for audience response, that Shakespeare use a widespread tradition. And it is a tradition, as Heckscher documents, in which the visual arts are related to a field of ideas including *Fortitudo* and *Patientia* as virtues that oppose *Melancholia-Tristitia-Acedia;* this is a central field of ideas used throughout *Pericles.*

The heightened moment when Marina's qualities suggest the inward virtue of Patience to Pericles is not only evidence of Shakespeare's fresh use of a familiar tradition but also of his mastery of visual craftsmanship in the late plays. The stage image in *Pericles* is founded on a freer and more forceful use of the commonplace of patience and her monument than Shakespeare gives to Viola: "She sat like patience on a monument/Smiling at grief" (2. 4. 113–14). And in *Twelfth Night* the verbal image is not strongly related to a stage image; in *Pericles,* the verbal image has a strikingly suggestive context in the visual composition on stage.

Stage images that draw on iconographical motifs are a recurrent feature of Shakespeare's plays; their centrality in *Pericles* suggests Shakespeare's emphasis, in the romances, on symbolic form. Stephen Orgel points out that visual experience in Shakespeare's late plays is integrally related to wonder "as the means to reconciliation and the restoration of losses."[24] In addition, visual experience is made thematic in *Pericles:* there is a recurrent problem of how we are to know truth from the appearance of things, and how we are to believe when faced repeatedly with the kind of deception Pericles met at Antioch and Tharsus.

Toward the end of the play, spectacle is used to intimate an ideal order beyond the flux of particulars, an order glimpsed only at rare moments. At such a "right time" Pericles is given the theophany of Diana. At Ephesus, when we see Pericles reunited to Marina and Thaisa, the gods themselves seem makers of spectacle.[25] The final tableau, which includes the figures of Cerimon and Helicanus, suggests how the gods work: through specific human virtues in action.

The epilogue invites us to see the characters, and the action of the play itself, as symbolic.

In Antiochus and his daughter you have heard
Of monstrous lust the due and just reward.
In Pericles, his queen and daughter, seen,
Although assail'd with fortune fierce and keen,
Virtue preserv'd from fell destruction's blast,
Led on by heaven, and crown'd with joy at last.
In Helicanus may you well descry
A figure of truth, of faith, of loyalty.
In reverend Cerimon there well appears
The worth that learned charity aye wears.

[Epilogue, ll. 1–10]

Although these rhymed couplets are less moving than the final stage tableau, Gower's epilogue is appropriate to a play in which visual presentation is so closely related to moral vision. Throughout *Pericles*, speaking pictures have been presented "to the judgement of your eye" (1. Ch. 41).

Notes

1. I am indebted to Mary Davison's work, "The Metamorphoses of Odysseus: A Study of Romance Iconography from the *Odyssey* to *The Tempest*," (Ph.D. diss., Stanford University, 1971), for information on this subject. I am also grateful to Peter M. Daly of McGill University, in a privately circulated paper, "Shakespeare's Eye: Iconographical and Emblematic Effects in the Plays: A Review of Recent Scholarship," for a critique of the term *emblem* in dramatic criticism that helped in my revision of this paper, and to Alan R. Young of Acadia University for his skillful leadership of the seminar "Shakespeare's Eye" at the Second Congress of the International Shakespeare Association, in which participants considered the difficult problem of relating terms from art history to dramatic criticism.

2. See, for example, critical comments in F. D. Hoeniger, ed., *Pericles*. The Arden Shakespeare (London: Methuen, 1963), p. lxxvii.

3. *Stage imagery* is defined as follows by Martha Hester Golden [Fleischer] in *The Reader's Encyclopedia of Shakespeare*, ed. Oscar James Campbell and Edward G. Quinn (New York: Cromwell, 1966):

> Stage imagery is created by the persons, properties, and actions visible and audible on stage when a play is in production. Its function is analogous to that of the allegorical picture in the emblem books of the Renaissance: to present the essential truth for instantaneous comprehension by the eye; while the dialogue, like the emblem book's verses, explicates and elaborates the image for the benefit of methodical, discursive reason.

I accept this definition in part but agree with John Doebler that it "seems to make all stage action symbolic"; and I also query the emphasis upon static presentation. See Doebler, *Shakespeare's Speaking Pictures* (Albuquerque: University of New Mexico Press, 1974), p. 7. Furthermore, the analogy to the emblem book tradition has limitations; emblems often create an ingenious image *not* for "instantaneous comprehension" but to force thought by wit.

4. I am grateful to Inga-Stina Ewbank for her emphasis on the crucial importance of language in relation to other elements in Shakespearean theater in her paper "The Word in the Theater," published in the present collection. See also her "'My name is Marina':

The Language of Recognition," in *Shakespeare's Styles: Essays in Honour of Kenneth Muir,* ed. Philip Edwards, Inga-Stina Ewbank, and G. K. Hunter (Cambridge: At the University Press, 1980), and her "'More Pregnantly than Words': Some Uses and Limitations of Visual Symbolism," *Shakespeare Survey* 24 (1971): 13–18.

5. There is a clear example in Peacham, *Minerva Britanna* (London: Wa. Dight, 1612), p. 113, *Sic nos Dij.*: a hand in the heavens strikes a ball onto an earth drawn to resemble grids of a tennis court.

6. *Pericles* 2. 1. 59–61. All references to *Pericles,* unless otherwise indicated, are to The Arden Shakespeare, ed. F. D. Hoeniger.

7. The death's heads are probably already on stage when Gower speaks—see 1. Ch. 40—and can remain throughout the exchange between Pericles and Antiochus—see 1. 1. 40, 44. They could be borne away when Antiochus exits (l. 121); they may remain until Pericles' exit (l. 143) or even throughout the exchange between Antiochus and Thaliard (1b).

8. Hallett Smith, *Elizabethan Poetry: A Study in Conventions, Meaning, and Expression* (Cambridge, Mass.: Harvard University Press, 1968), pp. 293–99, gives references to the story of Hercules' choice from Hesiod through its representation in Renaissance art and literature. I am indebted to Doebler's *Shakespeare's Speaking Pictures,* pp. 22–29, 98, and 192–93 nn. 2–3, for his references to this theme in another context and for the representation of the woodcut from Sebastian Brant, *The Ship of Fooles,* trans. Alexander Barclay, 2d ed. (London, 1570?), fol. 239v. Mario Praz notes that Brant's very frequently translated and edited *Narren Schyff* (1494?) is not, strictly speaking, an emblem book. See *Studies in Seventeenth-Century Imagery,* 2d ed., enl. (Rome: Edizione di storia e letteratura, 1964), p. 286.

9. See the verse to Peacham's emblem with the motto *Nec metuas nec optes,* p. 8. Peacham's marginal notes to this emblem refer to James I's *Basilicon Doron* (London, 1603), Bk. 1, p. 17. James links his advice to live so that one is ready for death to the "vertue of true Fortitude." Fortitude is a virtue central to *Pericles.* The *memento mori* tradition is also clear in Geoffrey Whitney, *A Choice of Emblems* (Leyden: Christopher Plantyn, 1586), p. 229, and is documented by Roland Mushat Frye, "Ladies, Gentlemen, and Skulls: *Hamlet* and the Iconographic Tradition," *Shakespeare Quarterly* 30 (1979): 15–28.

10. "Enter Pericles wette" is the stage direction of the 1609 first quarto. References in my paper to the first quarto are to the facsimile reprint introd. by P. Z. Round (London: C. Praetorius, 1886).

11. See Douglas Peterson, *Time, Tide and Tempest* (San Marino, Calif.: Huntington Library, 1973), p. 83 and p. 106 n.14, who refers to a figure of *caritas* in Adolph Katzenellenbogen, *Allegories of the Virtues and Vices in Medieval Art* (New York: Norton, 1964), p. 76. Lawrence J. Ross, "Art and the Study of Early English Drama," *Research Opportunities in Renaissance Drama* 6 (1963): 35–47, notes (p. 44) that by the time of the Renaissance there was an established tradition that singled out clothing the naked "as the symbol of the idea of Charity itself." I have noticed a representation of clothes being given for those in need in Bruegel's engraving "Charity," in his series of the Seven Virtues. See reproduction in H. Arthur Klein, *The Graphic Worlds of Peter Bruegel the Elder* (New York: Dover, 1963), p. 229.

12. See Davison, "The Metamorphoses of Odysseus," pp. 169–70, for the suggestion that the spectacle of fishermen hauling in their nets is used in this scene to "express the older Homeric tradition that a virtuous man can exercise his virtue, skills, and foresight to overcome worldly misfortune." Dramatic timing when the armor is discovered suggests that Shakespeare also balances this view in the scene with the one she cites in the proverb "Quod ars negat, Fortuna praestat," used by Jean Cousin in *Le Livre de Fortune* (1568), Plate 157, for a scene of fishermen bringing in fish with a net. A fisherman fishes in a raging sea in Bruegel's engraving of "Hope." See reprint in Klein, *The Graphic Worlds of Peter Bruegel the Elder,* p. 225.

13. See Edgar Wind, "Platonic Tyranny and the Renaissance Fortuna: On Ficino's Reading of Laws IV 709 A-712 A," in Millard Meiss, ed., *Essays in Honor of Erwin S. Panofsky* (New York: New York University Press, 1961), 1: 491–92. See also Rudolph Wittkower, "Chance, Time and Virtue," *Journal of the Warburg and Courtauld Institutes* 1 (1937–38): 313–21.

14. Praz, *Studies in Seventeenth Century Imagery*, p. 58, gives a cogent definition of courtly devices: "For the device is nothing else than a symbolical representation of a purpose, a wish, a line of conduct (*impresa* is what one intends to *imprendere*, i.e., to undertake) by means of a motto and a picture which reciprocally interpret each other."

15. Ibid., p. 57. Henry Green, *Shakespeare and the Emblem Writers* (London: Trübner, 1870), is sometimes naive in his attempt to locate sources for these *imprese*; we can, however, identify analogues. The devices of the third, fourth, and fifth knights can be closely paralleled in *The Heroicall Devises of M. Clavdivs Paradin*, trans. P. S. (London: William Keamey, 1591), as well as in other sources. The respective references to Paradin are: sig. V3, p. 309; sig. Z3, p. 357; sig. O3, p. 213. The devices of the fourth and fifth knights can also be paralleled in Whitney, *A Choice of Emblems*, pp. 183 and 139 respectively. The second device, as cited by Green, *Emblem Writers*, p. 165, can be seen in a somewhat similar form in Corrozet's *Hecatomgraphie* (1540), Emblem 28. There is no close known parallel to the first device, although the motto is also that of the Blount family (see Green, *Emblem Writers*, p. 160).

16. Peterson, *Time, Tide, and Tempest*, pp. 84–85, comments on Pericles' emblem and motto: "The meaning of the symbol and its accompanying moral were misread by Simonides." But Simonides' comment is perfectly suited to the action and in any case *implies* the reading that Peterson suggests: "the living though seemingly dead branch that represents the family of whom he is the only survivor."

17. I am indebted to Gerhart B. Ladner, "Vegetation Symbolism and the Concept of the Renaissance," in Meiss, ed., *Essays in Honor of Erwin S. Panofsky*, 1:303–22, for his excellent article that discusses these concepts in another context.

18. William S. Heckscher, "Shakespeare in His Relationship to the Visual Arts: A Study in Paradox," *Research Opportunities in Renaissance Drama* 13–14 (1970–71):5–17, discussing *Pericles*, notes (pp. 41–42; 67, n 29) that in scholastic thought *tristitia* (a mixture of sorrow and despair) was seen as part of the sin of *acedia*. But since, as he says, "sloth" or *acedia* was identified in Christian theology with loss of faith in the mercy of God, I have not emphasized *acedia* and have stayed as close as possible to the language used in the text. The word *despair* is not used; Shakespeare uses *sorrow* (4. 4. 25); *grief* (5. 1.26, 29, 87); *griefs* (5. 1. 131); *woe* (5. 1. 105); *distemperature* (5. 1. 27); and *melancholy* (5. 1. 219).

19. See the two most widely recognized immediate sources of *Pericles*, John Gower's *Confessio Amantis*, Bk. 8, ll. 1600–1601, and Lawrence Twine's *The Patterne of Painefull Adventures*, chap. 11, p. 540, in Geoffrey Bullough, *Narrative and Dramatic Sources of Shakespeare*, vol. 6 (London: Routledge, 1966).

20. My argument here differs substantially from Peterson's, *Time, Tide and Tempest*, pp. 52 and 81, although in many other respects I greatly admire his analysis of *Pericles*.

21. I am indebted to Inga-Stina Ewbank, in "'My name is Marina,'" for her valuable emphasis on a conditional quality in the exchanges between Pericles and Marina up to l. 142 of the recognition scene; for stressing, in "'More Pregnantly than Words,'" that Shakespeare does not set up a merely illustrative relationship between words and visual images; and for her exploration of these points in a fresh way in her paper "The Word in the Theater." See note 4, above. For his vivid realization that Pericles continues to test what he sees and hears, I am also grateful to Paul Whitworth, in an interview (15 March 1975) he gave me about his performance as Pericles in the then-current Oxford University Dramatic Society production.

22. John B. Bender, "Affinities between Jacobean Masques and Plays," *Research Opportunities in Renaissance Drama* 17 (1974):9–12, suggests a distinction between the way symbolic intimation (the term is his) in plays, as opposed to statement in Masques, was influenced by iconography.

23. Heckscher, "Shakespeare in His Relationship to the Visual Arts," pp. 36–56.

24. "The Poetics of Spectacle," in *New Literary History* 2 (Spring 1971): 382–83.

25. I am indebted to Samuel Lee Wolff's *The Greek Romances in Elizabethan Prose Fiction* for this idea; he points out that Heliodorus, in the *Aethiopica*, for example, conceives of his story "as a series of theatrical spectacles arranged by superhuman agency" (p. 183). By "right time" I am alluding to a Renaissance understanding of καιρός. See Wind, "Platonic Tyranny and the Renaissance Fortuna," pp. 491–92.

The Sense of Occasion: Some Shakespearean Night Sequences

by EMRYS JONES

The festive element in Shakespeare's plays is familiar to us from the work of a number of recent scholars. I want to approach this large subject by taking a single topic—Shakespeare's presentation of night—which may at first seem somewhat remote from the notions of festival and occasion.

The dramatists contemporary with Shakespeare make surprisingly little use of night as a dramatic occasion. There are of course a few night scenes in the plays of his immediate predecessors and early contemporaries, but most of them are different in kind and distinctly more primitive than those I want to discuss. One such notable night scene is that of Horatio's murder in *The Spanish Tragedy*. Kyd, who appears to have been such an innovator on so many fronts, may have struck his contemporaries as doing something boldly original here. Certainly, in *The Jew of Malta*, Marlowe, who in this play takes up several suggestions from *The Spanish Tragedy*, also sets a scene—or rather, not one scene but two scenes—at night, something he had altogether abstained from doing in the two Tamburlaine plays. (Indeed even in *Dido, Queen of Carthage*, which is possibly earlier, he includes no night scene, though Virgil had supplied him with a famous night-piece for Dido.) In these early Elizabethan plays (and one might add to the two I have just mentioned *Arden of Feversham* and Shakespeare's own *2 Henry VI*), the dramatization of night is rudimentary. Night is usually announced with a simple three- or four-line *chronographia*, a periphrastic way of saying "It's dark," as in Kyd's

> Black night hath hid the pleasures of the day,
> And sheeting darkness overhangs the earth.

But once it has been announced in this wordy but bluntly summary way, little is done with it dramatically: night is not much more than a period of imagined blackout, under whose protection crimes of various kinds can be safely committed.

Against this background of relative lack of interest on the part of Elizabethan dramatists, the originality of Shakespeare's own subsequent treatment of night stands out. Most of these other dramatists—and Shakespeare himself in *Henry VI*—treat night in the simplest way as a time of blankly conventionalized darkness, an effect unmodified by any other qualities or features. But for the first time in *Richard III*, Shakespeare created a new form of scene that evokes the temporal phenomenon of night as it is actually experienced in life. Night now becomes not just a matter of saying "It's dark," but of registering a whole series of temporal phases into which and through which and out of which one passes; not simply a static background labeled "darkness" or a locality with the effect of conferring invisibility. Night is here not a state but a process, a sequence of moments, beginning with evening and ending with morning. This is (after all) how it is experienced in life, and this is how it strikes an audience watching the scene in *Richard III*.

There are some contemporary plays—Peele's *Old Wives Tale* and Marlowe's *Faustus* among them—which certainly contain comparable forms of night sequence, though the time-plotting is much more sporadic and irregular than in Shakespeare and always less tightly systematized. What Shakespeare did was to convert the form into a type of sequence that he must have felt to have unusual potential, since he was to use it so variously in so many later plays.

So in *Richard III*, in the long scene before Bosworth, we are taken steadily, rhythmically, uninsistently yet highly allusively, through the successive stages of the night, beginning with sunset, and moving from evening to midnight to the small hours and through to dawn and cockcrow. This way of dramatizing night as a sequence of scenes or short episodes with its own beginning, middle, and end, seems to be peculiarly Shakespearean. It is a form of dramatic construction with great theatrical power. The Bosworth sequence is the earliest occurrence of the form in Shakespeare; in later plays—in tragedy, comedy, and history—it undergoes any number of modifications. In some of these plays the nocturnal occasion may be broken up into several discrete scenes, as it is in the first and second acts of *Romeo and Juliet,* where the Capulets' feast is preceded by scenes introducing first Juliet and her Nurse and then Mercutio and is followed by the even more powerfully knitted sequence of Mercutio's invocation of Rosaline, the balcony scene itself, and the early morning encounter between Romeo and Friar Lawrence. The entire sequence is divided by editors into several (half a dozen or so) distinct scenes, yet the impression of temporal continuity, from evening through night to morning, is quite clear and seems to me vitally important to the effect not only of this part of the play but of the play as a whole.

The chief significance of this form of night scene—the all-night night sequence—is that it is an extraordinarily powerful aid to establishing realism. It helps to convey—and often in a very short space of time—a profound sense of reality. One remembers the sequence in *Romeo and Juliet* as if it had occurred in a novel, or rather as if it were an episode from one's own life. Similarly in *Julius Caesar*, the night before the assassination and the early morning of the day itself, the Ides of March, receive emphatic dramatization. (One might note the moment when the conspirators fail to agree where the sun is to rise.) *Hamlet* opens with a brilliantly truncated version of the night-morning sequence: the Ghost appears at midnight, and shortly after—or so it seems—comes sunrise. But it is in *Othello* that the complete version of the night sequence, as initiated in *Richard III*, is adapted for the last time. This is in the second act, the night of Cassio's cashiering; and again the passage of time through the hours of darkness is carefully plotted, here with a scrupulous regard to evoking what it actually feels like to stay up all night and greet the dawn, stretching and yawning, with a slight feeling of hangover: "By th'mass 'tis morning;/Pleasure and action makes the hours seem short." And in a few moments' acting-time the musicians are playing an aubade for the newly married couple. In *Macbeth*, the night of Duncan's murder is treated much more allusively in terms of the temporal sequence, but the usual stages are marked, from the time when Duncan has, we are told, "almost supp'd," to the meeting of Banquo and Fleance around midnight ("I take 't, 'tis later," says Fleance), through the dead-of-night murder itself to the early morning knocking at the south entry—early, presumably, though Macduff reproaches the Porter for lying in bed "so late."

Shakespeare's choice of night for such scenic occasions as these (as well as others I have not mentioned, from the comedies and comic histories) has the effect of grounding the action in a socially specific context; and it is this socially circumstantial dimension that is important for achieving realism. A nocturnal occasion may bring social realities to mind in a way that temporally neutral occasions—actions done by daylight—may not. Day is a neutral value; day is the unstressed norm. And since night is, dramaturgically speaking, a departure from the norm, it may acquire in itself an expressive value. For the Elizabethan dramatist, night is time written in italics; it seems more emphatic than ordinary daylight time. Merely to begin an action at nightfall and end it at sunrise is to appeal to an audience's memory, enlist its imaginative cooperation: hence (in part, at any rate) the power of these evening-night-morning sequences, the quality they have of seeming to belong to one's own past. This is no doubt one of the reasons why the long evening-night-morning sequence in *Romeo and Juliet,* centering on the feast scene and the balcony scene, makes such a profound impact; something that can be brought out in a comparison with Brooke's poem, where the temporal sequence is strung out over several weeks and where the balcony scene does not take place at night at all. Looking back on the play—or so I find—one cannot fail to remember that evening followed by that night followed by that morning.

I want now to look at one example in particular of this kind of night sequence, and in doing so relate what I have just been saying to ideas of feast and festival.

The festive mood is especially strong in *Henry V*: so strong that one might call the play a festive history. (In this it pairs with *Henry VIII,* another festive history; whose last word is literally "holiday": "This little child shall make it holiday.") In *Henry V*, the role played by the Chorus is indispensable. More than anything else, the Chorus generates the excitement and expectancy aroused by the approach of a great occasion: it is the Chorus who infuses the audience with his own elated festive mood and ensures, in a way unique in Shakespeare, that the audience will rise to that occasion. For all its concern with war and battle, *Henry V* comes across in performance as a high-spirited holiday play. The play must culminate, however, in Agincourt; yet the famous battle with its armored knights on horseback is unstageable in any obvious way. Or rather, it *can* be staged, but only by adopting a very special imaginative strategy, which in the end works so well that no audience will feel a sense of disappointment. By the time we have reached the end, we will have been persuaded that the play has somehow encompassed the great battle—that we ourselves have somehow witnessed the battle of Agincourt.

But the witnessing is of a special nature. The Agincourt sequence takes the form of an all-night night sequence of the kind I have been describing. And in terms of stage duration, it is the longest such sequence in Shakespeare. Henry announces that "it now draws toward night": "Beyond the river we'll encamp ourselves, / And on to-morrow"—tomorrow will be the day. With that word "now"—"it now draws toward night"—the play drops to a slow tempo: time drags its feet; for the next 700 lines or so of text we are made to wait. The scenes alternate between the enemy camps, but after the first of the French scenes, with its refrain "Will it never be morning?", the Chorus interposes with the longest, most evocatively descriptive, of his speeches. And this speech disrupts the strict dramatic sequence by making our minds play freely over the entire night-morning sequence before that sequence has been enacted, ending with the next morning's battle:

> And so our scene must to the battle fly,
> Where—O for pity!—we shall much disgrace,
> With four or five most vile and ragged foils,
> The name of

—and for the first time since the prologue he speaks the famous name: "The name of Agincourt." So even while re-creating, with an unusual degree of immediacy, the night before the battle, the Chorus is appealing to the fame in history which that battle is going to acquire and which the audience of this play has already received as part of its inheritance. The night sequence, already begun, is now resumed: the long scene follows of Henry in disguise among his soldiers, where the play achieves its most extreme effect of *rallentando* —it slows down almost to a halt. Yet early in the scene the morning's approach is noted—". . . is not that the morning which breaks yonder?"—so that the movement of time is not forgotten and in any case the subject of converse between king and soldiers is the day's outcome, though not just in terms of the military event but of the ultimate fate of their immortal souls—the most *serious* question conceivable to men of Shakespeare's world. The momentousness of the coming occasion seems to grow as the scene progresses, an oppressive weight of imminent event, given final definition by Henry's very human reluctance at the end of the scene to abandon his self-communing and face the day's demands: "The day, my friends, and all things wait for me." But even now we are not allowed to move forward to the battle: we are taken back once again to the French ("The sun doth gild our armour: up, my lords!"), and only then do we at last see the English army at the moment before battle.

"Enter Gloucester, Bedford, Exeter, Erpingham with all his Host: Salisbury and Westmorland": the tableau is completed only with Henry's late entry. The great speech that follows is a prebattle oration, of course, though of a special sort: it boosts the morale of the troops, making them rejoice in their small numbers, but its greater function is to engage not the stage army but the theater audience—and in such a way as to make clear the imaginative strategy of the the whole play. "This day is called the Feast of Crispian": the idea is developed first of veterans remembering, and then of posterity commemorating, and in commemorating celebrating:

> He that shall see this day, and live old age,
> Will yearly on the vigil feast his neighbours
> And say, "Tomorrow is Saint Crispian."

Saint Crispin's Day will become Agincourt Day; and the night before will become an Eve or Vigil in that special festival sense. It will become (to use a phrase of Ben Jonson's) a "holiday eve," a convivial occasion, a night of drinking and feasting. And this realization—that the battle will ultimately issue in a feast—is what the entire play is leading up to. The prophecy made by Henry—

> And Crispin Crispian shall ne'er go by,
> From this day to the ending of the world,
> But we in it shall be rememberéd

fulfills itself whenever the play is performed, the play's audience constituting that very posterity invoked by Henry. For while Henry's speech is unfolding, we have changed our stance with regard to the battle: we have moved forward to that moment in history in which the play is being performed so that we are no longer imagining the eve and morning of Agincourt as it was at the time, but remembering it long afterwards. But more than remembering it: what every performance of the play makes its audience do is commemorate it, thereby making of the play itself a dramatic ceremony of remembrance and celebration.

When Henry says that the survivor of Agincourt

> Will yearly on the vigil feast his neighbour

his phrase points to the formal model that Shakespeare presumably has somewhere in his mind. The Agincourt sequence gives by far the greater part of its time to the eve of the great occasion, or (to use Shakespeare's own word here) the *vigil*, when the celebrants stayed up, watched, in preparation for the festival. This form—a vigil or eve followed by a holy day—was of course the traditional form taken by festivals in the church calendar: following Jewish practice, Christians regarded a feast-day as beginning at sunset on the calendar day preceding it. (Even today we have something approximating a weekly festival with a similar form: the modern "weekend"—"Saturday night and Sunday morning"—is the secularized version of an earlier Christian usage, whereby labor was desisted from during the latter part of Saturday so that the Christian might prepare for the Lord's Day.) In *Henry V*, Shakespeare has, with whatever degree of conscious awareness, adapted this festival form for that part of his play which has become Agincourt Eve: the long, anxious prebattle vigil has become the other festive, memorial vigil that is at the heart of the play itself.

Shakespeare's all-night night sequences, not only in *Henry V* but in the other plays I have mentioned and others that I have not, seem to owe something essential to older traditions of festival. One may finally postulate a specifically dramatic prototype for this form of all-night sequence. Shakespeare may have known sequences of mystery plays that presented the Gospel-narrative of the evening, night, and early morning that saw the arrest of Jesus. This would be the supreme instance of the all-night sequence, beginning with the Last Supper, proceeding to the events in the Garden of Gethsemane—the agony, the betrayal, and the arrest—and ending with Peter's thrice-repeated denial marked by the crowing of the cock. Here perhaps Shakespeare might find a precedent and an inspiration for his own practice.

"Conjectures and Refutations": The Positive Uses of Negative Feedback in Criticism and Performance

by HARRIETT HAWKINS

> To conclude, upon an enumeration of particulars, without instance
> contradictory, is no conclusion, but a conjecture.
>
> Bacon

If he were to be judged solely in terms of certain critical and directorial interpretations of his plays, Shakespeare, as a professional "Man of the Theater," would have to be accounted a failure.

To give an extreme example, in a recent book on Shakespeare's tragedies the author has announced to a (hitherto) unsuspecting world that Antony never *really* loved Cleopatra; that his passion for her was feigned in order to cover up his real reason for staying out of Rome (his terror of Caesar); and that he intended to betray her "in the worst way possible" through that final, misdirected warning, "None about Caesar trust but Proculeius." According to this critic, Antony's attempted betrayal was prompted (a) by his desire for revenge, and (b) by the knowledge that, "displayed in Rome," Cleopatra's charms "would do more to verify the legend of his enslavement than any number of reports."[1]

Now regardless of whether one credits or rejects it, this interpretation of *Antony and Cleopatra* raises the following questions—neither of which is either posed or answered by the critic who propounded it.

1. *If* they are valid, why have such crucially important points concerning Antony's motivation gone unnoticed for nearly 400 years?

105

2. So far as performance is concerned, in the absence of any soliloquies or series of asides so stating, how on earth is the actor portraying Antony supposed to inform everybody in the audience that he is only faking it, and *simultaneously* convince Cleopatra, Octavius, Enobarbus, and everyone else on the stage that his passion is absolutely genuine?

After all, the public nature of the drama requires that motivation be established and necessary information be got across to a mass audience with maximum impact during the two or three hours' traffic of the stage. Shakespeare, who showed no interest in their publication, could not have taken for granted that anyone would see his plays more than once or read them countless times in order to ponder their subtleties. Nor could he have assumed that his true meaning would finally reveal itself to generations yet unborn. As a popular dramatist, he had to write *for* the general public, and *against* the deadline set by a single performance. And the critical and theatrical verdict of centuries is that the passionate affinity between Antony and Cleopatra—not the lack of it—is what has manifested itself in their countless one-night stands.

It therefore follows that, if this critic is right in arguing that Antony never actually loved Cleopatra, then we have to charge the playwright himself with a virtually complete failure of communication—we must blame Shakespeare for having so long, so grievously, and (worse still) so unwittingly misled so many of us concerning the emotional and sexual relationship between Cleopatra's "man of men" and his "lass unparalleled." And this would be a pity considering (in the immortal words of Robert Benchley) "the hard work that Shakespeare must have put in on his wording" when he was writing this particular play. Be that as it may, the point here is that this critic's interpretation of Antony's motivation obliges us to make one of two decisions. If we credit it, Shakespeare must be deemed technically incompetent. Conversely, if we credit Shakespeare's competence as a playwright and poet—to say nothing of the critical and theatrical testimony of centuries—then this critic's conjectures must be rejected as false. We, therefore, have to decide whether this critic's interpretation, or the evidence against it, is the more powerful.

In the book from which my title and main lines of argument were lifted,[2] Karl Popper has observed that while there are no absolute criteria by which scientists may conclusively prove a conjecture or theory to be true, there *are* various ways to test theories, to refute them, to prove them suspect, incomplete, or false. And what Popper has to say about scientific conjectures has obvious relevance to critical and directorial interpretations of Shakespeare's plays. Of course, the natural tendency of individual scientists, critics, and directors alike is *not* to look for ways to falsify them, but to verify their theories by seeking to apply and confirm them. Human nature being what it is, we are all prone to disregard or underestimate any arguments against our own pet theories and conclusions. And the fact is that given the richness of Shakespeare's plays, it is easy to find in them *some* evidence that would seem to support almost any theory or interpretation we care to posit—that is, if we refuse to take into account any evidence against it. The alternative is to adopt the method advocated by Popper; and that is to actively seek out the best evidence against our own theories (not just those of others). This does not rule against the various methods of inquiry—quite the contrary: any and all sources of insight into, or knowledge concerning the plays— imagination, reason, personal experience, previous discussions or productions of the plays, other literature, Elizabethan documents, and so on—are most welcome. But all interpretations—whatever their origins— should be open to critical challenge. Therefore we could agree that there can be no definitive interpretation, any more than a definitive production, of a play by Shakespeare, and, simultaneously, acknowledge that interpretations which can stand up to the strongest arguments leveled against them are likely to be sounder than conjectures that require acceptance, purely on faith, of the authority who propounded them.

The texts themselves, the responses they have elicited from audiences down through the centuries, and the facts of theatrical life, provide our most obvious sources of "negative feedback" concerning critical interpretations of the plays. The common laws of theatrical communication that call into question the interpretation of *Antony and Cleopatra* described above also render suspect the views propounded by another critic, who has seen fit to inform us that Claudio was lying when he said he had a true pre-contract with Julietta, and that Kent and Cordelia were prejudiced when they reported that Goneril and Regan threw King Lear out into the storm. In this instance, Shakespeare's characters are said to tell the truth *only* when their statements confirm this particular critic's theories. Otherwise, characters are alleged to be speaking on the basis of a vested interest, lying, or deceived. For instance, Enobarbus is said to speak with the "voice of the play" when he criticizes Antony (criticisms with which this critic agrees). But those passionate lines lauding Antony's magnanimity (praises that this critic rejects as unfounded) are alleged to demonstrate that "even Enobarbus dies deceived."[3]

Now if we cannot credit Claudio's expository lines informing us about his relationship with Julietta, and cannot trust even Kent and Cordelia— characters whom Shakespeare took some pains to establish as spokesmen for truth at any cost—and if we cannot credit the last words of Enobarbus, then who, in the whole of Shakespearian drama, can we believe? If one rejects all the rules of the game whereby certain characters communicate to a mass audience the information or sentiments necessary for a basic understanding of the situation involved, then guess who becomes sole judge of truth, the omniscient authority who determines which characters speak with the voice of the play, which ones are lying? The literary critic, who thus usurps the authority of the playwright himself. It is *Shakespeare's* duty to let us know which of his characters are the deceivers, which are deceived, which are liars and hypocrites, and which are not. And if he fails, he fails. There is nothing any critic can do about that.

The fact that, without turning them inside out, Shakespeare's plays *cannot* be performed, and his speeches *cannot* be read in certain ways, renders certain interpretations of them suspect. For instance, a recent critic has argued that in *All's Well That Ends Well*, Shakespeare commends Bertram's rebellion against the "pious platitudes" and "nearly suffocating restraints" of the countess and the king.[4] Thus, the countess's advice, "Love all, trust few/Do wrong to none" is said to be "blandly conventional," the "kind of advice young people will react against." One wonders just how they will react—by loving none, trusting few, and doing wrong to all? This critic's arguments will not persuade those who find his elders far more attractive than Bertram, who—given (for instance) his behavior towards Diana—might best be defended as Shakespeare's most definitive portrayal of a stinker. If Shakespeare intended our sympathies to go to Bertram but failed in his efforts to elicit them, no critic can put things right for him without rewriting the text.

As a rule, the more drastic the alterations to the text required to produce it, the more likely a directorial or critical interpretation is to be wrong. It is, for instance, possible to imagine a performance of *Romeo and Juliet* conceived in terms of those scholarly arguments in fashion several years ago that dismissed the prologue and denied the emotional impact of the poetry to argue that Shakespeare's hero and heroine got what was coming to them for their passionate misdeeds. Still, the prologue and the poetry would have to be cut, radically adapted, or spoken in very peculiar ways in order to turn the play into an indictment of the young lovers. Similarly, the opening scenes of *Hamlet* had to be radically revised in the Royal Court production that was designed to conform to certain scholarly and directorial theories about the Ghost. Cases like these require the substitution of some scholar's or critic's or director's—or psychoanalyst's—frames of reference for the dramatic coordinates provided by Shakespeare's own expository scenes, prologues, and poetry.

For those who set out to interpret them in conformity to a reigning theory, the richness of the individual plays is an obvious source of difficulty. As Edith Holding concluded in her discussion of Charles

Johnson's adaptation of *As You Like It,* "The variety of intellectual and emotional life which Shakespeare offers" may be more than a given adapter—or director or critic—can handle. The selective version of the play produced may be coherent and effective in its own right, but nonetheless represents an "enormous reduction of Shakespeare's own breadth of vision."[5] Our knowledge of the texts themselves is our best check against one-sided or reductive interpretations of them on the stage. After all, to adopt an uncritical attitude towards the loony interpretations sometimes posited in performance (remember seeing Mariana swilling booze on the haystack at the moated grange?) seems just as absurd as to adopt an uncritical attitude towards all theories propounded in scholarly books and journals. The odds are that other people's brain-children, as well as one's own, are more likely to be Gonerils and Regans than true Cordelias. Why, though, are Shakespeare's works so consistently richer than so many critical and directorial interpretations of them?

Although I have paraphrased Popper in describing it, the method whereby one presents the evidence against one's own best arguments, as well as those of others, is the method most commonly employed by Shakespeare himself, who is forever confronting the best possible case in favor of something with the strongest (not the weakest) case against it— and vice versa. If, say, in *King Lear* he affirms the humane values of kindness, generosity, self-sacrifice, he does so by taking into account, as opposed to denying, the fact that those who act with best meaning may, therefore, endure the worst. Whole plays and poems, as well as any number of characters, are constantly asking, or finding out, "If this be error." Hamlet, for instance, considers himself obliged to seek out evidence against the insights of his own "prophetic soul." Thus, even though he passionately hates Claudius, he decides to subject the spectral evidence against his uncle to a critical test. If Claudius's "occulted guilt" does not manifest itself in the play-scene, then Hamlet himself will admit that his own "imaginations" were as "foul as Vulcan's stithy." Of major concern throughout Shakespeare's comedies, tragedies, and sonnets are the manifold human problems arising from the fact that "men may construe things after their fashion / Clean from the purpose of the things themselves."[6]

Perhaps for this reason, Shakespeare's own dramatic purposes are, for the most part, anyway, made obvious to his audience. In this sense, at least, Shakespeare seems more classical than some of his avowedly neo-classical contemporaries and successors: like the ironies of a Greek tragedy, Shakespeare's dramatic ironies tend to depend on information possessed by—not withheld from—his audience. In Shakespeare's works, as compared to Jonson's or Beaumont's and Fletcher's, surprise is the exception, not the rule. Indeed, given the point of view of the most dimwitted of groundlings, Shakespeare could be given full marks for making his main points emphatically, clearly, and often enough to penetrate even the thickest of skulls. This is why Richard Levin is surely right to argue that the "burden of proof" should rest upon those who reject the most obvious and reasonable hypothesis in interpreting a given play. "This does not mean," Levin adds, "that an informed and sensitive spectator will not see more in the play than a groundling," but for the most part, anyway, we would expect these further insights "to represent an enrichment of the common experience of the play—not something quite different from that experience and certainly not its opposite."[7]

Speaking of groundlings, in spite of the midtwentieth-century controversy about it, one wonders if even an Elizabethan numbskull would have had serious difficulty with the exposition in *Hamlet*. That Ghost is *there* to tell him what he needs to know about past events, about carnal, bloody, and unnatural acts, and deaths put on by cunning. Its independent existence is affirmed by the soldiers and Horatio, and its testimony is later confirmed by the murderer himself. For the purposes of tragic irony, Shakespeare thus makes certain that his audience, like Hamlet, knows that Claudius is as guilty as Cain. Having identified Claudius as the murderer of Hamlet's father before the end of the first act, Shakespeare contrives to set other obstacles in Hamlet's way. Indeed, he may have raised serious questions about the validity of spectral evidence in order to keep things from being too easy for Hamlet or for the audience. For although the Ghost tells us what we need to know about what has already happened, Shakespeare makes certain that, like Hamlet, we remain uncertain what will or should happen next, not knowing how or when the right moment for retribution will come. Should the Ghost's primary function as an instrument of exposition be totally disregarded, as it is in certain recent interpretations and performances? In the Royal Court production, for instance, the relationship between Hamlet and the Ghost was portrayed as one of demonic possession, and thus the Ghost spoke from Hamlet's belly. This interpretation, of course, mandated cutting the opening scene of the play, wherein Shakespeare himself gives the Ghost a larger symbolic significance that underscores its technical function.

One might argue that what Chekhov has to say about the artist's obligation to his public applies to critics and directors as well. "You are," wrote Chekhov, "confusing two concepts: *The solution of a problem and the correct posing of a question. Only the second is obligatory for an artist*."[8] As a rule, surely, Shakespeare's exposition serves to make certain that the various problems in his plays are correctly posed. Had Hamlet learned about the murder from another source—say the testimony of a human eye-witness—he would still have to make up his mind what to do about Claudius and when to do it. But what better instrument of exposition, in a tragedy obsessed by the past, than a Ghost? Rather like Queen Margaret in *Richard III*, or the ghost of Banquo in Macbeth, this compound, familiar Ghost simultaneously recalls and embodies truths about the past that cannot be permanently suppressed. It thus may be seen as the perfect dramatic manifestation of past passions and past crimes that, in life itself, may sometimes rise, "though all the earth o'erwhelm them, to men's eyes." "Remember me," it urgently, repeatedly, insists. And thus, from the outset, and precisely like its hero, this particular tragedy is haunted by the remembrance of things past, by the *status quo ante.* Indeed, various characters in this ghost-ridden play seem to be wraiths or specters of their former selves. Rosencrantz and Guildenstern, Hamlet's old friends, are now the instruments of his enemy. Gertrude, so loving to Hamlet's father, now honeys and makes love with his murderer. Hamlet, who loved Ophelia, treats her rudely and cruelly. Images from the past filter through the action like ghosts, suddenly intruding upon the present, or like Yorick, grimacing from the grave. These buried truths may be tragic, but there is no way of making certain that they will not, for the bane and the enlightenment of the present, break loose from their confines. Thus, the influence of the ghost of Hamlet's father seems dramatically more analogous—and certainly more richly analogous—to the pressures exerted upon the present by the past than to the instances of demonic possession portrayed at the Royal Court or in *The Exorcist.* To cut the opening scene and give the Ghost's lines to Hamlet is to deny Shakespeare his due credit as a Man of the Theater, in whose hands even the instruments of exposition may be instruments of revelation, contributing to the meaning of a play designed not only to imitate but also to explore, to discover, to inquire into the essential nature of our own most strange estate.

There are, of course, obvious arguments against some of the views I have propounded here, but there is time to mention only the most purely negative use of negative feedback. And that is to call attention to some of the dangers and anxieties of influence. Productions of Shakespeare's plays often represent developments of, or reactions against, previous productions. By the same token, many critical interpretations too often represent (a) a wholesale application of, or (b) a kind of chain reaction against, previous interpretations. Thus, on the one hand, we have a critical cognate to what Thomas Kuhn calls "ordinary science"— wherein a reigning paradigm is simply applied to the point where it is exhausted and replaced by another paradigm.[9] On the other hand, criticism (including my own worst work) seems equally formulaic and sterile when it is *simply* a reaction to other criticism. To give an historical exam-

ple, reading through the collections of Elizabethan critical essays com-
piled by Joel Spingarn and Gregory Smith very quickly becomes a bore
precisely because the arguments in them are so obviously derived from
and directed at each other, rather than the human or literary problems
posed in the individual works discussed. Moreover, we can take it for
granted that today's interpretations will be reacted against by the next
generation: "We think our fathers fools, so wise we grow;/ Our wiser
sons, no doubt, will think us so." Last year, a conference was devoted to
Shakespeare's characterization, but not so long ago, as William Empson
recalls, "There was a fashion for attacking character analysis, especially
in Shakespeare," which it has taken some time to get out of. "Maybe it
had a kind of truth," Empson concluded, but it was "dangerously liable
to make us miss points of character."[10]

Perhaps the best way to tackle the common problems of influence,
fashion, overreaction, dogma, and taboo is, like Empson, to acknowledge them as problems. One way to see where these problems arise
might be, as Morris Weitz has argued, to look to Shakespeare's plays
themselves not as subjects for commentary, but as primary sources of
wisdom and, like Dr. Johnson, to use them as such to evaluate reigning
assumptions, fashions, and taboos. For although there may be a limit to
what, of genuine and lasting validity, any one of us can think of to say
about Shakespeare, there is, after all, no limit to what we may learn from
him. How many lifetimes would it take for us (as playgoers, directors, or
critics) to discover, for ourselves, anything like as much about "the real
state of sublunary nature"—or the drama that mirrors it—than we can
learn from those "scenes through which a hermit may estimate the trans-
actions of the world, and a confessor predict the progress of the passions"?

Notes

1. Bertrand Evans, *Shakespeare's Tragic Practice* (Oxford: Clarendon Press, 1979), pp.
241–69.

2. K. R. Popper, *Conjectures and Refutations: The Growth of Scientific Knowledge* (London:
Routledge and Kegan Paul, 1969). And see also Bernard Beckerman, "Explorations in
Shakespeare's Drama," *Shakespeare Quarterly* 29 (1978): 133–45: "Feeling at liberty to interpret a role or scene in unlimited ways is not truly being free imaginatively. It is far more
thrilling and emancipating to discover the limits within which a given work allows legitimate interpretation."

3. A. L. French, *Shakespeare and the Critics* (Cambridge: At the University Press, 1972),
see pp. 17–19, 152–54, 220–21.

4. John Edward Price, "Anti-moralistic Moralism in *All's Well That Ends Well*," *Shakespeare Studies* 12 (1979): 95–111.

5. Edith Holding, *"As You Like It* Adapted: Charles Johnson's *Love in a Forest,"* Shakespeare Survey 32 (1979): 37–48.

6. I have more fully developed some of the points scattershot from here to the end in *Poetic Freedom and Poetic Truth* (Oxford: Clarendon Press, 1976), chap. 4; "What Neoclassical Criticism Tells Us About What Shakespeare Does Not Do," in *Comedy: New Perspectives,* ed. Maurice Charney (New York: New York Literary Forum, 1980); and in "The Morality of Elizabethan Drama: Some Footnotes to Plato," *English Renaissance Studies Presented to Dame Helen Gardner,* ed. John Carey (Oxford: Clarendon Press, 1980).

7. Richard Levin, *New Readings vs. Old Plays* (Chicago: University of Chicago Press, 1979).

8. See the *Letters of Anton Chekhov,* ed. Aurahm Yarmolinsky (London: Jonathan Cape, 1974), p. 86.

9. See Thomas Kuhn, *The Structure of Scientific Revolutions* (Chicago: University of Chicago Press, 1970), and *Criticism and the Growth of Knowledge,* ed. Imre Lakatos and Alan Musgrave (Cambridge: At the University Press, 1970).

10. William Empson, *Milton's God* (Cambridge: At the University Press, 1965), p. 69.

Some Approaches to All's Well That Ends Well in Performance

by ROGER WARREN

In what seems to me far and away the most interesting book about Shakespeare in the theater, Richard David describes how, at a conference in Stratford, a "lecturer, and his chairman, took much pleasure (and time) in demolishing" a production they had just seen, and he suggests that to try to be receptive to what a production "may have to show us about the play, however unexpected that may be, is a better recipe not merely for enjoyment in the theatre but also for the acquisition, if only through negatives, of a richer understanding of the play."[1] There in a nutshell Mr. David sums up what seems to me the most valuable critical approach to Shakespeare in the theater. With this in mind, I should like to suggest ways in which stagings of *All's Well That Ends Well*, including controversial ones, have contributed at any rate to my understanding of some important aspects of Helena, Bertram, and especially of the king and his court. John Wilders, literary consultant to the BBC Television Shakespeare, says in his introduction to the *All's Well* volume that this "is a difficult, elusive play and theatre audiences have, understandably, never learned to like it."[2] But then audiences have had precious little opportunity to learn to like it since they so rarely get a chance even to see it: the Royal Shakespeare Company's 1981 production is the first in Stratford for fourteen years. In the face of such neglect, critical accounts of past productions assume a greater importance than usual, and I shall draw on some of those, as well as on critical interpretations by the directors involved.

Richard David's own account in *Shakespeare Survey* of *All's Well* at the Old Vic in 1953 is a good example of what he means when he suggests that even an unpromising approach may illuminate a text. He describes without flinching how "Michael Benthall resorted to all the most disreputable tricks of the trade—drastic cutting, transposing . . . outrageous buffoonery": "The King became a figure of fun and the affairs of his court pure farce" so as to "play down the awkward facts of life" in the Helena/Bertram story and give it "the remoteness of a fairy-tale" in which "it was appropriate that Claire Bloom should play Helena as Cinderella." But instead of resting content with merely demolishing these things, Mr. David was able also to make the positive and much more interesting point that

> it was not only in spite of these tricks but partly *because of them* [italics mine] that the producer was able to offer a coherent, convincing, and, as far as I know, a new view of Shakespeare's play. . . . This lightening and de-personalizing of the story . . . suddenly revealed [the play's] kinship, not, as is usually supposed, with *Measure for Measure* and *Troilus*, but with the last romances.[3]

But whereas this interesting result had to be achieved by "lightening and de-personalizing" the complexity of the characters, especially Helena— "Helena as Cinderella," as Mr. David puts it—other productions have been *based* on this complexity and have attempted to give tangible substance to Helena's situation.

Tyrone Guthrie's aim at Stratford in 1959, for example, was quite contrary to Benthall's:[4] he said that he used "nearly contemporary" dress specifically to *avoid* "a realm where normal human manners and conduct do not operate" in order to emphasize that "the characters are careful and accurate portraits of human beings": he created an instantly recognizable Edwardian court of rigid protocol in which class distinctions *mattered;* this vividly emphasized the crucial social gulf between Bertram and Helena, and so provided a solid context to motivate Helena's despair.

The king of France, though an invalid in a wheelchair, nevertheless maintained the formalities, determinedly showing a bravely upright public front in the grip of pain, surrounded by officers in formal military dress snapping to attention, ever-responsive to his whims. In this context, one line in particular made a big impact, and several reviewers commented on it. This was the king's response to the assurance that he will be missed when he is dead: "I fill a place, I know't." For John Russell Brown in *Shakespeare Survey* it illustrated what he called "deliberate and effective mis-speaking of Shakespeare's lines" (i.e., these "mis-speakings" were the result not of incompetence but of deliberate distortion). He found this king "a tetchy princeling," lacking in assurance, who "strives continually to exert himself"—perhaps Professor Brown meant "to *assert* himself"; anyhow, he thought that the king's lines were "ingeniously spoken so that 'I fill a place, I know't' is a petulant rebuke."[5] Muriel

St. Clare Byrne in *Shakespeare Quarterly* also found that line important in describing this king, but she took it in a very different way:

> Robert Hardy . . . combined the quiet, assured dignity of age and office with . . . individual, perhaps slightly hypochondriacal, irritability . . . shrewd[ly] . . . summing up . . . his own petty importance when faced by the imminence of death: "I fill a place, I know't."[6]

It is interesting (and reassuring) that both critics concur about the *way* the line was delivered, but whereas one critic dismissed it as merely an eccentric "mis-speaking," the other looked for the reason: "Nothing could have been more acutely appreciative of the quality of the man and the monarch than the quiet, semi-ironic, realistic delivery." Harold Hobson, in his review, also singled out this line as "one of the outstanding moments of the play," and his description supports Miss Byrne's view that the delivery *contributed* to the impression of royal authority rather than, as Professor Brown thought, detracting from it: "'I fill a place, I know't' is superbly dismissive, marking the immense distance that separates a man of kingly mind from . . . his subjects."[7]

This consensus of concentration, if not of opinion, is a useful reminder of how accounts of performances emphasize the dramatic potential of what might seem at first sight inconspicuous lines; it also provides an interesting example of how theater criticism and literary criticism can support each other, for Nicholas Brooke claims that "I fill a place, I know't"

> defines admirably the play's pitch: no more, and no less. . . . The language of the play never strays very far from this pitch, and its most impressive moments share this striking bareness. . . . The blank verse does not soar nor the couplets resonate.[8]

This applies particularly to the couplets in which Helena persuades the king to try her cure. What exactly does that cure consist of? Nicholas Brooke points out that

> we are left with hints at four different explanations; hints rather than affirmations precisely as the couplets are couplets but not fully resonant. It may be drugs, or miracle, or magic—or it may simply be sexual response (miracle or magic in nature). (P. 82)

What is certain is that Helena herself is the crucial factor in the cure. Guthrie brought this out in a characteristically striking way. Her couplets, he says, "suggest a charm, suggest a hypnotism, suggest exactly what the situation demands, that Helena is beginning to dominate the sick old King by the supra-rational suggestion of faith-healing" (p. 82). Muriel St. Clare Byrne describes the effect in this performance:

[Helena] stands behind the King's [wheel-]chair, and places her hands on his brow. He makes an impatient gesture as if to brush aside her insolent presumption . . . stops at her invocation of "the greatest grace," relaxes, closes his eyes and listens, while . . . she speaks the couplets . . . as an incantation, a charm . . . and wrings from the so-called fustian rhymes a moment of pure theatre magic and spell-binding. (P. 563)

Here, then, the stress was on "magic" and "spell-binding." Other productions have sought other solutions for this scene.

Nicholas Brooke points out that when Lafew says that Helena's "simple touch / Is powerful to araise King Pippen," "a bawdy sense is fairly obvious. So is Lafew's excited hope that Helena's sexual attractions—'Doctor she'—will revive the King's spirits." They certainly did so in no uncertain terms in the BBC television version. This production was based visually on seventeenth-century Dutch paintings in order to place the characters in a vivid context, "the feeling of an inner life of a household going on," as the designer put it.[9] So the sick king was liberally "bled" in a darkened, claustrophobic room surrounded by attendants, after Rembrandt's "Anatomy Lesson of Dr. Tulp"—no wonder he felt "worn . . . out / With several applications"; and to have Helena shut in alone with him in that dark room strikingly emphasized the point which Barbara Everett makes in her New Penguin introduction, that "Helena speaks as though the cure incurred the risk of indelicate imputations being made against her,"[10] especially since the king here clearly reponded to her very specifically as a woman, fondling her face and finally kissing her. This arguable interpretation had the merit of focusing attention on the ambiguities surrounding the cure itself. Barbara Everett adds that Lafew "twice describes the King himself, after his cure, as one who has specifically gained in 'lustiness,'" and that while Helena's complicated self

is far from being simply sexual . . . sexual it certainly is. . . . It would be a mistake to question her claim . . . to be moved by "grace" . . . but it would be an equal mistake to lose sight of the "nature" that animates her. As a character, Helena has *power*.

And it is to that *power*, left ambiguous but certainly in part sexual, that the king responds. Donald Sinden's overt interest in Helena also had another dramatic advantage later on, since his immediate attraction to her, and particularly his actually *kissing* her, lent additional force by contrast to Bertram's cruelty in denying her the kiss she asks for in the scene of their parting.

The Polish director Konrad Swinarski had an interestingly similar approach. Interviewed by Ralph Berry,[11] he tells us that he "edited the scene *showing* how Helena cures the King; she does a kind of massage."

When Ralph Berry asked if the massage had "specifically sexual over-
tones," Mr. Swinarski replied that "like every massage it was half sexual!", adding carefully, "only half." "But anyhow," he continues, the
king

> discovers that he can move, and Helena . . . helps him to stand up. It
> continues like this: she starts to walk with him, then all of a sudden she
> starts dancing with him, counting the steps one, two, three, four, one,
> two, three, four, then it turns into a kind of Court dance with the
> whole cast

and Lafew comments, "Why, he's able to lead her a coranto."

Tyrone Guthrie also took this line as the basis for his staging, not
merely of this episode, but of the entire following scene. The danger of
setting the play in what T. C. Worsley called "Merry Widow country,"
with the court orchestra "playing *valses* that just remind one of Franz
Lehar"[12] was that this setting might by association trivialize, for instance,
Bertram's public humiliation of Helena; but Harold Hobson thought
this in fact "the most striking instance" of the way that "Guthrie's elaborate decorations of the text work with the play, and not against it. They
. . . reinforce the effects implicit in the words." The cured king led
Helena, if not a coranto, then into one of those waltzes that reminded
Worsley of Lehar. This developed into a full-scale formal dance sequence that corresponded exactly to the formal couplets in which the
eligible wards are presented to Helena. Her last partner was Bertram,
but it was one thing to dance with her, quite another to marry her.
Harold Hobson describes what followed: Bertram

> shatters the formality by rushing to the steps of the throne, and un-
> folding the horror by which he has been overcome. The effect is very
> great; the artificiality that Mr. Guthrie has deliberately induced is
> smashed by the reality of Bertram's assertion of individual indepen-
> dence,

an effect intensified when Bertram defied *this* king and humiliated
Helena in front of *this* court, which froze in icy disapproval at his blatant
disregard of protocol. A local newspaper reviewer captured the effect
vividly. Because this king was able to "whip the court scenes into moments of extraordinary frenzy,"

> The great scene which . . . ends with the dying fall of Bertram stand-
> ing broken in the centre of the darkened stage, leaves one with the
> sense that here was a "scene" indeed . . . which battered at the senses
> and left behind it echoes of wrath and ruin.[13]

But if Guthrie brought out things about these court scenes that I have
not found in other productions, it was the very difficult final scene that

especially distinguished the BBC television version. Elijah Moshinsky says that whereas "it was fashionable in the sixties to play those scenes very ambivalently—Bertram would look round guiltily, etc.," it is for him "a happy ending" (p. 28). And he makes two interesting comparisons. For Helena's final appearance, "returned from death"—"she has fulfilled the contract, she is expecting a child—[he] said he wanted a feeling of Rembrandt's *Jewish Bride*" (p. 24). This figure—quietly loving, yet also enigmatic—seems a significant parallel to his sympathetic understanding of Helena, especially at the end. As for Bertram, says Moshinsky,

> It's like *The Marriage of Figaro*: when the Count apologises to the Countess it doesn't mean that he's really going to change his sexual habits, but the *apology* is genuine and the music floods out! He has achieved a *potential* for change. Bertram has reached that potential at the end of *All's Well*—and he didn't have that potential before.

A problem with this comparison is that the phrase with which the count begs forgiveness ("Contessa, perdono") is so *expansive* that it is capable of being developed into a serenely hymnlike ensemble of reconciliation, whereas Bertram's spare, cryptic, conditional couplet is the very reverse of expansive. But in practice, the director's willingness to find human potential in that spare language led to a very successful realization of the scene: instead of showing Helena herself when she finally appeared, Moshinsky moved the camera from the face of one amazed onlooker to another, seen from Helena's point of view, and finally focused on Bertram, to whom she now appears a deliverer. As a result, that final couplet seemed less an outrageous condition than a real wish to know how this had happened, as he finally gave her the kiss that he had denied her earlier. This effect could, of course, only have been achieved on film, but it seems to me a good example of using the advantages of the medium to emphasize the individual psychology that is so important in this play, showing us the climax through Helena's eyes, yet in the process concentrating on Bertram's response as well.

What Harold Hobson said of Guthrie's interpretation could be said of Moshinsky's also: that it was a "personal vision" inspired by the "words of the text." It seems to me that individuality is an especially appropriate quality in directors of *All's Well* in view of that "element of . . . the intensely individual," which Barbara Everett rightly isolates as characteristic of both the heroine and the play (p. 8).

Trevor Nunn's 1981 production opened after the Congress had ended. Set in 1910, it followed Guthrie closely in the court scenes: the sick king was in a wheelchair; Helena chose Bertram during a court dance from which the other suitors were eliminated as in a game of musical chairs; the court shrank from Bertram as he humiliated Helena. The tall metalwork arches and sliding glass panels of John Gunter's set suggested, with equal ease, an Edwardian court; a station platform as the troops arrived in Florence; a café run by the widow and much frequented by the military, in which Bertram wooed Diana and Parolles was interrogated; and, most important, an airy conservatory for Rossillion. For, taking its cue from Peggy Ashcroft's exquisitely bittersweet countess ("this thorn/Doth to our rose of youth rightly belong" very tender), the general tone of this production was intimate and conversational, since Trevor Nunn sees *All's Well* as "Shakespeare's most Chekhovian play" (quoted in *The Times*, 19 November 1981). So whereas Guthrie emphasized Helena's white-hot passion, here she had the muted despair of Varya in *The Cherry Orchard*, right down to the keys at the waist of her severe black dress. And in place of Guthrie's rigidly maintained court protocol, Bertram and the king even settled down casually in the wickerwork chairs of the conservatory at Rossillion for the final interrogation. Left alone, Bertram and Helena took hands awkwardly, but as they walked upstage, their hands drew apart again, final image of an unequal marriage.

Notes

1. Richard David, *Shakespeare in the Theatre* (Cambridge: At the University Press, 1978), p. 9.

2. *All's Well That Ends Well*, British Broadcasting Corporation Television, 1981, p. 9.

3. Richard David, "Plays Pleasant and Plays Unpleasant," *Shakespeare Survey* 8 (1955): 134–35.

4. Tyrone Guthrie, "A Modern Producer and the Plays," in *The Living Shakespeare*, ed. R. Gittings (London: Heinemann, 1960), pp. 79–82.

5. John Russell Brown, "Three Adaptations," *Shakespeare Survey* 13 (1960): 140.

6. Muriel St. Clare Byrne, "Shakespeare at Stratford and the Old Vic, 1959," *Shakespeare Quarterly* 10 (Autumn 1959): 561.

7. Harold Hobson, *The Sunday Times* (London), 26 April 1959.

8. Nicholas Brooke, "*All's Well That Ends Well*," *Shakespeare Survey* 30 (1977): 75, 81.

9. BBC TV, *All's Well*, p. 24.

10. Barbara Everett, *All's Well That Ends Well*, New Penguin Shakespeare (Harmondsworth: Penguin Books, 1970), p. 20.

11. Ralph Berry, ed., *On Directing Shakespeare* (London: Croom Helm, 1976), p. 45.

12. T. C. Worsley, *The Financial Times*, 22 April 1959.

13. N. T., *The Leamington Spa Courier*, 24 April 1959.

Between a Sob and a Giggle

by G. R. HIBBARD

The title of this paper is, to be quite frank, what Ben Jonson's egregious Lantern Leatherhead would call "a get-penny," and, like many another "get-penny" title, its connections with most of what will appear under it, including this initial reference to Jonson, are somewhat tangential. All the same, there is at least one important respect in which the disreputable purveyor of hobby-horses in *Bartholomew Fair* has something in common with William Shakespeare: when he metamorphoses himself into Lantern, "the master o' the motions," in act 5, he has to ventriloquize all the words that appear to come from the mouths of his puppet actors. Shakespeare—and here I get on to a hobby-horse from my own stable of wooden hacks—did, I am convinced, much the same thing. As he wrote, he heard every word he gives his characters to speak resounding, in its proper accent, tone, pitch, and emphasis, within his own head. By the time a play of his was complete, it had also received its first authentic performance, in so far as the spoken word is concerned—setting, movement, decor, and the like are clearly another matter—in the mind of its creator, a Platonic ideal of performance, one is tempted to say, towards which every subsequent performance, whether in the theater or in the imagination of the reader, strives, usually in the knowledge that it can, at best, be but an approximation to, a shadow of, that "true and perfect" original production.

I say "usually" because there are occasions, rare and precious occasions, when a play not merely receives a production that measures up to what the playwright heard, one imagines, with his inner ear, but may even go beyond it. Such an occasion, for me, was John Barton's 1969 production in Stratford of *Twelfth Night*, with—to mention only the two performances that linger most vividly in memory—Donald Sinden as Malvolio and Judi Dench as Viola. "One speech in it I chiefly loved." It was Viola's soliloquy, at the end of 2. 2, immediately after Malvolio has thrown Olivia's ring at her feet, and it begins, you will recall, thus:

121

I left no ring with her; what means this lady?
Fortune forbid my outside have not charmed her!
She made good view of me; indeed, so much
That methought her eyes had lost her tongue,
For she did speak in starts distractedly.
She loves me, sure: the cunning of her passion
Invites me in this churlish messenger.
None of my lord's ring! Why, he sent her none.
I am the man. If it be so—as 'tis—
Poor lady, she were better love a dream.

[2. 2. 15–24]

Miss Dench's rendering of that last line in particular was unforget-table, and quite inimitable, leaving one with the conviction that this, indeed, was how the words should be said, though one had never heard them said like this before. "Poor lady," filled with womanly sympathy for Olivia's plight, came out as predominantly a sob but with a faint touch of mischief in it, the merest ghost of a giggle. And then, as the line pro-gressed, that ghost materialized, took the words over, and had "a dream" almost, but not quite, to itself, for underneath the giggle of amusement still lingered an echo of the initial sob, barely audible yet indubitably there.

In this instance Miss Dench, I am inclined to think, probably improved on Shakespeare, for the voice he heard with his inner ear is most likely to have been the voice of a boy actor; and no boy could possibly achieve the "heavenly mingle" of concern and amusement that she brought to bear on the line, and, for that matter, on the part as a whole. If it was an "improvement," by which I mean something even better than what Shakespeare had in mind when he wrote the speech, it was one that he would, I think, have entirely approved of, for it catches and condenses, as it were, the very essence of this extraordinary play, or at least of that part of it which deals with Orsino, Olivia, Viola, and Sebastian. The "mingle" I have referred to is there from the outset. There is pain, the pain of love melancholy springing from unrequited passion, in the lyr-ical grace and beauty of the lines with which Orsino opens *Twelfth Night;* yet, at the same time, there is just a touch, a slight suggestion, of in-dulgence and self-consciousness in their exquisite phrasing and modula-tion that invites not a giggle, that would be much too much, but the almost imperceptible flicker of a smile. Established thus at the very be-ginning, the "mingle" persists throughout the play to reach its culmina-tion in the reunion of Viola and Sebastian, where the dominant tone of wonder and rapturous joy is shot through and through with those mock-ing little parodies of romance conventions, such as "My father had a mole upon his brow"—"And so had mine" (5. 1. 234–35). Thinking along these lines, I was, at first, tempted to describe "Poor lady, she were better love a dream" as the keynote for all that part of the play to which it belongs, but it can best be regarded, perhaps, as providing a kind of sliding scale for it, limited at one end by the sob and at the other by the giggle. I should, incidentally, if I were asked to think up a similar kind of scale for the rest of *Twelfth Night,* settle on "Between a hiccup and a hangover," the hiccup denoting the irresponsibly spontaneous hilarity, slightly leavened with malice, that sets the plot against Malvolio in train, and the hangover, the rather sour disillusionment with a bright idea that has got out of hand and run to excess in which that same plot ends.

Miss Dench's handling, or perhaps voicing would be more accurate, of that line which I have said so much about already, leaves one thankful that the speech direction, as distinct from the stage direction proper, had not been invented in Shakespeare's day. The only thing remotely resembling it that I remember coming across in Elizabethan drama is John Marston's stage direction in *The Malcontent,* to the effect that *"BILIOSO entering, Malevole shifteth his speech"* (1. 4. 43.1), meaning that the hero drops the manner and the accent that are his as Duke Alto-fronto and assumes those he has adopted for his disguised self, Malevole. The nearest Shakespeare comes to doing this is in a rather similar situation, but, characteristically, he includes the direction in the dialogue. After Feste has been playing the role of Sir Topas, Sir Toby eggs him on to further fooling by saying "To him [Malvolio] in thine own voice" (*Twelfth Night,* 4. 2. 64). Indeed, speech directions that are half concealed in the dialogue are fairly common in the plays. To remain with *Twelfth Night* for the moment, we know before Sir Toby enters in 1. 5, and so does he, that he will speak "nothing but madman," since Olivia tells us so (1. 5. 101). Similarly, Viola as Cesario, is given a broad hint about the manner she is to adopt in her first exchanges with Olivia when Malvolio informs his mistress that the messenger at the gate "speaks very shrewishly" (1. 5. 152), meaning, I think, *pertly* rather than *sharply.* This method of controlling and directing the actor's delivery seems to me a better one than those very explicit speech directions with which Ibsen and Shaw, for example, spatter their pages. It is unobtrusive; it invites the actor to look out for it; to make the discovery of it for himself. Above all, it does not rest on the assumption that the actor is rather less than half-witted, which is the only reason I can see for the italicized phrases that Shaw interpolates between the speech headings and the speeches themselves in a passage such as this from *Pygmalion.* It is early in the first act. Liza, the Flower Girl, has just been creating a great hubbub, because Higgins, the Note Taker, has been recording every word she has said. Higgins now steps forward to ask, "What do you take me for?" This is what follows:

The Bystander. It's all right: he's a gentleman: look at his boots. *[Explaining to the note taker]* She thought you was a copper's nark, sir.

The Note Taker [with quick interest] Whats a copper's nark?
The Bystander [inapt at definition] It's a—well, it's a copper's nark, as you
   might say. What else would you call it? A sort of informer.
The Flower Girl [still hysterical] I take my Bible oath I never said a
   word—
The Note Taker [overbearing but good-humored] Oh, shut up, shut up. Do I
   look like a policeman?
The Flower Girl [far from reassured] Then what did you take down my
   words for? How do I know whether you took me down right? You
   just show me what youve wrote about me.

If I were any one of the three actors there, I should, I think, bitterly
resent the slur on my general intelligence and my professional competence that Shaw casts under the pretense of being of assistance.

Shakespeare's helpful hints for actors are then, I would suggest, more
tactful, and therefore more acceptable, than Shaw's categorical imperatives. They can also be more compelling. He often avails himself of his
supreme gifts as a poet to put the question of how a line or sentence is to
be spoken beyond all doubt. Even the richly endowed Bottom would be
hard driven so to "aggravate" his voice as to roar out Hotspur's line "To
be so pestered with a popinjay" with a gentleness that would do credit to
"any sucking dove." But not every character, even in the plays of Shakespeare, has such a distinctive and highly individualized way of speaking
as does a Hotspur, a Mistress Quickly, or a Coriolanus, who establishes
his voice and presence in his first sentence, consisting of the one word
Thanks. It is not an expression of heartfelt gratitude, but rather, as the
rest of the speech that it prefaces makes abundantly plain, a polite yet
incisive order to Menenius to shut up. Once the actor has read the rest of
the speech, he knows exactly how to say *Thanks.* He may well, however,
find himself in difficulty when he encounters a short speech, amounting
to no more than a line or two and couched in the simplest of words, with
little or nothing before it or after it to guide him in his enunciation of it,
and coming from the lips of one who has no special voice of his own, or
of one such as Hamlet, who has indeed a voice of his own, but a voice
that is an amalgam, as it were, of many voices.

Here is a very familiar example of what I have in mind. Early in 3. 4.
of *Hamlet,* the prince kills Polonius. Gertrude's reaction is to cry "O me,
what hast thou done?"—a question that Hamlet answers (and I try to
keep my reading as neutral as possible) with these words:

> Nay, I know not:
> Is it the King?

[3. 4. 25–26]

On the face of it, nothing could be simpler or clearer than those eight little monosyllables in a row. A child can understand them. But can we be sure what they mean when spoken by Hamlet at this precise point in the play? I do not think we can, because what they mean depends largely, perhaps entirely, on how they are said; and that, in turn, depends on how we have been led to regard Hamlet and his role by all that has happened so far. One possibility is that they come out wearily, as the quick-witted prince, having satisfied his impulse to act, begins to realize that he may have made a mistake. "Nay, I know not:/Is it the King?" can mean "Why ask me? I have no idea. Could it be the King?" Another way of rendering those same words is with an abrupt change in tone from plain statement, "Nay, I know not," to a sudden access of hope and elated eagerness: "Is it the King?" Both ways are possible, but both seem to me inadequate, because neither conveys anything of the sense of outrage and disillusion that Hamlet must feel on discovering that his own mother has betrayed him by concealing an eavesdropping spy in her private apartment to listen in to his interview with her. So I offer a third rendering, which goes thus: "Nay," uttered as an angry reproof and meaning "None of that!" or "Come off it!" Then, "I," said very emphatically, "know not," implying "I don't know. How could I? But you most certainly do. So why ask me?" And, finally, with the tired disgust of one who has been forced to see a truth even worse than his strongest suspicions could have led him to, "Is it the King?" meaning "That bloody Claudius again, I suppose? It would be."

As you have probably realized by now, I prefer my third version to either of the other two, partly for the reasons I have given already, but also because it, alone of the three, takes proper account of the queen's natural but none the less foolish outcry, which looks so suspiciously like a plea of ignorance. But, while I think it is right, I have no way of proving it is right. The eight monosyllables remain an enigma. I can state it, and leave it at that. The actor and his producer are in a less enviable position; they have to make up their minds.

They are spared that task in my next example from the same play, because its bearing is a textual one. The decision that has to be made will already have been made by the editor of whatever text they have chosen to use. Line 21 of act 1, scene 1, is a question: "What, has this thing appeared again tonight?"; but the three earliest texts disagree about who asks it. The Second Quarto of 1604/5 gives the line to Horatio; but the Folio and the First Quarto of 1603 both assign it to Marcellus. There are two further complications. The evidence that the compositor who set this page of Q2 had a copy of Q1 in front of him and made extensive use of it is very strong. His departure from it in giving the line to Horatio (*Hora.*) should therefore be a deliberate one, the result of his following the manuscript he was copying. But, on the other hand, there is a wide

agreement among editors that the reporter responsible for the text of
the first scene in Q1 was the actor who played Marcellus. So he should
have known which speeches were his own. It is a pretty conundrum.
Faced with it, Dover Wilson sought a solution in the nature of the line
itself. Calling it a "contemptuous question" (*The Manuscript of Shakespeare's "Hamlet" and the Problems of Its Transmission* [Cambridge: At the
University Press, 1934], p. 37), he unhesitatingly allots it to the appropriate speaker, "the sceptical Horatio," the man who does not believe in
ghosts and who, therefore, dismisses the apparition with "the contemptuous word 'thing'" (note *ad loc.* in Wilson's edition). His decision may
well be the right one; but, if it is right, it is despite the reasons he gives,
not because of them. The line can be spoken in two ways, not one as he
assumes; and the way in which it is spoken will depend entirely on the
speaker of it. *Thing* can indeed be a word of contempt. It is so when
Hamlet shocks Rosencrantz by telling him "The King is a thing— . . . Of
nothing" (4. 2. 27–29). But it is by no means restricted to this sense; it
can equally well be used of the monstrous, the uncanny, or the admirable. I detect no sign of contempt in Banquo's question to Macbeth about
the witches:

> Were such things here as we do speak about?
> Or have we eaten on the insane root
> That takes the reason prisoner?
>   [*Macbeth*, 1. 3. 83–85]

Nor do I find contempt in Prospero's description of Caliban, the offspring of a witch and a devil, as "this thing of darkness" (*The Tempest*, 5.
1. 275). Least of all do I find it when Cominius says of Coriolanus, "He
was a thing of blood" (2. 2. 107). If we only knew what Shakespeare
heard with his inner ear as he wrote that line in *Hamlet*, we should know
for certain to whom it belongs. But we do not. We must have grounds
more relative than Dover Wilson's before we can decide to whom it
should go.

I end with a question about three simple words. How does Claudio say
"Thanks, dear Isabel" at 3. 1. 104 of *Measure for Measure*? Isabella has
worked very hard on her brother for the best part of fifty lines before
revealing Angelo's conditions to him, and worked on him so effectively
that his immediate response on hearing them is "Thou shalt not do't." It
would seem the right moment for her to say "Thanks, dear Claudio."
Instead, she replies:

> O, were it but my life!
> I'd throw it down for your deliverance
> As frankly as a pin.

It is not easy to think of a more tactless and ungenerous answer. The only "thanks" it deserves is a sarcastic one. But *Measure for Measure*, despite its title, is little concerned with either the giving or the receiving of deserts. So perhaps Claudio's expression of gratitude is genuine after all, a turning of the other cheek in keeping with the teaching of the Sermon on the Mount. If it is, Isabella knows what to do about it. She slaps that other cheek mercilessly: "Be ready, Claudio, for your death tomorrow." It is kinder to her, I think, to assume that Claudio's "Thanks, dear Isabel" does have a sharp edge to it.

Characterization through Language in the Early Plays of Shakespeare and His Contemporaries

by A. R. BRAUNMULLER

In his edition of *The Works of Shakespear,* Alexander Pope claimed:

> His *Characters* are so much Nature her self, 'tis a sort of injury to call
> them by so distant a name as Copies of her. Those of other Poets have
> a constant resemblance, which shews that they have receiv'd them
> from one another, and were but multiplyers of the same image. . . .
> But every single character in *Shakespear* is as much an Individual, as
> those in Life itself; it is as impossible to find any two alike; and such as
> from their relation or affinity in any respect appear most to be Twins,
> will upon comparison be found remarkably distinct. To this life and
> variety of Character, we must add the wonderful Preservation of it;
> which is such throughout his plays, that had all the Speeches been
> printed without the very names of the persons I believe one might
> have apply'd them with certainty to every speaker.[1]

Exaggerated as Pope's words are, many audiences and critics have
agreed and continue to agree with him.[2] I would like to explore Pope's
assertion and examine how Shakespeare leads us to infer a character's
nature through the style of that character's speech. In a sense, this pro-
ject may mean rehabilitating "character" as a valid subject for discussion.
My focus will be on Shakespeare's early plays—on the plays, that is,
where rhetoric and verbal ornament begin to be subordinated to the
individualized dramatic speaker and to other theatrical demands.[3] As an
experimental "control," and as illustrations of critical method, I have
chosen several short passages from George Peele's plays.

128

There are, of course, numerous historical and theoretical problems in linking dramatic language with dramatic character. A basic and debatable assumption is that the dramatists of the 1580s and '90s do show action originating within individualized dramatic agents or characters. Plays will certainly work very well without making characters responsible for the drama's action: Tudor moral drama and some plays of Beckett and Pinter, for example, often do not attribute actions to a psychologically framed and represented human agency. Nevertheless, Renaissance English plays frequently invite us to hypothesize qualities of their characters, and they often do so through language. A motto for this point might be a sentence from Puttenham's *Arte of English Poesie:*

> man is but his minde, and as his minde is tempered and qualified, so are his speeches and language at large, and his inward conceits be the metall of his minde, and his manner of utterance the very warp and woof of his conceites. [3. 5: "Of Stile"]

Very generally, the rhetoricians' treatment of *ethos* justifies investigating "character" in English Renaissance drama. Historically, we know, it has been claimed that specifiable features of language have specific emotional sources and effects. Thus, certain poetic meters most legitimately express and evoke certain emotional states. Similarly, rhetorical figures gained emotional specializations (asyndeton for anger, antimetabole for wit, etc.), although the rhetoricians did not always agree on the details. Finally, of course, there were some fairly elaborate ascriptions of diction to "characters," as defined by age, social class, nationality, and so forth.

The practice of any great poet explodes the systematizers' rules, but the rules were invented on the valid premise that we share, or can be led to share, some broad assumptions about language's relation to its emotional and psychological origin. Without that principle, a group art would be impossible, and the audience's reactions would be a congeries of divergent and idiosyncratic responses. Thus, the good rhetoricians always used the reality-criterion: their experience of ordinary people speaking validated a figure's special appropriateness to a given mental-emotional state. At the same time, we may well agree that rhetorical figures "are flexible, and can be effective channels for quite varied states of mind or levels of argument,"[4] just as monosyllables may express both deep emotion and stupidity and iambic pentameter suits both comedy and tragedy. Moreover, any stylistic analysis that hopes to infer "character" from speech must consider both the specifiable linguistic features and a broadly defined dramatic context. Sometimes the coincidence of figure, or diction, or meter with the inferred source will fit the "rules," sometimes not.

Three features of Renaissance English dramaturgy tend to make dra-

matic speech homogeneous rather than individualized. Stylistic decorum
is one, of course, and another is the very rapid and full development of
conventional speeches for the commonest dramatic occasions. As early
as the prologue to *Damon and Pythias* (c. 1564), Edwards writes that "In
Commedies, the greatest Skyll is . . . to frame eche person so, / That by
his common talke you may his nature rightly know"; this sounds promis-
ingly like a counsel of individualization until he continues, "correspondent to their kinde their speeches ought to bee."[5] Slightly later,
Whetstone's preface to *Promos and Cassandra* (1578) complains about
other playwrights who "use one order of speach for all persons: a grose
Indecorum, for a Crowe wyll yll counterfet the Nightingales sweet voice:
even so, affected speeche doth misbecome a Clowne."[6] The verbal clues
are all quite clear: "correspondent to their *kind*," "grose *Indecorum*," and
the antithesis between "affected speech" and "clown." Edwards, Whetstone, and their peers ask only that all kings should be kingly, bishops
ecclesiastical, and clowns "low"; they do not stipulate that one king (or
bishop, or clown) should sound different from another and perhaps
would not want, even if they had the necessary artistic resources, such
differentiation. No easy method can be found for distinguishing between "decorous" characterization and individualized character. Any
dramatic character is an abstraction created from the generalizing and
particularizing forces in the drama and in the audience's experiences
and expectations. The critic must deal with degree, not absolute distinction.

Tradition also supplies a second impetus toward homogeneous
speech. Every genre produces a limited, if large, number of repeated
situations: lovers vow fidelity or lament infidelity; kings command execution, battle, or freedom; tragic heroes decide for ambitious risk, or
learn of desperate failure; and so on. These repetitive necessities naturally harden into convention. Writers become, as Pope says, "multiplyers
of the same image." Thus, Wolfgang Clemen conclusively demonstrates
the existence of patterns of speeches, speeches that all sound more like
one another than they sound either like an individual sensibility responding to a specific fictive situation or like other speeches in their
immediate vicinity.[7] Here again, the critic seeking to find the evidence
and the methods of characterization through speech must admit the
interplay of tradition and individual talent and try, even on an *ad hoc*
basis, to estimate quality rather than to rely on some well-defined "test."

A third force making dramatic speech unindividualized is the way
Elizabethan dramatists cheerfully violate what Pope called "the wonderful Preservation" of the "life and variety of Character." *Contra* Pope,
Elizabethan playwrights will sacrifice virtually any inferred fictional
character in order to get things said that need saying. Any character may

at any time serve as "a kind of running implicit chorus"—the phrase is John Holloway's—and in such moments, the characters often employ language from "a common 'pool' of blank verse," as B. Ifor Evans called it.[8] The consequences of all three forces—decorum, conventional speeches in conventional situations, and inconsistent characterization— are much the same. We have to remain aware of the entire dramatic enterprise and adjust the interpretation of any single character's speech for its contribution either to that larger entity, the play, or to the equally fictitious construct, the character's "character." Understanding a play in the theater and understanding any part of it consist of a constant move- ment between generalization and specificity. In each case, our thoughts and tentative conclusions are influenced by what we bring from tradi- tion, from our individual experiences, and from the very process of comprehending a specific text.

As practicing dramatists (rather than technical rhetoricians or critics), Shakespeare and his fellows variously employed language to charac- terize their imagined persons. The most obvious if not very refined method is the distribution of meter, rhyme, and prose. The fullest Shakespearean example is *A Midsummer Night's Dream*.[9] At a similarly basic level comes characterization through choice of jargon, dialects, unusual vocabularies, or foreign-sounding jibberish. Jonson, Heywood, and Dekker exploit this method much more than Shakespeare.[10]

Another simple characterizing device involves repetition, either of some phrase (the "Barkis is willing" method), or of verbal formulae (proverbs, for example),[11] or of some linguistic error (malapropism in Dull, Bottom, Elbow, and Dogberry, for example, or anacoluthon in Juliet's nurse), or the exploitation of the four types of pun by the fools, the clowns, and Falstaff. While Shakespeare grew more and more adept at manipulating the wit-combats and suggesting their very serious conse- quences for both language and reality,[12] repetition and malapropism, like the use of catch phrases and jargon as characterization, have the major drawback of inelasticity. Once established, these forms of verbal characterization must be continued. They do not offer any opportunity for change in the character's perception or reflection. We can neither anticipate how such a character will respond to a new stimulus nor be retrospectively enlightened when we find an unexpected coherence in diverse reactions (i.e., when we formulate the character's "character"). This method excludes diverse reactions on principle. Consequently, these techniques tend to be reserved for small, usually comic, roles. More complex values will arise only when the dramatist contrasts these linguistic formulae with more flexible styles or places them in situations that exploit their rigidity for other ends (e.g., Parolles in *All's Well*).

Three more sophisticated methods of characterization through language include modeling a character's speech on some recognizable external standard, distributing specific classes of imagery to a character or group of characters, and attributing a consistent pattern of response to an individual character. Initially, Shakespeare appears to have regarded a character who sacrificed his linguistic independence to some external pattern as comic. Thus, Armado and Holofernes. In *As You Like It*, however, Silvius' unhappy Petrarchanism makes him both comic and more disturbingly enslaved, a proto-Caliban reciting the delimiting words tradition gave him. Falstaff's ridicule of euphuism falls into this more complicated category, where the diction bares potentially disastrous limitations of sensibility and predicts the character's inflexibility. When the external model is not a traditional style (like classroom rhetoric, Petrarchanism, or euphuism), but the language of another character, the results are complex and rarely comic, as Othello's adoption of Iago's language concisely illustrates.

Othello is also one of the handful of examples that have been found to support the suggestion that Shakespeare uses a speaker's choice of imagery as a method of characterization.[13] Wolfgang Clemen, like Richard David and many other critics, claims that Shakespeare moves from an imagery of situation to imagery that is "the characteristic manner of expression of the chief character."[14] Here Clemen means not imagery defined by its vehicle, but "figurative language."

Finally, at a very general level, a speaker's language and style may invite the audience to infer an individual cast of mind, an habitual viewing of many different circumstances from a single perspective. Thus, Shylock's mind first analyzes any situation for its implied economic benefits and losses ("I'll have my bond—I will not hear thee speak / I'll have my bond and therefore speak no more," *Merchant*, 3. 3. 4–5), and Falstaff thinks first of self-preservation, whether awakened from a nap in the tavern or informed of Hal's accession to the throne. Such very general habits of mind do indeed have implications for the character's style, although it is exceedingly difficult to describe the ways that influence might operate, especially since our perception of the habit of mind arises largely from the style rather than vice versa. That is, one is returned to the general/concrete problems we encountered before. For critical purposes, however, we may justifiably reverse the process as we experience it in the theater and discover how the dramatist brought about that theatrical effect in the first place. We may try to extrapolate principles of characterizing a "mind set" through language, even though our postulated knowledge of that mentality depends upon the style in which it is expressed.

A few examples from George Peele's plays will illustrate the theoretical issues and demonstrate briefly a method for discussing the problem.

They also provide a benchmark for the Shakespearean texts. Peele was a very accomplished stylist, but his work seems paradoxically to have had rather little impact on other dramatists. His plays were all probably written in the crucial decade from about 1582 to 1592, and they often show a surprising range of verbal experiment, from the metrical variety of *The Araygnement of Paris* to the mixed verse and prose and astonishing structural inventiveness of *The Old Wives Tale.* Peele's dramatic style had the misfortune to be crushed between the millstones (or milestones) of Lyly's comic prose and Marlowe's iambic pentameter. The first he did not choose to imitate, even in the vital and exciting prose of *The Old Wives Tale,* and the second he apparently could not imitate, if *The Battle of Alcazar* is a representative showing. While *The Araygnement of Paris* and *The Old Wives Tale* might have fashioned later styles, then, they had little influence except perhaps on Greene (in *James IV* and *Friar Bacon and Friar Bungay*) and thus, only obliquely, upon Shakespeare himself. Peele's one thorough-going success in a serious, blank-verse drama for the public stage, *David and Bethsabe,* belonged to a genre from which few plays survive.

The general critical view holds that Peele wrote good lyric poetry, but could not make it "dramatic." The opening scene of *David and Bethsabe* confirms this judgment: Bethsabe and David have some splendidly complex and legato speeches, but the speeches, like the actors on stage, remain separate. Language does not intersect as dialogue, although shared imagery and emotion do help create an atmosphere of sensuality and threat. Peele compounded his problem when he chose to imitate the formality of Biblical narrative (for example, the characters often discuss themselves in the third person, most are addressed by title, and nearly every place-name garners an epithet) and to recall the imagery of his Biblical sources.[15] For the most part, the play's lines display their "proud full sail" in a way that makes differentiation by character virtually undetectable, although Peele manages some startling iterative imagery and, in Absalom's death, some crafty kinetic language.[16]

The superficial simplicity of *The Old Wives Tale* almost required that the characters be types. The three witty pages would be at home with their cousins in Lyly, and Huanebango the braggart soldier-poetaster might just survive in *Love's Labour's Lost*'s gallery of stylistic freaks, but none develops unpredictably and individually. When Madge the old wife begins her jumbled narrative, she sounds very like Juliet's nurse:

O Lord I quite forgot, there was a Conjuror, and this Conjuror could doo anything, and hee turned himselfe into a great Dragon, and carried the Kinges Daughter away in his mouth to a Castle that hee made of stone, and there he kept hir I know not how long, till at last all the Kinges men went out so long, that hir two Brothers went to seeke hir.

> O I forget: she (he I would say) turned a proper yong man to a Beare
> in the night, and a man in the day. . . . [Ll. 119–26]

Chronological inconsistency, precision in minor detail and vagueness in
significant facts, the backing and filling along the narrative path, irrelevant association, all imitate an amateur raconteur and—taken together—
create an appropriately vague fairy-tale or folktale ambiance. Decorum
created this character, not the pressure of an individual precisely imagined and conveyed as an individual. Occasionally we hear a speaker who
does not have scores of parallels elsewhere. When Madge's husband,
Clunch the smith, finds the three lost pages, his dog barks at them:

> Hearke this is Ball my Dogge that bids you all welcome in his own
> language, come, take heed for stumbling on the threshold, open dore
> Madge, take in guests. [Ll. 53–55]

A cheerful anthropomorphizing and country superstition mingle well
with Clunch's genuine friendliness and rural asyndeton to produce a
peasant character less artificially constructed than Madge. So, too, the
rustic conflict over the burial of "Jack," the supernatural character who
will help the hero gain his romance princess, also blends rhetorical artistry with a sense of individual speech:

> You may be ashamed, you whorson scald Sexton and Churchwarden,
> if you had any shame in those shamelesse faces of yours, to let a poore
> man lie so long above ground unburied. A rot on you all, that have no
> more compassion of a good fellow when he is gone. [Ll. 454–58]

Peele uses crude oaths and polyptoton for emphasis, tautology ("above
ground unburied"), and the speaker's chance association (the idea of an
unburied man produces "rot on you all") to convey simple outrage confronting bureaucratic stubbornness. When the Sexton replies, "Parish
me no parishes, pay me my fees, and let the rest runne on in the quarters
accounts," we infer a long series of quarrels among obstinate and vocal
adversaries.

The thumping, bombasted blank verse of *The Battle of Alcazar* allows
fewer opportunities for individualized expression than *The Old Wives
Tale*'s verse and prose. Occasionally, the stiffness weakens, and
Stukeley's skeptical English nature appears when he confides to an unnamed companion:

> Sit fast Sebastian, and in this worke
> God and good men labor for Portugall,
> For Spaine disguising with a double face,
> Flatters thy youth and forwardnes good king
> Philip whome some call the catholike king,

I feare me much thy faith will not be firme,
But disagree with thy profession.

[Ll. 806–12]

Stukeley for once eschews the other characters' gaudy abstractions, and the syntax is fairly direct, but even here the clumsy third-person addresses remain and Peele's alliterative mania touches all but two lines. The style characterizes the speaker very badly. When Peele does approach a conventional occasion for rhetorical display, the curse, he employs the devices very cleverly and very openly:

Where shall I finde some unfrequented place
Some uncouth walke where I may curse my fill,
My starres, my dam, my planets and my nurse,
The fire, the aire, the water, and the earth,
All causes that have thus conspirde in one,
To nourish and preserve me to this shame,
Thou that wert at my birth predominate,
Spit out thy poison bad, and all the ill
That fortune, fate or heaven may bode a man.
Thou Nurse infortunate, guiltie of all:
Thou mother of my life that broughtst me forth,
Curst maist thou be for such a cursed sonne,
Curst be thy sonne with everie curse thou hast,
Ye Elements of whome consists this clay,
This masse of flesh, this cursed crazed corpes,
Destroy, dissolve, disturbe, and dissipate,
What water, earth, and aire conjeald.

[Ll. 1268–85][17]

Peele handles the mathematical development of the topics expertly: he synchronizes two parallel sets of terms (stars/planets, dam/nurse) with a third category, the elements. First, he develops stars and planets as influences and sums them with an alliterative triplet, "fortune, fate, or heaven." The next section develops the other set of parallel terms but reverses their original order, "Nurse infortunate . . . mother of my life." Anaphora on "curst" then makes the transition from the two sets of terms to the four elements, which are not initially repeated, but instead summed in a series of parallel clauses describing the body they constitute, "this clay . . . This masse . . . this cursed crazed corpes." The implicit four-ness of the elements reappears in the line that consists of four alliterating verbs—"Destroy, dissolve, disturbe, and dissipate"—and Peele almost manages to recite all four in the final line. The poet can not quite conclude his striking interplay of paired terms against quadruple elements, but the slight collapse in the last line does not invite us to think about the speaker's imagined psychology. Instead, we hear only a smart manipulation that does not finish on all fours.[18]

Peele had clearly read *The Shepherds Calendar* before he wrote *The Araygnement of Paris.* He borrows many pastoral names from Spenser, and he learned what F. P. Wilson felicitously called "a virtuosity in metrical experiment and in variety of tone, a decorum of style, a melody more than ordinary."[19] Peele displays a precocious command of literary tradition, and his architectonic skills easily manage parallel and contrastive plots. Reading Spenser would not teach, nor would Peele's courtly audience demand, however, a differentiation among characters.

A few simple distinctions may be found: the pastoral humans and their rural gods employ homely, rustic images, for example, and the social designators in their speeches mark them as inferior to the play's Olympian gods. Paris has some of the suavity of a young courtier, and even fourteeners can convey his guilty anxiety when he realizes he may be held responsible for abandoning Oenone:

> *Venus:* Sweete sheepeherde, didst thou ever love.
> *Paris:*   Lady, a little once.
> *Venus:* And art thou changed.
> *Paris:*   Faire queene of love I loved not al attonce.
> *Venus:* Well wanton, wert thou wounded so deepe as some have ben,
> It were a cunning cure to heale and rufull to be seene.
> *Paris:* But tell me, gracious goddesse, for a starte and false offence
> Hath Venus or her sonne the power, at pleasure to dispence.
>
> [Ll. 678–83]

When arraigned before the gods, Paris will claim entrapment: Venus, Pallas, and Juno forced him to make a choice and then reneged on their agreement. But naiveté, the common human condition when confronting the gods, also played its part in Paris's choice, and these lines convey the surprise and wheedling tone ("Faire queene of love" and "gracious goddesse" indeed) Paris adopts when he begins to understand the consequences of his actions. Having seen and heard the splendid love scenes between Paris and Oenone, the audience knows that Paris is shading the truth with "Lady, a little once." After Venus has delivered her homily on the "drops of firie Phlegiton" that will "scorch false hartes," Paris may well ask in astonishment and apprehension, "Is Venus and her sonne so full of justice and severity" (line 696).

As the excerpt shows, the fourteeners represent dialogue very effectively. They rarely have the padding and excessive alliteration that infect other poets' long lines and even bother Peele's own iambic pentameter. He has the good sense to divide the fourteeners among several speakers and will sometimes use the rhyme as a way of linking successive scenes.

Lengthier speeches usually go into the play's most common meter, iambic pentameter couplets. The playwright reserves the dignity of blank verse for the play's most important moments: the prologue, Paris's oration before the gods (suitably interrupted by pentameter couplet-commentary from the jury), and Diana's resolution of the conflict through awarding Queen Elizabeth the fatal golden ball.

Given the court-setting and *The Araygnement*'s pageantlike qualities, the most obvious explanation for the lack of characterization through verbal style is that Peele composed his verse according to a scene's emotional tone or substance rather than according to some idea of the characters' individual natures. Only from time to time might he wish to show character issuing in action and thus feel the need to supply the agent's quality. More important for the play were the sequences of semi-emblematic "shows" and the interplay of lightly incarnated abstractions. In their different ways, *David and Bethsabe* and *The Old Wives Tale* also prize other dramatic qualities above characterization: religious pageantry and fairy-tale whimsy, for example. Generically, *The Battle of Alcazar* might appear the play likeliest to reveal characterization through language, because Peele sought to give historical events a tragic pattern. Yet the play's obvious imitation of *Tamburlaine* and Peele's habitual interest in elaborate ceremonial scenes and occasions for set speeches all lead away from an individual characterization.

These examples show how a fine verbal artist often remained within decorous convention (in Madge) or within the limits of a set-piece speech (in *The Battle of Alcazar*). On other occasions, Peele can manipulate the rhetorical and metrical patterns to imply an individual mentality as in *The Araygnement of Paris* and *The Old Wives Tale*. At almost the same time, or even perhaps exactly the same time, as Peele's mixed success with verbal characterization, Shakespeare was writing his earliest plays. Two soliloquies from *Two Gentlemen of Verona* and two episodes from *Titus Andronicus* illustrate how Shakespeare differed from his adept and popular contemporary.

The soliloquies from *Two Gentlemen* are both Proteus's; one comes from the end of act 2, scene 4, and the other from the very beginning of act 2, scene 6. We learn that he has fallen out of love with Julia and in love with Valentine's lover, Sylvia. The play is notoriously full of inconsistencies of locale, nomenclature, and facts of the plot, and these two scenes plus the intervening scene of Launce and Speed (2. 5) have been studied as evidence for what Clifford Leech called "a conjectural reconstruction of the stages of composition."[20] Leech's theory is too complex for easy summary. He suggests that a new scene (2. 5), written after other surrounding scenes had been completed, introduced Launce into the play; this addition required a second, new soliloquy for Proteus (the

one in 2. 6), essentially repeating the one in 2. 4. I do not think the
theory necessary, nor do I think that the soliloquies are the same. Indeed, they work principally to characterize Proteus.

The relevant portion of 2. 4 shows us Proteus's first meeting with
Sylvia. As Valentine leaves the stage, he confides that Sylvia and he are

> betroth'd; nay more, our marriage hour
> Determined of: how I must climb her window,
> The ladder made of cords, and all the means
> Plotted, and 'greed on for my happiness.
>
> [2. 4. 175–78]

Rather than joining Valentine immediately to aid him "in these affairs,"
Proteus lingers behind and delivers this soliloquy:

> Even as one heat another heat expels,
> Or as one nail by strength drives out another,
> So the remembrance of my former love
> Is by a newer object quite forgotten.
> Is it mine eye, or Valentinus' praise,
> Her true perfection, or my false transgression,
> That makes me reasonless, to reason thus?
> She is fair; and so is Julia that I love—
> That I did love, for now my love is thaw'd,
> Which like a waxen image 'gainst the fire
> Bears no impression of the thing it was.
> Methinks my zeal to Valentine is cold,
> And that I love him not as I was wont.
> O, but I love his lady too-too much,
> And that's the reason I love him so little.
> How shall I dote on her with more advice,
> That thus without advice begin to love her?
> 'Tis but her picture I have yet beheld,
> And that hath dazzled my reason's light;
> But when I look on her perfections,
> There is no reason but I shall be blind.
> If I can check my erring love, I will;
> If not, to compass her I'll use my skill.
>
> [2. 4. 188–210]

The slightly modernized punctuation emphasizes, but does not create, a
pattern visible in the Folio text. The speech proceeds through a sequence of three- and four-line groups: proverbial expressions and their
application (ll. 188–91); Proteus's questions about the source of his emotions ending with a phrase introducing the self-argument proper, "to
reason thus" (ll. 192–94); a statement of the case, "She is fair; and so is
Julia that I love," immediately followed by a parenthetical and confused
contradiction, "that I did love . . ." (ll. 195–98); two short reflections on

what the change means for his relation with Valentine and the reason for that change (ll. 199–202); a slightly longer passage, sketching the way to pursue his love, "How shall I dote on her with more advice . . ." (ll. 203–8); a clinching couplet, with one line devoted to checking, the other to compassing, his love (ll. 209–10).[21]

We can see an underlying structure vaguely recalling a sonnet's quatrains, but the soliloquy lacks a sonnet's structure "to reason thus." The opening section does not quite establish the antitheses typical of an argumentative speech: "former" is carefully separated from "remembrance," which in turn is not quite antithetical to "newer object." The line beginning "Is it mine eye" is textually very suspect, although it may originally have had some antithetical structure; the first surviving antithesis is "true perfection" / "false transgression" and the see-saw is continued in a polyptoton, "reasonless, to reason." The compressed image that the Folio surrounds in a parenthesis ("my love is thaw'd . . .") again defeats antithesis or rhetorical structure. B. Ifor Evans discerns here "the beginning, in a very tentative way, of that mounting imagery where one idea is rejected before it is developed but made the basis of a new association and comparison."[22] This imagery laps over into the suggestion that Proteus's "zeal to Valentine is cold" (cf. "thaw'd . . . fire"). Two more antitheses appear—"love him not" / "love his lady too-too much" and "with more advice" / "without advice"—but the fulcrum of the contrasts shifts through the line and over the line-division, reducing the see-saw effect. The final contrast ("picture" / "perfections") would be almost unhearable without the alliteration.

The closing couplet, like the twin proverbs at the start, shows Proteus scrambling to impose some verbal order on his feelings. While the couplet clinks satisfactorily on will:skill, it hardly grows out of the preceding and confused "argument." Similarly, the proverbs sound as if they introduce apomemonysis, a type of argument discussed by Peacham, in which proverbial wisdom confirms the speaker's view.[23] The proverbs' tidy categorization and the planning visible in the "Even as . . . Or as . . . So . . . is" construction of the first four lines soon break down into the chaos of the "mounting image" in lines 195ff. Although the precise definition of "proverb" is debatable, Proteus uses proverbial language more than any other "serious" character, proportionately almost as much as the clowns, who are addicted to it as a platform for their wit.[24] Proteus often uses these sayings as a way of denying his slippery character, or of trying to fix it in some stable shape. Thus, while the soliloquy employs sonnet-language and some sonnetlike structure, it chiefly reveals an uncertain speaker responding to an unexpected emotion. Proteus's love is "erring," and so is his speech. We hear a speaker who has not marshalled his thoughts and feelings. Proteus has yet to consider their implications for himself or for any other character.

When we next hear Proteus, it is after the clowns have mocked their respective masters' love affairs (see especially 2. 5. 10ff. and 36ff.). Anaphora, isocolon, parison, and epistrophe now have their way:

> To leave my Julia, shall I be forsworn;
> To leave fair Silvia, shall I be forsworn;
> To wrong my friend, I shall be much forsworn.
>
> [2. 6. 1–3]

Proteus shortly asserts that "my oath / Provokes me to this threefold perjury" (ll. 4–5), and Clifford Leech rightly observes that "a straining for rhetorical structure takes command of the thought" (new Arden edition, p. xxiii) because three perjuries are hard to find logically, but very satisfying rhetorically. Antithesis riddles the speech:

> Love bade me swear, and Love bids me forswear
>
> At first I did adore a twinkling star,
> But now I worship a celestial sun:
>
> I cannot leave to love; and yet I do;
> But there I leave to love, where I should love
> Julia I lose, and Valentine I lose;
> If I keep them, I needs must lose myself;
> If I lose them, thus find I by their loss:
> For Valentine, myself; for Julia, Silvia.
>
> [2. 6. 6, 9–10, 17–22]

Unlike the many fewer antitheses (even on a per-line measurement) of the first soliloquy, these oppositions are tightly grouped within the lines and within the heavy end-stopping. Parison and isocolon add to the rigid, predictable, building-blocklike qualities of many lines.

The soliloquy hunts letter and word relentlessly. Although the speech presents itself as a deliberative one, Proteus has already reached a decision. Sister Miriam Joseph chose this speech and Berowne's in *Love's Labor's Lost*, 4. 3, as examples of sophistic argument, but the difference in context is crucial.[25] Berowne's fellow sinners explicitly request his speech: "now prove / Our loving lawful and our faith not torn . . . some flattery for this evil . . . O some authority how to proceed / Some tricks, some quillets" (4. 3. 279–83). Berowne responds to the challenge, and no one doubts that his speech is a rhetorical display piece, showing how anything may be made into anything else. Proteus's second soliloquy has no audience except himself, and he never acknowledges his rationalizing design. Rather than Berowne's confident "Have at you, then, affection's men-at-arms," Proteus makes Love responsible: "if *thou* hast sinn'd" (2. 6. 7; my italics). Different as this speech is from Berowne's, it is also very different from Proteus's first soliloquy. Both have the tag that signals an exercise in chop-logic: compare "me reasonless, to reason thus" with "O sweet-suggesting Love. . . . Teach me (thy tempted subject) to excuse it."[26] In the first case, Proteus does not "reason" and we perceive it; in the second case, he has learned Love's lesson well, and he does "excuse" his attitudes.

Proteus finally announces, to his own satisfaction, that "I cannot now prove constant to myself, / Without some treachery us'd to Valentine" (2. 6. 31–32), and the verse immediately becomes much less heavily patterned when he explains his plan:

> This night he meaneth with a corded ladder
> To climb celestial Silvia's chamber-window,
> My self in counsel, his competitor.
> Now presently I'll give her father notice
> Of their disguising and pretended flight. . . .
>
> [2. 6. 33–37]

The closing couplet emphasizes how the speech has been a result of Love's education in deceit and self-hypnotism: "Love, lend me wings to make my purpose swift / As thou hast lent me wit to plot this drift" (ll. 43–44). "Drift" describes both the betrayal of Valentine's plan and the teaching of how to excuse that betrayal.

However they came about, the two soliloquies could hardly be more different. The first expresses a mind surprised and uncertain, the second a mind determined and rationalizing. While Shakespeare never facilely associated overt rhetorical structure with insincerity, the barrage of clipped and tense patterns in the second soliloquy manifests a mind using verbal structure as a substitute for honesty. The comparative ease and directness of the speech's final section, when Proteus announces his plan to cross both Valentine's elopement and "Thurio's dull proceeding" (2. 6. 41), again imply a decision already made, merely awaiting the fits and starts of self-justification to be concluded. Act 2, scene 5 smooths the transition from Proteus surprised to Proteus decided: he now has sufficient dramatic time to invent both excuse and course of action. Perhaps the closest Shakespearean analogy is Leander's eager rationalizing when he awakens after Puck's irresponsible anointing *(A Midsummer Night's Dream,* 2. 2. 110ff.).[27] In *Two Gentlemen,* Proteus's change and subsequent rationalization take slightly longer, and while the source may also be love's irrationality, no external mechanism (like the fairy juice) purports to explain it. Proteus's second soliloquy, moreover, displays calculation without self-mockery (as opposed to Berowne's similar speech). Shakespeare may have proceeded as he did because an abstract issue, the love-friendship conflict, interested him or, of course, the text may have developed in layers as Clifford Leech believed. Whatever their origin, the two soliloquies now convincingly define a fairly individualized shift from emotional bewilderment to self-justification.

As these soliloquies show, Proteus's language has a narrow range of diction and accepts only a schematic model for the mind's and heart's operation. The reverse is true of my other Shakespearean example, Aaron the Moor in *Titus Andronicus*. He can speak very Marlowe in a Tamburlaine-ish mood—"Now climbeth Tamora Olympus' top . . ."—a line J. C. Maxwell thought might be Peele's—and frequently, he recalls Barabas, the Jew of Malta.[28] He can soften—but not sentimentalize—his usual callous language when talking about his infant son ("Look how the black slave smiles upon the father, / As who would say, 'Old lad, I am thine own'").

Above all, Shakespeare has given Aaron an ability to move from one register or tone to another, and this quality sets his speeches apart from the rant and lament most characters use. Thus, he changes very smoothly from the placating servant-tone when be breaks up the fight between Chiron and Demetrius into a magnificently contemptuous and matter-of-fact tone when he realizes the princes are not "lovers" as he first thought (2. 1. 37), but sexual vandals (or, rather, Goths). Initially, Aaron assumed the princes were honorable competitors with Bassianus for Lavinia's love: "are ye mad? or know ye not in Rome / How furious and impatient they be, / And cannot brook competitors in love?" (2. 1. 75–77). He applies the conventional dissuasions:

> think you not how dangerous
> It is to jet upon a prince's right?
> What, is Lavinia then become so loose,
> Or Bassianus so degenerate,
> That for her love such quarrels may be broach'd
> Without controlment, justice, or revenge?
>
> [2. 1. 63–67]

The truth dawns, and it is marked by a verbal clue:

Chiron: Aaron, a thousand deaths
          Would I propose, to achieve her whom I love.
Aaron: To achieve her! how?

                                        [2. 1. 79–81][29]

When he hears first "achieve" and then Demetrius's series of crude proverbs (2. 1. 85–87), Aaron realizes the truth and responds with an equal crudity: "Why, then, it seems some certain snatch or so / Would serve your turns" (2. 1. 95–96). The line is as casually vulgar as Second Gentleman's remark about Evadne: "'Tis a fine wenche, weele have a snap at her one of these nights as she goes from him" (*The Maid's Tragedy*, ed. Bowers, 5. 1. 115–16). When Chiron caps the play on "turn" and "serve" ("Ay, so the turn were served") and Demetrius exclaims, "Aaron, thou hast hit it," the Moor ripostes:

> Would you had hit it too!
> Then should not we be tir'd with this ado.
> Why, hark ye, hark ye, and are you such fools
> To square for this? Would it offend you then
> That both should speed?
>
> [2. 1. 97–101]

His verbal and immoral superiority comes through the rhyme; the re-peated "hark ye, hark ye" is incredulous contempt and cajolery. Aaron can hardly believe the princes' stupidity in fighting over a woman they merely lust for. Like the witty fool, Aaron pays close attention to others' language (as in "achieve") because it allows him a grim humor—the Vice's humor and Barabas's—and also gives him the evidence he needs to exploit and control.

The second example comes from a much later scene when it appears that Chiron and Demetrius will kill Aaron's newborn bastard. Demetrius declares, "I'll broach the tadpole on my rapier's point: / Nurse, give it me; my sword shall soon dispatch it." Aaron replies with an extraordi-nary soliloquy:

> Sooner this sword shall plough thy bowels up.
> Stay murtherous villains! will you kill your brother?
> He dies upon my scimitar's sharp point
> That touches this my first-born son and heir.
> I tell you, younglings, not Enceladus
> With all his threat'ning band of Typhon's brood,
> Nor great Alcides, nor the god of war,
> Shall seize this prey out of his father's hands.
> What, what, ye sanguine, shallow-hearted boys!
> Ye white-limn'd walls! ye alehouse painted signs!
> Coal-black is better than another hue
> In that it scorns to bear another hue
> For all the water in the ocean
> Can never turn the swan's black legs to white,
> Although she lave them hourly in the flood.
>
> [4. 2. 87–102]

Here Aaron ranges through many of the styles hitherto kept separate, but we can see how effectively separate the rhetorical sections are. The first two lines accompany Aaron's physical response (the men draw their weapons on "sword" in lines 86 and 87) and prepare for the speech with a rhetorical question, freezing his listeners. Aaron follows with two four-line enjambed sentences: first the romantic oath ("burning tapers of the sky" may be cliché, but it *is* romantic and the image serves Banquo well enough), then the grandiloquent classical allusions, introduced with a contemptuous epithet, "younglings." Each section ends with a demonstrative *this*-clause:

> this my first born son and heir
> this prey out of his father's hands.

Aaron's contempt, his astonishment that such feeble opponents as Demetrius and Chiron should challenge him, breaks into gutter-vilification of the princes' color, introduced with his characteristic repetition: "What, what, ye sanguine, shallow-hearted boys! / Ye white-limn'd walls! ye alehouse painted signs!" Calmer after this outburst, Aaron proceeds to praise "coal-black," supporting his praise with proverb and anecdote.

Most of Aaron's styles are here, and much of his character: romanticism, pompous pride in his own strength and the fact that he shared an empress's bed, the language of the streets so familiar to a slave and villain, the quieter confidence of the self-made outsider (cf. the Nurse's insulting "fair-fac'd breeders of our clime"). Perhaps less obvious is the way the speech moves the speaker himself towards resolution. Moments before, Aaron had seemed to capitulate:

> *Chiron:*   It shall not live.
> *Aaron:*   It shall not die.
> *Nurse:*   Aaron, it must; the mother wills it so.
> *Aaron:*   What, must it, nurse? then let no man but I
>   Do execution on my flesh and blood.
>
> [4. 2. 80–84]

After the swan-anecdote, however, Aaron's pride in his color and his fatherhood changes his mind: "Tell the empress from me, I am of age / To keep mine own, excuse it how she can" (4. 2. 104–5). The speech turns the scene's energy to Aaron's side, and the Nurse, Chiron, and Demetrius are reduced to feeble objections and finally to:

> Advise thee, Aaron, what is to be done,
> And we will subscribe to thy advice:
> Save thou the child, so we may all be safe.
>
> [4. 2. 129–31]

If we compare Shakespeare's use of language as characterization with Peele's, we may well agree that Peele had little help to offer Shakespeare when he sought contemporary examples of dramatic characterization.

Yet Peele's dramatic technique illuminates some analogous qualities in *Two Gentlemen* and *Titus Andronicus*, qualities that lead away from verbal characterization and the larger technique of locating action in character. The feeling of patterned action in *Two Gentlemen* is strong, so strong that it often overrides at least a modern audience's sense of verisimilar human behavior. The play's urge toward symmetry encourages such compositional theories as Leech's because it appears likely that every Jack needs not only a Jill but a comic servant as well. When the pattern requires that a character change, as Proteus does in act 2, Shakespeare can give the moment psychological nuance, but the pattern initiates the change. In *Titus Andronicus,* the characters themselves frequently acknowledge Shakespeare's own classical sources and seem deliberately to take such classical antecedents as models for their own "modern" actions.[30] Characters and situations align themselves with preexistent attitudes, values, and events. As a result, the dramatic need to situate cause in character diminishes, and events gain their meaning through echo, not immediate origin. Later in his career, Shakespeare found ways to represent both the overriding patterns and a vision of life in which character and action define one another reciprocally. Whether from conviction or ineptitude, Peele never did develop this double capacity, and preferred (if he had a choice) to work through patterned situations, employing—for the most part—stock characters.

Notes

1. "Preface" to *The Works of Shakespear,* 6 vols. (London: J. Tonson, 1723–25), 1: ii–iii. Unattributed quotations of Shakespeare in my text refer to *Complete Works,* ed. Alfred Harbage (Baltimore, Md.: Penguin, 1969). Michael J. B. Allen, Charles Forker, G. R. Proudfoot, and David S. Rodes kindly read and criticized this essay.

2. See, for example, F. E. Halliday, *The Poetry of Shakespeare's Plays* (London: Duckworth, 1954), p. 15.

3. Cf. Richard David, *The Janus of Poets* (Cambridge: At the University Press, 1935), pp. 3 and 31.

4. Brian Vickers, *Classical Rhetoric in English Poetry* (London: Macmillan, 1970), p. 121; the entire section on "The Theory of Rhetorical Figures: Psychology and Emotion" (pp. 93–112) is very useful.

5. Arthur Brown and F. P. Wilson, eds., Malone Society Reprint (Oxford University Press, 1957), A2r; black letter in original.

6. Quoted from *Narrative and Dramatic Sources of Shakespeare,* comp. Geoffrey Bullough, 8 vols. (London: Routledge, 1957–75), 2:443.

7. See Wolfgang Clemen, *English Tragedy Before Shakespeare,* trans. T. S. Dorsch (London: Methuen, 1961).

8. See John Holloway, *The Story of the Night* (1961; reprint ed., Lincoln: University of Nebraska Press, 1963), pp. 21–22 and 24 and B. Ifor Evans, *The Language of Shakespeare's Plays* (London: Methuen, 1952), p. 94.

9. See Frederick W. Ness, *The Use of Rhyme in Shakespeare's Plays* (New Haven, Conn.: Yale University Press, 1941), pp. 81–82.

10. See, for example, Hilda Hulme, "Shakespeare's Language," in James Sutherland and Joel Hurstfield, eds., *Shakespeare's World* (London: Arnold, 1964), p. 164.

11. See "Shakespeare and the Diction of Common Life," in F. P. Wilson, *Shakespearian and Other Studies,* ed. Helen Gardner (Oxford: Clarendon Press, 1969), p. 115.

12. See esp. Brian Vickers, *The Artistry of Shakespeare's Prose* (London: Methuen, 1968), chap. 3, and Terence Eagleton, "Language and Reality in *Twelfth Night,*" *Critical Quarterly* 9 (1967): 217–28.

13. See M. Morozov, "The Individualization of Shakespeare's Characters through Imagery," *Shakespeare Survey* 2 (1949): 83–106, and the blunt statement in Walter Raleigh, *Shakespeare* (New York: Macmillan, 1907), p. 224. In "Shakespeare's Imagery: The Diabolic Images in *Othello,*" *Shakespeare Survey* 5 (1952): 62–80, S. L. Bethell usefully discusses characterization through imagery, noting that it is basically a naturalistic device that Shakespeare rarely pursued unilaterally (see esp. pp. 63–65). See, also, the discussion in Maurice Charney, *Style in Hamlet* (Princeton, N.J.: Princeton University Press, 1969), pp. 215–20.

14. Wolfgang Clemen, *Development of Shakespeare's Imagery* (New York: Hill and Wang, n.d.), p. 54 (concerning *Richard II*); he elaborates his views on p. 81. Clemen ignores the distinction between "objective" and "subjective" imagery (cf. Vickers, *Artistry,* pp. 20 and 26–27).

15. Peele certainly could write excellent narrative blank verse: see *David and Bethsabe,* lines 282–300 in *The Dramatic Works of George Peele,* gen. ed. C. T. Prouty, 3 vols. (New Haven, Conn.: Yale University Press, 1952–70), from which all quotations are taken, and George Smart, "English Non-Dramatic Blank Verse in the Sixteenth Century," *Anglia* 61 (1937): 391, on Peele's long poems, *The Honour of the Garter* (1593) and *Anglorum Feriae* (1595).

16. The imagery of music, harp, lute, ivory, and gold links David, his sons, his kingship, and his divinely mandated mission; for the stage directions implicit in Peele's lines, see T. W. Craik, "The Reconstruction of Stage Action from Early Dramatic Texts," *Elizabethan Theatre V,* ed. G. R. Hibbard (Toronto: Macmillan, 1975), pp. 79–91.

17. The Yale edition makes several major errors in this speech; I have corrected them from the Huntington Library quarto.

18. It is quite true, as Gary Taylor and G. B. Shand pointed out to me, that Peele's apparent lapse may in truth be the compositor's.

19. F. P. Wilson, *Marlowe and the Early Shakespeare* (Oxford: Clarendon, 1953), p. 10.

20. See Clifford Leech, ed., *The Two Gentlemen of Verona,* new Arden edition (London: Methuen, 1969), p. xxx. I quote this text throughout. In *Shakespeare's Apprenticeship* (Chicago and London: University of Chicago Press, 1974), pp. 193–95, Robert Y. Turner discusses this portion of the play and the characterization of Proteus.

21. Since writing this paragraph, I have found Karl-Heinz Wendel's analysis of the speech in *Sonettstrukturen in Shakespeares Dramen* (Bad Hamburg v.d.H.: Gehlen, 1968), p. 56. Wendel sees a "sonnet" in lines 188–91, 195–98, 205–10; lines 192–194 and 199–204 are interpolated verses used "als Reflexion über Valentines Bedeutung ausserhalb der Sonetteinheit." Overall, Wendel finds the speech "ein markantes Beispiel, wie Shakespeare die traditionelle Kunstform zugunsten des dramatischen Effektes zerbricht."

22. Evans, *Language of Shakespeare's Plays,* p. 26.

23. See Sister Miriam Joseph, *Shakespeare's Use of the Arts of Language* (New York: Columbia University Press, 1947), pp. 309–10.

24. My calculations are based on R. W. Dent, *Shakespeare's Proverbial Language: An Index* (Berkeley and Los Angeles: University of California Press, 1981), a private communication from Professor Dent, and the lines-per-role given in T. W. Baldwin, *The Organization and*

Personnel of the Shakespearean Company (Princeton, N.J.: Princeton University Press, 1927). Proteus averages one proverb per eighteen lines, more than twice as many as Valentine; Speed uses about one proverb per nineteen lines and Launce one in seventeen. Julia's speeches have a high average (about one proverb in twenty-four lines), but more than half of her proverbs occur in 2. 7 (her dialogue with the witty maid, Lucetta), while Proteus's proverbs are quite evenly distributed through the play.

25. Joseph, *Shakespeare's Use of the Arts of Language*, p. 203.

26. The "tag" may be the remnant of the older method of direct self-questioning: compare Tamburlaine's "What is beauty, saith my sufferings then?" for example.

27. See Harold Brooks's new Arden edition (London: Methuen, 1979), pp. cxii–cxiii and his citations of R. W. Dent, "Imagination in *A Midsummer Night's Dream*," *Shakespeare Quarterly* 15 (1964): 115–29. Richard Proudfoot points out to me the similarity between the sequence of Proteus's soliloquies and Angelo's in *Measure for Measure*, 2. 2 and 2. 4.

28. For both the Tamburlaine and Barabas parallels, see Nicholas Brooke, "Marlowe as Provocative Agent in Shakespeare's Early Plays," *Shakespeare Survey* 14 (1961): 35–36; the subject has been reexamined in M. C. Bradbrook's "Shakespeare's recollections of Marlowe," in *Shakespeare's Styles: Essays in Honour of Kenneth Muir*, ed. Philip Edwards, Inga-Stina Ewbank, and Stanley Wells (Cambridge: At the University Press, 1980), pp. 191–204. Several other essays in this volume bear on my topic; see esp.: G. K. Hunter, "Poem and Context in *Love's Labour's Lost*," pp. 25–38; Stanley Wells, "Juliet's Nurse: The Uses of Inconsequentiality," pp. 51–56; Nicholas Brooke, "Language Most Shows the Man. . . ? Language and Speaker in *Macbeth*," pp. 67–78. I quote J. C. Maxwell's new Arden edition (1961; reprint ed., London: Methuen, 1968) of *Titus* throughout.

29. Maxwell revises the Q and F punctuation here, but F's "her, how?" would do, if we assume that ? represents exclamation.

30. I am thinking, of course, of the elaborate references to the Procne-Philomela legend, but also of the English morality-style treatment of the Murder-Revenge-Rapine scenes. In *Shakespeare and the Allegory of Evil* (New York: Columbia University Press, 1958), Bernard Spivack finds Aaron himself a "hybrid" of literary typology (the Vice) and individualized characterization (see esp. pp. 379–86 and, more generally, pp. 337–39).

Shakespeare and Kyd

by PHILIP EDWARDS

The purpose of this paper is to ask what the significance may be of the absence of the Ghost at the conclusion of *Hamlet*. I think Kyd may be able to help in this inquiry. I should like to begin, however, with a few uncontroversial comments on the similarity between *Hamlet* and *Julius Caesar*. Shakespeare surely calls attention to this similarity in the curious exchange between Polonius and Hamlet in 3. 2.

Hamlet.	. . .My lord, you played once i' th' university, you say?
Polonius.	That did I, my lord, and was accounted a good actor.
Hamlet.	What did you enact?
Polonius.	I did enact Julius Caesar. I was killed i' th' Capitol. Brutus killed me.
Hamlet.	It was a brute part of him to kill so capital a calf there.

"Brutus killed me." Shortly after the tumultuous and premature ending of the court play, Polonius is killed by Hamlet, who mistakes him for the king.

Shakespeare had written his own play of *Julius Caesar* about twelve months before *Hamlet*. It is generally assumed that John Heminges acted both the old-man parts, Caesar in the first play and Polonius in the second, and that Richard Burbage acted both Brutus and Hamlet. There seems to be a private joke here, as Heminges says to Burbage, "Here we go again! Last year you killed me when I was Caesar and you were Brutus; now you're going to kill me when I'm Polonius and you are Hamlet." Is there not also here an identifying of the two killers, Brutus and Hamlet? Twice John Heminges is an old-man victim; twice Richard Burbage plays the well-intentioned murderer.

Both *Julius Caesar* and *Hamlet Prince of Denmark* are studies of an intellectual in the world of action. In each, a bookish, reflective man is summoned to a major political task requiring complete personal involvement and the use of violent physical force. The play of *Julius Caesar* shows us, to use one of Polonius's phrases, how an "unproportioned thought" is given his act. Brutus is an immensely high-minded man, given to the highest ideals of personal conduct and political aims; a man who measures everything against the teachings of the sages. From the highest motives he agrees to assassinate Caesar. The assassination is quickly decided on and quickly carried out. The greater part of the play is devoted to the disastrous consequences of the "unproportioned thought." *Julius Caesar* portrays the consequences of the deed done; *Hamlet* the consequences of the deed not done.

We recognize that the play of *Hamlet* is, like *Julius Caesar*, a political play, a play about the individuals whose business it is to run the state, a play about a nation during a period of perplexity and transition. The hero of the play is a man whose propensity for reflection and cogitation has become proverbial. And however we try to answer that most difficult of our questions—to what extent did Hamlet succeed?—there can be little disagreement about the terrifying cost of the course of action or inaction which he pursues. At the end of the play, Denmark is in a worse state than at the beginning. The play opens in fear and uneasiness as the kingdom is threatened with war by Fortinbras; it ends with the foreigner, Fortinbras, taking over the kingdom without having to fire a single shot. As Dr. Johnson grimly remarked: "The apparition left the regions of the dead to little purpose." Claudius is dead, but so is the rightful inheritor of the kingdom, Hamlet; so are Gertrude, Polonius, Laertes, Ophelia, Rosencrantz, Guildenstern.

The extent and quality of Hamlet's triumph is teasing to ascertain; the extent of his failure is abundantly clear. *Julius Caesar* and *Hamlet* are studies in political failure. A noble Roman and a noble Renaissance prince. Each man of books and deep thought; each overcome by the sea of troubles he takes arms against.

You would perhaps grant these similarities. You might however balk at the speculation that *Hamlet* is an attempt to rewrite, or better to rework the basic theme of *Julius Caesar*. *Julius Caesar* is a beautifully controlled and beautifully articulated play, whose central ambiguity (our view of Brutus) is a deliberately worked perspective which does not confuse us.

A strange dissatisfaction, you would say, that made Shakespeare unlock that symmetrical and harmonious artefact, *Julius Caesar*, and create that perturbed, confused, bewildering tangle, *Hamlet Prince of Denmark*. But perhaps the writing of *Hamlet* was a purposeful move away from the simplicity of *Julius Caesar*, from a too-easy ordering of the complexities it so confidently deals with.

What was it, then, that attracted Shakespeare in the old play of *Hamlet,* which had been doing the rounds in the 1590s, as a vehicle for a second and more subtle working out of the problem of the meditative man summoned to the field of political action?

My own guess is that it was the presence of the supernatural. The supernatural happenings in *Julius Caesar* do not affect the fact that the play is firmly placed in the world of men. This is not true of *Hamlet.* Heaven, earth, and hell are the setting of the play. The world of man is poised within a vast transcendental world of spirit to which it belongs, is an integral part of a cosmos containing places of eternal suffering and eternal bliss.

The original story of Hamlet, as it appears in Saxo Grammaticus or in the much later rendering by Belleforest, contains no ghost coming from the other side of the grave to tell Hamlet of a secret murder and of the need to take revenge. The murder was known to all, and Amleth needed no one to instruct him that it was his duty to take revenge.

But there *was* a ghost in the play which Shakespeare knew. That play, which we surmise to have been by Thomas Kyd, is irrevocably lost. The only thing we know about it is that it had a ghost, and that the ghost appeared to Hamlet, urging him to revenge. This is from Thomas Lodge's famous remark, "pale as the vizard of the ghost which cried so miserably at the Theatre, like an oyster-wife, Hamlet, revenge!"

To the old story, Kyd (if he is the author) had added a ghost, a voice from the spirit world communicating with human beings, urging the hero to a duty. This single fact which we know about the old play may indeed have been the element that beckoned Shakespeare towards it.

In Thomas Kyd's extant play *The Spanish Tragedy,* we find that the world of man is set within and surrounded by a spirit world. On stage, watching the action during the entire play, is the ghost of a dead man and his conductor from the underworld, aptly named Revenge. In this play the gods control but they do not communicate. Their control is complete, and their silence—towards the living—is complete. All that we see acted out by the humans on stage—all aspirations and contrivances and errors—are cheerfully accepted by the gods as contributions to a previously concocted divine plan, rigid and undeviating. At the end of the play, the dead are dismissed without hesitation to their everlasting abodes, whether of suffering or of bliss.

Totally rejecting the heroic myths of his fellow-lodger Marlowe, for whom the human scene centers on the actions and passions of remarkable individuals, Kyd in *The Spanish Tragedy* took a collection of rather unremarkable individuals and made his plot an intricate network or web of colliding aspirations. One person's plan collides with another's, and both career off in another direction to collide with a third. Bel-imperia takes Horatio as a new lover to spite her would-be lover Balthazar. But this action infuriates her brother Lorenzo, who plans to kill the new lover. In the meantime Balthazar's marriage to Bel-imperia is being planned by the authorities as a means of uniting the kingdoms of Spain and Portugal. Bel-imperia and Horatio never have a chance. He is murdered before her eyes. But, by removing Horatio, Lorenzo brings a new factor into existence, the revenge of a bereaved father, Hieronimo. (There is a great similarity here with *Hamlet,* in which in the middle of the play, the unintended killing of Polonius generates the counter-movement of Laertes' revenge, which eventually destroys Hamlet before he can exact *his* revenge.)

Kyd's characters are passionate people who act with fierce determination, sometimes impulsively, sometimes with careful premeditation. But, one and all, they are born to frustration. Their thoughts are theirs, their ends none of their own. This frustration takes place entirely within the sphere of human society, in the encompassing, entangling network of conflicting plans and aspirations in Spain and Portugal.

But all this struggling of the will, and deflection of purpose, become the means by which transcendental decrees are fulfilled. Hieronimo craftily plans that Bel-imperia shall use a real dagger in the court play and so actually kill her fellow-actor Balthazar. By this, unwittingly, is the initial decree of Proserpine fulfilled, that Andrea should see Balthazar "deprived of life by Bel-imperia." But Hieronimo did *not* plan that Bel-imperia should then stab *herself.* "Poor Bel-imperia missed her part in this." In this voluntary act of suicide, Bel-imperia exercises her free will and alters Hieronimo's scheme. But this act restores her to the waiting spirit of Andrea. There is nothing that men and women do that does not contribute to the divine plan. Revenge may fall asleep, but it does not matter. Whatever men do, it will turn out as the gods decree.

But who *are* these powers who direct human affairs? Proserpine and Pluto; Aeacus, Minos, and Rhadamanthus; Revenge. What does Kyd's classical pagan machinery signify? These are dark gods whose destinies require for their fulfillment the existence of human hatred and the rankling desire for retribution.

In the early days after the murder of Horatio, Hieronimo asks the heavens to help him towards a justice which he thinks his king will carry out. Every step forward in his mission to discover the murderers and bring them to justice he regards as the work of heaven. But in the extremities of frustration, he thinks that "justice is exiled from the earth" and talks of applying to the infernal gods for help. When he has decided to undertake revenge for himself, though he knows that the heavens disapprove of private revenge, he does *not* see himself as an agent of those infernal powers. On the contrary, he believes he must be enjoying the support of heaven.

> Heaven applies our drift,
> And all the saints do sit soliciting
> For vengeance on these cursed murderers.

But, as Kyd makes abundantly clear, it's the infernal gods who are running things. At the conclusion of the play, the ghost of the dead Andrea, who had been so apprehensive that things were taking the wrong course, rejoices at the fulfillment of the revenge that he was promised and happily surveys the carnage on the stage: "Ay, these were spectacles to please my soul." And he helps to apportion eternal sentences, whose "justice" makes our blood run cold.

How different it all is in Shakespeare's *Hamlet*! A ghost, whose status and authority are by no means certain, appears three times, trying to communicate with the living. The first time he is silent; the second time he unveils the secrets of the past to Hamlet and urges him to action. The third time he intervenes in the scene between Hamlet and his mother, and tries—unsuccessfully—to change the course of Hamlet's activity. He does not appear again; at the end of the play he is absent and no one speaks of him. There is the carnage on the stage; Horatio, Fortinbras, and Osric are the only survivors. What does the Ghost think of it all? He has disappeared. There is no word of approval, or sorrow, or anger. He neither praises his dead son nor blames him. Or, if he was a devil, he does not reappear to gloat over the great devastation that he has caused. The rest is silence indeed.

It is a striking fact that the Ghost is not there at the end of the play to tell us what he thinks. It is possible that he was absent also at the end of the old pre-Shakespearian *Hamlet*. But it is also possible that the absence is Shakespeare's innovation; a challenge to the Kydean certainty as we find it in *The Spanish Tragedy*. Shakespeare perhaps went to his source because of its supernatural element, but he transformed it. Now it is to be the audience's task, not the dramatist's, to decide what the relationship of Hamlet's actions is to those who rule our destinies.

Hamlet himself in the last scene is convinced that in trying to kill Claudius he is doing the will of heaven, that he better understands the divine will than he did earlier in the play, and that to neglect the duty imposed on him by the Ghost is to incur damnation.

A. C. Bradley, while acknowledging Hamlet's failure, sees it that way, too:

The Ghost affects imagination not simply as the apparition of a dead king who desires the accomplishment of *his* purposes, but also as the representative of that hidden ultimate power, the messenger of divine justice set upon the expiation of offences which it appeared impossible for man to discover and avenge, a reminder or a symbol of the connexion of the limited world of ordinary experience with the vaster life of which it is but a partial appearance. . . . The apparent failure of Hamlet's life is not the ultimate truth concerning him.

[*Shakespearean Tragedy*, 1904, p. 174]

Kyd might have said, and perhaps did say in the old play of *Hamlet*, that Hamlet was deluding himself. That in pursuing his vengeance he was actually fulfilling the decrees of darker forces than those of a Christian providence, forces quite unnameable except by some device of using the mythology of classical writers—"thrusting Elysium into hell," as Nashe remarked with an unnerving accuracy which may or may not have been intended.

The whole tendency of modern literary criticism, since the seminal essay of George Wilson Knight in 1930, has been to treat *Hamlet* as a tragedy of delusion or obsession, or some kind of satanic infiltration. Whoever the Ghost is, it is constantly argued from one point of view or another that he is doing Hamlet no good. This is to view Shakespeare's play with a Kydean certainty.

Hamlet asks Horatio, "Is't not to be damned/To let this canker of our nature come/In further evil?" Horatio, prudently, returns no answer. The question indeed, is quite unanswerable. It is awful to be asked to say yes or no to this. Yet it is the question which the whole play of *Hamlet* places before us. It is put to us by another baffling Dane, Kierkegaard, in his *Fear and Trembling*. Abraham heard a voice, which he assumed was God's, telling him to sacrifice his son Isaac. Isaac was not killed, but Abraham was ready and willing to kill him. Either he was a murderer, or he was an obedient child of God. Faith, says Kierkegaard, is "a paradox which is capable of transforming a murder into a holy act well-pleasing to God." But, he asks, "If the individual had misunderstood the deity— *what can save him?*"

The presence of the Ghost in the early part of *Hamlet* suggests the possibility of making a higher truth active in a fallen world. During the course of the play we may well feel that the attempt to import the values of a higher world into Denmark causes nothing but physical and moral damage to all concerned. We may be tempted to deduce from this that there is no world of higher truth or values. But this deduction is not warranted by the text.

The absence of the Ghost at the end of *Hamlet* leaves the play, and us, in a hazardous, precarious point of balance. In an uncertainty which, however displeasing to us, is necessary for the tragic impact of the play.

You can never know whether the mission Hamlet so uncertainly carried out was divinely inspired. Yet one's response to the terrible cost of his mission depends on knowing. Perhaps this is what Hazlitt meant when he said, "It is we who are Hamlet!"

In *Hamlet,* Shakespeare gave a whole new perspective—the perspective of eternity—to the problem of the engagement of the philosopher in political action as he had treated it in *Julius Caesar.* The relationship between the hero and supernatural forces is in forceful contrast to the relationship established by Kyd's *Spanish Tragedy.* The supernatural forces are not clearly in control of worldly actions and events, as they are in *The Spanish Tragedy.* The identity of the forces is ambiguous, not certainly Christian nor certainly anti-Christian; nor positively non-Christian as they are in *The Spanish Tragedy.* It would be very interesting if Shakespeare had found in the old *Hamlet* a supernatural structure similar to that in *The Spanish Tragedy.* If he had, then the play that inspired him to deepen and spiritualize the conflict of Brutus also provoked him to challenge the certainty of its grim metaphysics, and so led him to the tragic uncertainties of Hamlet's commitment and achievement.

Shakespeare and Jonson

by ANNE BARTON

In 1618, when Ben Jonson made his famous journey to Scotland and talked with (or more properly, at) William Drummond of Hawthornden, Queen Elizabeth had been dead for fifteen years. Prince Henry, briefly cherished as Astraea's true heir, had been in his grave for six years, and William Shakespeare for two. The Jonson who conversed with Drummond had arrived, I want to argue, at a seeming impasse as a writer of comedy. Indeed, he may well have made a private decision to abandon the stage. *The Staple of News,* his next new play, did not appear until 1626, eight years after the meeting with Drummond and ten years after *The Devil Is An Ass,* the last of his Jacobean comedies. The Jonson of 1618 could afford to turn his back on the theater, or so it must have seemed. A famous and, of late, a much honored man, he had already published his Folio *Works,* including nine of his plays. He had powerful friends and patrons, was about to receive an honorary M.A. from Oxford University and, apart from his established position as chief masque writer to the court of King James, he was busy with various literary projects of a nondramatic kind. When his library was destroyed by fire in 1623, Jonson lamented, in "An Execration Upon Vulcan," the disappearance of a whole galaxy of precious, unpublished works: several translations, an English grammar, his history of the life of Henry V, a poetic account of his expedition to Scotland, what sounds like the original (and probably much larger) version of *Discoveries*—"twice-twelve-years stor'd up hu-

This lecture derives from a book, *Jonson and the Compass of Comedy,* to be published by Chatto and Windus in 1983. Two paragraphs and several sentences necessary for the argument have appeared in an article entitled "Harking Back to Elizabeth: Ben Jonson and Caroline Nostalgia," *English Literary History* 48 (1981): 706–31. Quotations from Jonson are taken from *Ben Jonson,* ed. C. H. Herford and Percy and Evelyn Simpson, 11 vols. (Oxford: At the University Press, 1925–52). Shakespeare quotations are drawn from *The Riverside Shakespeare,* ed. G. Blackmore Evans (Boston: Houghton Mifflin, 1974).

manity"—and, rather less expectedly, a number of theological writings. These were the losses that really hurt. He comes close to forgiving the lame god of fire for sweeping away something less consequential: "parcels of a Play."

In talking to Drummond that winter of 1618, Jonson with characteristic highhandedness dismissed a number of celebrated poets, both living and dead, who like himself had begun writing during the reign of Elizabeth. He expressed unqualified impatience at that time with Thomas Campion, Samuel Daniel, Sir John Davies, John Day, Thomas Dekker, Michael Drayton, Edward Fairfax, Sir John Harington, Gervase Markham, John Marston, and Thomas Middleton. Jonson had been for years a notorious dissenter from the mainstream of Elizabethan literature, and this blacklist was obviously far from complete. Anthony Munday, for instance, satirized as Antonio Balladino in the revised version of Jonson's early comedy *The Case Is Altered,* is absent. So is Thomas Kyd, the author of that stubbornly memorable play *The Spanish Tragedy,* a play which haunted Jonson even more persistently and cruelly than it did other dramatists of his generation. If Dekker is to be credited, Jonson had himself acted the part of Hieronymo during his days of lowly service "among the mimics," which would help to explain why he could never thereafter get it out of his head. Also, as I believe myself (although I do not want to argue the case here), Jonson *was* the skillful ventriloquist responsible for the famous "additions" to the play commissioned by Henslowe in 1601–2 and printed in Pavier's edition of 1602. And yet both the language and the revenge form of *The Spanish Tragedy* were peculiarly offensive to his artistic principles. Marlowe too, at least the Marlowe who wrote *Tamburlaine* and was indirectly responsible for so much of that *"scenical* strutting and furious vociferation" which Jonson later deplored in *Discoveries,* rather surprisingly seems to have escaped censure before Drummond in 1618.

For his friend George Chapman, for one lyric by Sir Henry Wotton, and for Robert Southwell's poem "The Burning Babe," Jonson did find words of unalloyed praise. But when he came to what seem to us now to be the four great names of Elizabethan poetry—Philip Sidney, Edmund Spenser, John Donne, and William Shakespeare—his response was significantly divided. Jonson had a shrewd sense of what the judgment of posterity on this quartet was likely to be. They were not poetasters. Whatever their faults, they were writers who mattered, which is why Jonson returns to them again and again. Yet the feelings they aroused in him had, for a long time, been contradictory and a little defensive.

Jonson's mixed attitude towards Shakespeare, the scandalous inventor of servant monsters, seacoasts in Bohemia and moldy tales; a man who wrote too glibly and "wanted Arte" but who was also the master of "well torned, and true-filed lines"; in tragedy the peer of Aeschylus, Sophocles, and Euripides, and in comedy of Aristophanes, Plautus, and Terence—"not of an age, but for all time"—is famous. Less attention has been paid to the fact that his response to Sidney, Spenser, and Donne displays a strikingly similar inconsistency. Sidney obviously obsessed Jonson as the realization of a personal ideal: the good poet who was also a conspicuously good man, who brought his life and his art into just that harmonious accord which Jonson prized and found it so difficult in his own case to achieve. In "To Penshurst," Sidney is the poet at whose "great birth . . . all the *Muses* met." Elsewhere in *The Forest,* and in the *Epigrams,* he is the great, the "god-like Sidney," who exhausted the wealth of the Muses' springs. *The Silent Woman* even turns him into a professional man of letters, admittedly by somewhat sophistical means. When Sir John Daw sneers at men who are obliged to live by their verses, Dauphine punningly slaps him down: "And yet the noble *SIDNEY* lives by his, and the noble family not asham'd."

But how much of Sidney's work did Jonson genuinely admire? The neoclassicism of *The Defense of Poesie* was predictably appealing. *Arcadia* and *Astrophil and Stella,* the fictions through which Sidney in fact "lives," were another matter. The Jonson who talked to Drummond disapproved of romance literature. Moreover, as he pointed out sourly, in *Arcadia* Sidney violated the principles of classical decorum, failing to distinguish the speech of princes from that of clowns. It is true that Saviolina and Fungoso in *Every Man Out of His Humour* are constantly reading *Arcadia* and introducing its choicer phrases into their discourse. They also happen to be half-wits, whose admiration in no way honors Sidney's book. As for *Astrophil and Stella,* it was largely responsible for the sonneteering vogue of the 1590s, and Jonson made it clear to Drummond that he deplored the sonnet, that tyrannical bed of Procrustes, as he called it, in which sense is distorted in the interests of form. It is all too tempting to dismiss as casual flattery Jonson's poem in *The Forest* in which he assures the Countess of Rutland, Sidney's daughter, that she is (or might become, with a little more effort) a poet quite as good as her father. Unfortunately, Jonson reiterated this opinion in talking to Drummond, and that is altogether more embarrassing.

As for Spenser, Jonson told Drummond that he did not like either his stanzas or his matter. But he also told him that he had troubled to work out an explication of the allegory of *The Faerie Queene,* which he sent to Raleigh. He crammed his own, personal copy of "*Spenser's* noble book" (as he called it in his epigram to Venetia Digby) with marginal annotations. And he not only advised young men, in *Discoveries,* to read Spenser *for* his matter, but informed a presumably bewildered Drummond that, after all, Arthurian material formed incomparably the best subject for an heroic poem. "In affecting the ancients," Jonson grumbled, "Spenser writ no language." Yet Drummond records that his guest liked to recite sections of *The Shepherd's Calendar* from memory. In his masque *The Golden Age Restored* of 1615, Jonson had already placed Spenser beside Chaucer as one of those "sons" of Apollo who accompany Astraea on her return to earth.

John Donne, like Shakespeare, was Jonson's personal friend. Jonson praised him in his *Epigrams* as "the delight of *PHOEBUS,* and each *Muse,*" and he told Drummond that Donne was "the first poet in the world, in some things." He clearly valued Donne's critical judgment, sent him his own poems with a trepidation that seems unfeigned and (again according to Drummond) introduced him as a speaker in his lost apology for *Bartholomew Fair,* under the name of Criticus. Interestingly enough, it was the Elizabethan and not the Jacobean Donne who appealed to Jonson: all Donne's best poems, he claimed, had been written before the age of twenty-five. He himself had memorized all of "The Bracelet" and parts of "The Calme." But this brilliant contemporary, "whose every worke," Jonson asserted in his *Epigrams,* "came forth example, and remaines so, yet," was also (it seems) a willfully obscure poet who "for not being understood, would perish," and who "for not keeping of accent, deserved hanging."

Jonson found it easy to condescend to the lesser stars of Elizabethan poetry. The four great planets—Sidney, Spenser, Shakespeare, and Donne—compelled respect. Their achievements, however, which he was too intelligent not to recognize, were disquieting. After all, the great men, as well as the poetasters and the lesser lights, had helped to define his own temperamental separation from the main current of late-sixteenth-century poetry and drama. During the 1590s Jonson developed a distinctive poetic and (more particularly) a distinctive comic mode by reacting against a generalized Elizabethan norm. In this respect, he was the exact opposite of Shakespeare, who forged his own style during the last decade of the sixteenth century by assimilating and then transcending the native tradition.

I do not want to deny the influence of Lyly, or of popular morality drama or the Elizabethan pamphleteers on Jonson's early humor plays. It is important to remember, too, that in 1598 Francis Meres was praising Jonson for tragedies, every one of which is lost. In 1618, after the publication of his Folio, Jonson told Drummond that half of his comedies were not in print. We will never know what Jonson's lost Elizabethan popular plays were really like: *The Isle of Dogs, Hot Anger Soon Cooled, Page of Plymouth, Robert II King of Scots, Richard Crookback,* and heaven knows how many more. Clearly Jonson was determined that this hackwork (much of which he was writing concurrently with those early humor plays that he did carefully preserve) should sink without trace. But the fact that he produced plays during the 1590s in collaboration with men like Nashe, Dekker, Porter, and Chettle—and we know from *Eastward Ho!* later just how proficient and adaptable a collaborator Jonson could be—makes it plain that he had, however reluctantly, served out a literary as well as an actor's apprenticeship to the popular dramatic tradition.

Jonson knew, then, exactly what he was reacting against as a writer of comedy. Shakespeare, a man some eight years his senior, must have seemed to him to exemplify and focus everything from which he himself was trying so hard to break away. And yet Shakespeare was not only a personal friend, very possibly the man who enabled Jonson to escape from his servitude to Henslowe: he was a comic dramatist who had somehow contrived to do most of the things of which Jonson disapproved, to follow false gods, and yet create plays that Jonson simply could not brush away and dismiss as he could work by Greene and Dekker, Heywood, Porter, Chettle, and Munday, even though they derived, apparently, from the same popular quarry. This is why, as I want to argue, Shakespeare was such a thorn in Jonson's flesh. It also, I believe, accounts (at least in part) for the fact that in later years Jonson, in effect, recanted that he worked out a kind of intelligent rapprochement with what for so long had been the rival comic form.

Almost invariably, comparisons between Jonsonian and Shakespearean comedy resolve themselves into a series of well-worn antitheses. Classical versus romantic, first of all. A comedy of specialized as against one of wide appeal. Jonson's meticulously created urban worlds, usually contemporary London, more or less thinly disguised, against those of a man who insisted upon ruralizing even his cities (Athens or Messina, Milan and Tyre) and upon blurring our sense of historical time. Jonsonian comedy displaying only the most perfunctory interest in love and marriage, tending (Queen Elizabeth always excluded) to debase or simply ignore women, against one presenting marriage as the most valuable of human relationships, and women, even the youngest and most inexperienced, as the natural embodiments and guardians of the values central to a good society. A rigidly moral if not positively punitive art, poised against something far more tolerant and forgiving. Stereotyped humor characters whose obsessions may be brutally shattered but who are fundamentally incapable of growth or change, measured against Shakespearean characters who learn from their experiences, becoming wiser and better in the course of five acts—or even, like Orlando's brother, overnight. Eddying, disjunctive Jonson plots, against an essentially linear and causal story line. Compression and the unities as natural features of comic form, as opposed to a relaxed and cavalier treatment of time and place. Plays which simply stop—because a situation has been fully explored, because "mischiefs feed / Like beasts, till they be fat, and then they bleed," because the time has come to apply the match to the fuse and blow the whole preposterous entanglement sky-high—against a comedy in which the end, characteristically, crowns all.

Like most literary generalizations, these are certainly open to qualification, from both the Jonsonian and the Shakespearean side. Yet they seem at least roughly accurate. I suspect, moreover, that Jonson would have endorsed them, and with some pride. Which does not mean that he could prevent himself from craning his neck from time to time to regard the alien territory on the other side of the fence, with a measure of personal unease. In *Every Man Out of His Humour* of 1599, perhaps the most extreme and defiantly idiosyncratic of all Jonson's Elizabethan comedies, one of the two chorus characters betrays at one point a hankering after a different kind of play. He wonders whether the argument of the satiric comedy they are watching might not have been "of some other nature, as of a duke to be in love with a countesse, and that countesse to be in love with the dukes sone, and the sone to love the ladies waiting maid: some such cross wooing, with a clowne to their serving man." From this alarmingly prescient account of *Twelfth Night,* a play Shakespeare had not yet written, he is haled away sternly by Cordatus, a character described as "the author's friend," who informs him that comedy should be what Cicero said it was: an imitation of life, a glass of manners and an image of truth—pleasant, ridiculous, and designed, above all, for the correction of social abuses. Anything else, and most certainly a romantic plot of the kind just outlined, is mere window dressing for the vulgar. So much for Shakespeare. And yet at the end of this very play, Jonson cannot forbear looking across the fence again in what seems to be an uncritical, indeed almost an admiring, fashion. He allows one of his characters to describe another as "a kinsman to Justice Silence," in full consciousness of the very different comic kingdom that reference will conjure up. While Macilente, that lean, raw-boned anatomy and uncompromising satirist, who to some extent speaks for Jonson himself, begs for applause in the last lines by suggesting that audience approval might have the power to transform him into his comic antitype rendering him, as he says, as fat as Sir John Falstaff.

Jonson's ten surviving Elizabethan and Jacobean comedies often seem to invoke conventions, themes, or situations associated with specific Shakespearean plays in a deliberately distorted form. So the mock combat between the two cowards Daw and La Foole in *The Silent Woman,* each one falsely convinced of the ferocity of his opponent, replays the reluctant encounter between Viola and Sir Andrew Aguecheek. The collegiate ladies in the same play, living apart from their husbands in a little

single-sex society that is rudely shattered by their sudden, collective passion for Dauphine, seem to glance uneasily not only at a contemporary feminist affectation but at Navarre's abortive scheme for an Academe in *Love's Labour's Lost.* It seems doubtful that Puntarvolo in *Every Man Out of His Humour* would have been accompanied by so palpably engaging and omnipresent a dog had Jonson not been remembering Launce and his friend Crab in *The Two Gentlemen of Verona.* (But, Jonson being Jonson, Puntarvolo's dog is poisoned in the end.) The balcony scene from *Romeo and Juliet,* as critics have long recognized, reappears in a most disturbing and dubious form in *Poetaster,* when Julia and her exiled lover Ovid are obliged to part. Indeed, I would argue that what appears to be the current critical deadlock over exactly how Jonson intends us to take this scene—whether as condemnation of the erring couple or celebration—derives precisely from our uncertainty as to what the dramatist's attitude really is to his Shakespearean model.

None of these echoes can be pinned down or dismissed as simple parody. They are odder and more mixed than that. Moreover, they associate themselves with other episodes, harder to relate to a particular Shakespeare play, which nonetheless seem to point stubbornly but ambiguously in the general direction of Jonson's great competitor. Only three characters in Jonson's twelve surviving Elizabethan and Jacobean plays could be said to transform themselves in a positive, Shakespearean manner, as a result of their experience in the course of the action, as opposed simply to being smashed (like Humpty Dumpty falling off his wall) or remaining, for better or worse, just what they were at the start. They are Kitely in the revised *Every Man in His Humour,* the miser Sordido in *Every Man Out of His Humour,* and the Banbury preacher Zeal of the Land Busy in *Bartholomew Fair.* The handling of all three suggests a Jonsonian desire to experiment with the rival mode, coupled with a weird failure of conviction at the crucial moment.

Kitely tells us, at the end of *Every Man In,* that he is now cured of causeless jealousy of his young wife, and then instantly undercuts this recantation by announcing that he has taken it, word for word, from "a jealous man's part, in a play." In *Every Man Out,* the heartfelt curses of the rustics when they discover the identity of the would-be suicide they have cut down, impel Sordido abruptly into blank verse and a resolve to spend the rest of his life doing good to his neighbors. The speech itself comes close to sounding plausible. But, again, Jonson cannot maintain a serious attitude towards this conversion. Moments later, the rustics are pointing out that Sordido's tears trill as softly down his cheeks as the vicar's bowls along his green. Absurdly, they plan to ask the town clerk to enter the miser's conversion in the Acts and Monuments. As for Zeal of the Land Busy's perfunctory and anticlimactic collapse before the up-

lifted garment of Leatherhead's puppet—"For I am changed, and will become a beholder with you"—neither in the theater nor in the study does it really convince as the effective reeducation of that terrific opponent of Baal, Dagon, and idolatrous groves of Images detected among the humble wares of a gingerbread stall. It is as though Jonson wants to flirt with another kind of comedy, but finds that when it comes to the point he cannot rid himself of the attitude he expressed in his "Epistle to Sir Edward Sackville":

> Men have beene great, but never good by chance,
> Or on the sudden. It were strange that he
> Who was this Morning such a one, should be
> *Sydney* ere night.

Jonson found a more characteristic, and also more successful, compromise solution to the problem in *The Alchemist*, a comedy in which a bewildering variety of people find their way to Subtle's house of illusions precisely because they are longing to be transformed, to discover a more spacious and glamorous way of life, whether as gallant, roaring boy, captain, great lady, or master of the philosopher's stone. The dreams all fail. These lives are about as likely to turn into gold as are Sir Epicure's andirons. But that is something Jonson can understand, and also (more than many of his critics have been willing to allow) something for which he has a kind of sneaking sympathy.

Jonson told Drummond that he had once begun to write a comedy based on the *Amphitruo* of Plautus, but abandoned it because, as he said, he could never find two pairs of actors so like each other in appearance that he could "persuade the spectators they were one." This is a revealing comment. Plautus had not had to worry about persuading his audience that Jupiter and Amphitruo, Mercury and Sosia were indistinguishable, for the simple reason that Roman actors wore masks. Elizabethan actors did not wear masks. Moreover, they performed in close proximity to the audience, usually in full daylight. Jonson's hesitation is entirely understandable. And yet Shakespeare, when faced with exactly the same difficulty, treated it with a joyous unconcern. I suppose it is just possible that there was one set of identical twins in the Lord Chamberlain's Company around 1593, when *The Comedy of Errors* was first performed—although T. W. Baldwin's researches certainly did not reveal them. The mind boggles at the thought of there being *two* sets. In effect, Shakespeare simply did not care that his two Dromios and his two Antipholuses were not visibly identical on the stage in the manner demanded by his plot. In a comedy largely concerned with the transformations effected by the mind, he was perfectly willing to let this blatant theatrical

incongruity take its place in the argument of the whole. Moreover, in *Twelfth Night* a few years later he did it again. Despite the chorus of wonder that breaks out when Sebastian finally appears to confront Viola his twin—"An apple cleft in two is not more twin," "How have you made division of yourself?"—most members of any theater audience will always be more struck by the *dissimilarity* in appearance of these supposedly identical twins than by the likeness everyone is hailing as so miraculous. Far from trying to minimize the inevitable discrepancy between verbal statement and visual fact, Shakespeare calmly called the attention of the whole theater to it. He did so, I think, in both *Twelfth Night* and *The Comedy of Errors*, for reasons that have to do with his interest in the complex relation between imagination and truth: in the extent to which, in fact, we create the world we say we perceive.

Ben Jonson refused, unlike Shakespeare, to have anything to do with the *Amphitruo* in a theater which could neither provide him with two sets of identical twins to play the parts nor bypass the problem of verisimilitude by way of the mask. He rejected, in fact, precisely that hinterland of experience, between fantasy and fact, sleep and waking, with which Shakespearean comedy is largely concerned. Jonson's Jacobean comedies deal extensively with deceit, with playacting, and pretense. But always as weapons of imposture. They are never, as so often in Shakespeare—in *The Taming of the Shrew*, for instance, in *As You Like It*, *Twelfth Night*, or *Much Ado About Nothing*—a means of uncovering truth. When Pertinax Surly in *The Alchemist*, or Justice Overdo in *Bartholomew Fair*, are so misguided as to try to use disguise in this sense, they not only make fools of themselves. They do so in ways that call certain fundamental assumptions of Shakespearean comedy into question. It was like Jonson to reverse Shakespeare's favorite device of the heroine who masquerades as a boy, in doublet and hose, as he does with Epicoene's pretense in *The Silent Woman*, or with Wittipol's disguise as an improbably gigantic Spanish lady in *The Devil Is An Ass*. When, in his Elizabethan and Jacobean plays, he does turn transvestism the Shakespearean way round, in Lady Would-Be's mistaken conviction that Peregrine is "the most cunning curtizan of Venice" merely posing as a man, or in the corrupt courtier Anaides's habit of forcing his punk Gelaia to wait on him in male attire, as his page, in *Cynthia's Revels*, we seem to be looking at Shakespearean comedy through a distorting glass.

By comparison with his own Elizabethan comedies, let alone with Shakespeare's, Jonson's Jacobean plays are strikingly pessimistic. For all their hilarity, their energy and inventiveness, the view of man and of social relations that they put forward is essentially despairing. And there are no longer any moral arbiters, characters like Justice Clement from *Every Man In His Humour*, or Asper, Crites, and Horace in the

Elizabethan comical satires, to affirm the possibility of other and better ways of behaving. And yet it is important to remember that, with time, even Shakespeare seems to have found optimistic comedy difficult to sustain. *Measure For Measure* is Shakespeare's most Jonsonian play. This is so not only because of its urban setting—Vienna is a city that we really do believe in as a surrogate for London—but because the play creates a sense of complex, ineradicable human evil beyond the capacity of its own comic conventions to control. The comedy may end with marriages in the usual Shakespearean way. Apart from the contract between Claudio and Juliet, two people who are given nothing whatever to say to each other in the final scene, none of these unions possesses any emotional reality. It is not even certain that Isabella accepts the Duke. Lucio's wedding is a punishment which he regards as equivalent to whipping and hanging. Angelo has no words of love, or even of ordinary thanks, for Mariana—to whom he owes his life. This is a comedy ending which goes through all the usual Shakespearean motions, but it does so in a way that robs them of vitality and conviction.

Measure for Measure seems to have been the last comedy Shakespeare ever wrote. After it comes an unbroken string of tragedies, halted only by *Pericles* in 1609. And *Pericles* is a very different kind of play. Like its three successors, *Cymbeline, The Winter's Tale,* and *The Tempest,* it represents a break with Shakespeare's earlier style so radical as to make the very word *comedy* seem inappropriate as a description. *Romances,* if you like, or *final plays,* but not *comedy,* or at least not in the sense in which we apply that word to *As You Like It* or *A Midsummer Night's Dream.* I want to argue that *Bartholomew Fair* turned out, in a sense, to be Jonson's *Measure for Measure.* With this play, he seems to have arrived at a crisis in the development of his own kind of comedy which parallels the one Shakespeare had experienced some years before, even though the reasons for it were very different.

Most recent critics seem to have agreed that *Bartholomew Fair* displays a tolerance and geniality new in Jonson's work. No one is punished. At the suggestion of Quarlous, they all go home to Justice Overdo's to a feast, and to hear out the remainder of Littlewit's play. This conclusion is certainly not punitive, but neither (as it seems to me) is it very sunny. This off-stage feast may be an improvement on the violent and disordered banquets in *Every Man Out of His Humour, Poetaster,* and *The Silent Woman,* but it still falls considerably short of being a Shakespearean "one feast, one house, one mutual happiness." Jonson has simply resigned himself to the fact that human beings are fundamentally ineducable, that appetite and a shared impulse towards aggression—symbolized respectively by the feast and by the knockabout and degradation of the puppet play—are the only things upon which a social order can be realistically based.

I should be prepared to maintain that *Bartholomew Fair* is Jonson's greatest play. Certainly it is his richest and most ambitious. But it was also the end of a road. Unlike Shakespeare, Jonson was a basically accumulative artist, who tended to reuse the same character types and situations in play after play. In *Bartholomew Fair*, he finally managed to get his entire comic world, painstakingly assembled over a period of years, on stage at once, to make a grand culminating statement. This is a play which stretches the capacities of Jonson's own achieved comic form to the breaking point. With well over thirty speaking parts, an enormous number for a Renaissance comedy, it maintains the most delicate balance between order and chaos, between structure and a seemingly undisciplined flow which is like the random, haphazard nature of life itself. All the world's a Fair, Jonson seems to be saying, and all the men and women merely angry children, even those like Winwife and Quarlous, Grace and Justice Overdo, who begin by regarding themselves as rational, superior beings in a society of thieves and zanies. Jonson aimed here at an inclusiveness he had never sought before. The result is brilliant, but it precipitated him into artistic bankruptcy.

Jonson's next play, *The Devil Is An Ass*, two years later in 1616, reveals just how crippling an overdraft was incurred by *Bartholomew Fair*. An astonishing amount of this comedy reworks earlier Jonsonian material. Indeed, it might almost be subtitled "The Further Adventures of Face and Subtle," except that here they happen to be called Merecraft and Engine, and they have obviously been listening, at some point, to the ravings of Sir Politic Would-Be. The situation of Fitzdottrel's wife, jealously mewed up at one moment by her appalling husband, forced by him in the next into the presence of her aspiring lover—all in the interests of financial gain—derives from that of Corvino's Celia. There are two gallants in *The Devil Is An Ass*, just as there were in *Bartholomew Fair*—Wittipol and Manly—and Wittipol repeats the ruse of Epicoene by getting himself up in female attire and mingling with another collegiate society of absurd and corrupt ladies. Guilt-head and his son Plutarchus, the careful citizen and the young man nourishing aristocratic ambitions, are versions of Sordido and Fungoso from *Every Man Out*, while Fitzdottrel himself combines the specific vices of Epicure Mammon, Corvino, and Politic Would-Be. At the end, he simulates diabolic possession in the manner of the advocate in *Volpone*. Even the words of this comedy often sound strikingly familiar. Wittipol, wooing Fitzdottrel's wife by her own husband's agreement, tells her bluntly that "you are the wife / To so much blasted flesh, as scarce hath soule / Instead of salt, to keep it sweet."

In *Bartholomew Fair*, Edgeworth had said just this of Cokes: "talke of him to have a soule? 'Heart, if hee have any more than a thing given him instead of salt, only to keep him from stinking, I'le be hang'd afore my time." Wittipol merely gives us a verse restatement of Edgeworth's original joke.

The Devil Is An Ass is compulsively repetitive of earlier work, as Jonson himself must have known. And yet it also strikes out bravely in some new and unexpected directions. Mistress Fitzdottrel, for instance, is the first woman in a Jonson comedy who can fairly be described as a heroine. She is beautiful, intelligent, passionate, and chaste. Significantly, the name "Fitzdottrel" does not fit her at all—in the way that "Otter" or "Would-Be," earlier, had accurately described both husband and wife. It is simply another degradation imposed upon her by her ghastly spouse. In exploring the hell of her marriage and the strength of her temptation to accept Wittipol as a lover, Jonson treats Mistress Fitzdottrel with sympathy and respect. For the first time, he enters the precincts of romantic love—the area central to Shakespearean comedy, but left untouched in his previous plays. His means of entry is unusual. Mistress Fitzdottrel is a married woman, not a maiden. There can be no question of canceling her wedding vows and uniting her with Wittipol, the man of sense and feeling who values her for what she is. But it matters that Jonson should take her predicament seriously, that he should lament the waste of so much feminine intelligence, as well as youth and beauty, on a fool. And that we should care, as we did not care about the future of Celia at the end of *Volpone*.

In exploring the Wittipol/Mistress Fitzdottrel situation, Jonson also took his first steps in the direction of a Shakespearean attitude towards play-acting and illusion. When Wittipol discovers that because of her promise to her husband, the lady cannot utter a word in reply to his lovesuit, he adroitly proceeds to change places with her, to impersonate her, and say in her imagined person what he hopes she is thinking and feeling. The result is startling. For a time, Mistress Fitzdottrel behaves as though the real woman has agreed to feel and be guided by the sentiments her imitation has expressed. The theater dictates to life, not because it is an agent of deceit, as it was in the hands of performers like Volpone, Face, or, in this play, Merecraft the projector, but because it has uncovered a hidden, emotional truth. It was an idea Jonson was to return to and greatly elaborate, years later, when he wrote *The New Inn*.

For the moment, however, he showed no signs of wanting to build on *The Devil Is An Ass*. I said at the beginning of this paper that the Jonson who talked to Drummond in 1618 may well have decided to abandon the public stage. He was busy as a masque writer, of course, but he had never found it difficult before to occupy himself both with royal entertainments and with the theater. I think myself that he turned away from the stage for a whole decade because he could not see his way artistically after *The Devil Is An Ass,* could not resolve the problem he had tackled there for the first time: that of forging a new comic style. Shakespeare, in a similar situation, had turned to tragedy. But Jonson had no real gift in this line. *Sejanus* is a very interesting play, but its real value seems to me to lie in the fact that Jonson was able to work through it to *Volpone,* that it was the means by which he broke out of that first, and far less acute, comedic perplexity which assailed him after *Poetaster. Sejanus* mediates between the comical satires and Jonson's greater and more somber Jacobean plays. *Catiline,* on the other hand, does not stand in this kind of relationship to its immediate successor, *Bartholomew Fair.* Nor is it in itself a work which suggests that even if audiences had liked it, which they conspicuously did not, Jonson had an untapped tragic potential left him to explore.

After his return from Scotland, Jonson engaged himself in a host of literary activities. He, after all, unlike Shakespeare, was not dependent upon "public means which public manners breeds." Or not for awhile. Then King James died, and Jonson, a man who could not establish with Charles I the relationship he had enjoyed with his father, found himself once again obliged to write for the theaters. His financial position was habitually insecure and, after a stroke left him partially paralyzed in 1628, it steadily became worse. It is tempting to wonder, indeed, how often Shakespeare, that solid citizen of Stratford, may have advised his friend to cut his expenditure on books and wine, invest in a sound country property and a parcel of tithes, and generally defend himself in a good, bourgeois way against the realities of old age. If he did, Jonson did not listen and so, having no real choice in the matter, Jonson returned to confront an artistic issue he would probably have preferred to avoid: that of a new style in comedy.

Shakespeare himself, when he stood at this same crossroad some years before, had reached back to those traditional dramatic forms with which his own art had always had a basic affinity. *Pericles* deliberately summons up the rambling, episodic plays of the early Elizabethan period: gallimaufries like *Sir Clyomon and Sir Clamydes, The Cobbler's Prophecy,* or the original *Mucedorus.* Jonson, understandably, turned at first to a different but equally obsolete form: morality drama. The young Jonson had ostensibly scorned these plays, even as Shakespeare had once felt free to mock the old romances in the Pyramus and Thisbe interlude of *A Midsummer Night's Dream,* but they lay close, all the same, to Jonson's particular temperament and way of seeing. In trying to make a fresh start in

comedy, both men began by resurrecting one specific part of their dramatic inheritance: romance and the morality play, respectively. The impulse was similar, and so were some of the consequences.

Here again, *The Devil Is An Ass,* with its subplot concerning the adventures of that much put-upon junior demon Pug during his one day's
holiday from Hell, had already pointed the way. But *The Staple of News* in
1626, Jonson's first Caroline comedy, is even more completely and
anachronistically a morality play. In telling the familiar story of the
prodigal son, Jonson employed an outworn Elizabethan dramatic device
in the disguise of Penniboy Canter, the father who feigns his own death
and then takes service with his son and heir in order to see "if power
change purpose," and "what our seemers be." Jonson had mocked Justice Overdo when he did something similar in *Bartholomew Fair.* But
there is no mockery of Penniboy Canter, even as there is none of the two
moral conversions (that of the prodigal himself and of the Canter's
miserly elder brother) with which the comedy ends. The scepticism
which served to undercut the earlier reformations of Kitely and Sordido
has no place in *The Staple of News.* Nor does there seem to be any irony
about the fact that the Prologue for the court performance takes the
very unexpected form, for Jonson, of a Sidneian sonnet.

When Jonson returned to the stage in 1626, both he and the world
around him were much changed. He himself was significantly older. He
had arrived at that time of life when men are naturally tempted to
review their own past, to reevaluate and assess the opinions and experiences of their youth. In Jonson's case, this tendency can only have been
reinforced by the crippling paralysis which confined him to his lodgings,
with time on his hands, and, as he outlived his old friends one by one, an
ever-diminishing number of visitors. Secondly, in 1623, Heminge and
Condell had produced Shakespeare's plays in Folio. Jonson had edited
his own plays in Folio seven years before, an enterprise which must have
encouraged them. He may have helped Shakespeare's fellow sharehold-
ers in their task in ways that went beyond the two poems he contributed
to the volume: "To the Reader" and "To the Memory of My Beloved,
The Author Mr. William Shakespeare and what He Hath Left Us." The
impact of those thirty-six Shakespeare plays, eighteen of them never
printed before, standing together to confront him as the completed
work of a friend whose art he had criticized, but the importance of which
he had always conceded, must have been enormous. The consequences,
as I have argued elsewhere (*English Literary Renaissance* 9 [1979]: 158–
79), first declare themselves in *The New Inn,* Jonson's second Caroline
play. Here, in 1629—an aging dramatist, "sick and sad," as he describes
himself in the epilogue—he turned away from morality drama to re-
think the premises of Shakespearean comedy: in effect, to come to terms

with its attitudes and, up to a point, make them his own. Moreover, this impulse is one that perpetuated itself in Jonson's last three Caroline plays: *The Magnetic Lady* (1632), *A Tale of A Tub* (1633), and *The Sad Shepherd*, the pastoral that Jonson left unfinished at the time of his death in 1637.

But it was not only sickness, the inclination of old men to reminisce, or the Shakespeare First Folio that impelled Jonson into what was really a kind of belated Elizabethanism. It was also a spirit abroad in the air around him, one that had been steadily gathering force since the early years of James's reign. Bishop Goodman, himself an apologist for King James, nevertheless found himself obliged to record the fact that although England at the end of Queen Elizabeth's life was

> generally weary of an old woman's government, after a few years, when we had experience of the Scottish government, then in disparagement of the Scots, and in hate and detestation of them, the Queene did seem to revive; then was her memory much magnified,—such ringing of bells, such publick joy, and sermons in commemoration of her, the picture of her tomb painted in many churches, and in effect more solemnity and joy in memory of her coronation than was for the coming of King James. (Godfrey Goodman, *The Court of King James the First* [London, 1839], 1:98.)

In the latter years of James's reign, and throughout that of his successor, more or less hagiographic accounts of the life of the great queen—often concealing a savage, implied comparison with the failures of the Stuart regime—poured from the press. The legend of Good Queen Bess's golden days, a legend containing a good deal of distortion and exaggeration, as such legends usually do, had been unleashed. In the end, it would bear a certain amount of responsibility for sweeping King Charles from his throne.

The whole question of late Jacobean and Caroline nostalgia for the reign of Elizabeth is immensely complex, and one that modern historians of the period are only now beginning to explore. For a number of reasons I cannot consider it at any length here. But it does seem to me important to remember that this attitude took literary, as well as political, forms. Revivals of old, seemingly outmoded Elizabethan plays—many of them at court—including the plays of William Shakespeare, are a feature of the 1630s. Moreover, two of Jonson's oldest and closest friends, Sir Robert Cotton (d. 1631), and William Camden (d. 1623), Jonson's former master at Westminster School, the man to whom he said he owed "All that I am in arts, all that I know," both moved, near the end of their lives, towards the conviction that Elizabeth, not James, had in fact been the Augustus Caesar of Britain, and her reign a direct parallel to the Golden Age of Rome. It was an opinion shared by Newcastle, Jonson's last patron.

Jonson had always been fascinated by classical myths of a golden age. They turn up again and again in his masques and plays. Ironically, during the last and (on the whole) fairly sour and disillusioned years of Elizabeth's reign, he had actually written a comedy about the Rome of Augustus. *Poetaster*, with its final establishment of the good poet Horace and the consummately great poet Virgil as acknowledged legislators of mankind, ruling side by side with a just and enlightened emperor, had fairly obviously been intended in 1600 as a contrast to the sorry state of affairs in the England of Elizabeth. At this time, Dekker identified Horace, the satiric poet newly elevated into favor and importance by Caesar at the end, as a flattering self-portrait of Jonson himself. He was right. *Poetaster* was the wish-dream of a disgruntled Jonson acutely conscious that this was not, in fact, the position he occupied in Elizabeth's court, and disinclined to see any connection between either the political or the literary splendors of the classical Rome he venerated and a degenerate contemporary world. But the whirligig of time brought in, if not exactly his revenges, at least a radical reconsideration of the recent past. Jonson was by no means the only old man who discovered during the decade of the 1630s, as the Puritans gathered strength, that he had actually lived in the Golden Age, without knowing it at the time.

I do not want to push Jonson's late change of heart too far. He associated himself with Horace in *Poetaster* but he would never, not even in his last years, have been able to recognize that the Virgil of the play was really William Shakespeare. Indeed, a late but persuasive tradition recorded by Gildon and Rowe has the old Jonson still arguing grumpily with Suckling and Davenant about the impurity of Shakespeare's art. That was only to be expected. What one could not have predicted were Jonson's four last plays, and the new understanding not only of Elizabethan literature but, more especially, the spirit of Shakespearean comedy that breathes through them all.

In *Bartholomew Fair*, back in 1614, Jonson had for the first time given English literature the role hitherto fulfilled in his comedies by the Greek and Roman classics. When Quarlous selects the name "Argalus," the knight of true and self-sacrificing love, from Sidney's *Arcadia*, and Winwife chooses "Palemon," from Chaucer's "Knight's Tale," as the words to be inscribed in Mistress Grace's table-book, the two men inadvertently damn themselves. The names are talismanic, summoning up stories in which love and friendship were difficult, demanding ideals but untainted by financial or prudential considerations. The contrast implied between the mutually distrustful fortune-hunting of Quarlous and Winwife, the cold, detached attitude of Grace Wellborn, and the passionate loyalty and commitment of Argalus and his lady Parthenia, Palemon, Arcite, and Emily is devastating. Moreover, when he came to the puppet play at the end of *Bartholomew Fair,* Jonson rubbed the judgment in. Here he used *Damon and Pithias,* an early Elizabethan play by Richard Edwards, and Marlowe's great poem "Hero and Leander" as the paradigms, works of art commenting not only upon Littlewit's travesty of them, but also upon the corresponding debasement of love and friendship in Quarlous, Winwife, and Grace. It is the memory of Edwards, Sidney, Marlowe, Fletcher, and Shakespeare, far more than the Ciceronian maxims so piously mouthed by Justice Overdo, which effectively mock the triumph of appetite and aggression at the Fair.

Jonson's four final plays, *The New Inn, The Magnetic Lady, A Tale of a Tub,* and *The Sad Shepherd,* carry this kind of Elizabethan nostalgia to a much further extreme. Significantly, three of the four have country settings. *The Magnetic Lady,* as Jonson is at pains to point out in his introduction, actually goes back and rewrites the humor plays of his youth. In doing so, it transforms a brand of comedy originally dedicated to judgment and destruction into one of reconciliation and accord. As for *A Tale of A Tub,* a play apparently set around 1560, early in the reign of the Virgin Queen, it is so filled with archaic words and constructions and with an outmoded early Elizabethan verse that Jonson's Oxford editors were impelled, despite its late position in the posthumous Folio of 1640, to argue for it as a misplaced piece of juvenilia: a play written even before *Every Man In His Humour* and hastily revised by the elderly Jonson to accommodate a satire on Inigo Jones. This early dating was attacked sharply, and I think entirely rightly, by W. W. Greg. In fact, *A Tale of A Tub,* with its fresh, country world, its entirely affectionate handling of a collection of positively Shakespearean local rustics (most of them nostalgically obsessed with parish records, genealogies, and the history of their community) could only have been written in Jonson's last years. The play's linguistic archaisms can be matched in *The Sad Shepherd* and in the two late entertainments commissioned by Newcastle, and only there. It looks very much as though the man who once girded at Spenser because "in affecting the ancients, he writ no language," came at the end of his life to do exactly this himself.

Although *The New Inn* uses two lines from John Donne's "The Calme," a poem written during the Essex expedition of 1597, as the pivot upon which its fifth act turns, the spirit which informs it throughout is Shakespearean. The hostelry of The Light Heart at Barnet, among the fields, is a place to which people journey, leaving the city behind them, and in which they are transformed, a place that is heightened and extraordinary. The agents of transformation are twofold: romantic love and theater. I said earlier that for the younger Jonson play-acting and deceit were almost always the weapons of imposters, not ways of discovering truth. In *The New Inn* this is no longer so. The comedy adopts a positively Shakespearean view of the imagination. Something odd, too, has happened to the usual Jonsonian charactonyms or "speaking names"— names like Politic Would-Be, Fastidious Brisk, or Volpone—which had tended to fix and define characters, depriving them of the freedom and flexibility that most of Shakespeare's people inherit with their more neutral names. In the high plot, they have either vanished, or they are names like Lovell and Frampull, possessing two possible meanings, into the positive one of which the character moves in the course of the action. These are people capable of change.

If the multiple discoveries of the last act of *The New Inn* are odd—the revelation that the supposed son of the Host, who has been acting the part of a girl called Laetitia in the revels, really *is* a girl and called Laetitia, or that a husband and wife estranged and separated from each other for years have both been living under the same roof all along without recognizing one another—they are no more implausible than the events of the final scene of *Cymbeline* or *The Winter's Tale.* Certainly Jonson handles these ostentatiously fictional consonances in an intensely Shakespearian way. Dryden dismissed *The New Inn* and all the rest of Jonson's late plays as "dotages." And the appellation, unfortunately, has stuck. But then it used to be common to denigrate *Pericles, Cymbeline, The Winter's Tale,* and *The Tempest* as the products of Shakespeare's boredom and creative decline in his last years. The last plays of Jonson, like the last plays of Shakespeare, are extreme and difficult works of art. They do not readily yield up their secrets. They constitute a remarkable achievement all the same, and one sorely in need of sympathetic reassessment. Quite as much as the commendatory verses to the Shakespeare First Folio, they can stand as Jonson's real tribute to the man whose different kind of art had both infuriated and haunted him for so long.

Beaumont and Fletcher's Hamlet

by H. NEVILLE DAVIES

Beaumont and Fletcher's *The Maid's Tragedy* is about a wedding. The play begins during the hiatus of jollification between public ceremony and private consummation that temporarily admits the uneasy paradoxes of a bride who is maid and wife, and the action focuses on the events of the wished-for night and the night thereafter. Presumably that is why the managers of mirth chose this as one of the fourteen plays to be performed by the king's company to celebrate the royal wedding of 1613, when James's daughter married the Elector Palatine.[1] But, like funeral baked meats served at a wedding banquet, it was a remarkably astringent choice, no more apt than the tragical mirth of *Pyramus and Thisbe,* no less disturbing than the grotesquery of Donne's *Epithalamion Made at Lincoln's Inn.* "The anguish of a torturing hour," as Theseus called it, gives way in this play not to the loving relief of a wedding night, but to the anguish of a torturing life. Evadne reveals to Amintor that she is the king's mistress, her bridegroom is merely "to bear the name of husband" that her "sin may be / More honourable." As for the nuptial bed that confronts them, Evadne bluntly declares

> I sooner will find out the beds of snakes,
> And with my youthful blood warm their cold flesh,
> Letting them curl themselves about my limbs,
> Than sleep one night with thee.[2]

Amintor's bewilderment ("Was ever such a marriage night as this!") becomes the king's some twenty-four hours later when Evadne visits the royal couch and substitutes for the thrills of bondage games the terror of involuntary restraint, for sexual passion the frenzy of revenge, and for the delights of copulation the horrors of ritual murder. Nor does the impropriety end here.

The final lines of the play, spoken when both Evadne and Amintor as

173

well as the king are dead, append a moral that assorts uncomfortably
with Jacobean notions of the divine right of monarchs:

> on lustful kings
> Unlook'd-for sudden deaths from God are sent;
> But curs'd is he that is their instrument.

What joy, or offense, there was in all this for King James and his eager
son-in-law we might well wonder. Certainly in the Restoration period
Waller chose to replace the killing of the king by a less objectionable
ending.[3]

The morning after the wedding night the lustful king, who cannot
now be sure that his mistress has a husband in name but not in deed,
questions Evadne and Amintor. "How lik'd you your night's rest?" he
says to the bride before interrogating Amintor, who dissembles too convincingly:

King.	Amintor, wert thou truly honest till thou wert married?
Amintor.	Yes, sir.
King.	Tell me then, how shows the sport unto thee?
Amintor.	Why, well.
King.	What did you do?
Amintor.	No more or less than other couples use; You know what 'tis; it has but a coarse name.
King.	But, prithee, I should think, by her black eye And her red cheek, she should be quick and stirring In this same business, ha?
Amintor.	I cannot tell; I ne'er tried other, sir; but I perceive She is as quick as you delivered.

[3. 1. 130–41]

I hope the Elector Palatine in 1613, who, like his bride, was seventeen
years old, was as adroit as this when responding to his royal father-in-law
the morning after *his* wedding. Court gossip relates that "the next morning the King went to visit these young turtles that were coupled on St.
Valentines day, and did strictly examine him whether he were his true
sonne in law, and was sufficiently assured."[4] Perhaps we can imagine
James slobbering and "fidling about his cod-piece,"[5] as was his wont, and
posing the same question: "What did you do?" But what I would like to
know is whether the audience who attended the play did so after this
interview had taken place, and were therefore alive to the parallel, or
whether James allowed his prurient (not, I think, dynastic) solicitations
to follow what he had seen enacted on stage.

However, it is not just the Royal Wedding production of *The Maid's
Tragedy* that raises questions of attitude and proper response. The play
challenges convention, anyway. Where, for instance, *Hamlet* includes an

inset play in the middle of the action, *The Maid's Tragedy* admits a substantial inset masque as a major feature of the very first act. In this
position the inserted entertainment vies for primacy with the main action itself, which, for a time, is virtually reduced to the status of an
induction. In *Hamlet,* the arrival of the players allows opportunity for
comment about drama and acting, and in *The Maid's Tragedy* the prepa-
rations for the wedding masque similarly prompt a discussion about
masques. It is with this, in fact, that the action begins, so establishing the
piece at once as a highly self-conscious, self-referential undertaking.
Lysippus, the king's brother, strikes a supercilious attitude that is
matched by the dismissive, mocking tone of Strato who converses with
him and who prepares us for the coming masque by pointing out how
predictably boring such productions "tied to rules of flattery" are. But
the conventional elements of the masque excite an eroticism that will be
unconventionally frustrated when the bride and groom retire for the
night. As Professor Ewbank has demonstrated, the flattery and expression of conventional sentiments in the masque provide an antithesis to
the corrupt reality, with a rich irony being engendered by the disparity.[6]
The mode of *The Maid's Tragedy* is not that of *The Knight of the Burning
Pestle*, but the intelligence that produced it is similar.[7]

When *The Maid's Tragedy* was performed in Stratford in 1980 by the
Royal Shakespeare Company at The Other Place, there was a rare and
memorable opportunity to enjoy the play. Even rarer was the chance of
seeing *The Maid's Tragedy* and *Hamlet* in repertoire at the same time, but
much as I valued Barry Kyle's exciting production I was disappointed by
the failure to explore the relationship between the two plays, though
Tom Wilkinson as an imposing Melantius and a retiring Horatio supplied, by chance, a common element. The presence of *Hamlet* in Beaumont and Fletcher's play has sometimes been cause for complaint,
sometimes reason for conscientiously listing parallels, but too rarely has
recognition given joy. Merely to list is uninteresting. To turn a blind eye
or wag a scolding finger is surely to miss the point.

At the end of the masque the king is praised as *le roi soleil* whose
brilliance turns night to day, but the disparity between the compliment
and the reality is immediately evident since the king has to call for lights
when the two last masquers, Night and Cynthia, wearing one of her
brightest moons for the occasion, exit. However, I suggest that a production would not be amiss in which the call for lights by a wicked king at the
end of a court theatrical reminded the audience of Claudius by some
similarity of staging with a production of *Hamlet* known to that audience.
Of course, the king's wickedness has not yet been revealed, even if there
is reason to suspect that something is rotten in the Isle of Rhodes, but
subtleties are possible in the derivative that are denied to the precursor.

Where *The Murder of Gonzago* simply reenacts Claudius's crime, the masque is proleptic and hints at trouble to come, while the king's good wishes to the newly married couple as they go to bed can take on a disturbing or sinister quality when spoken by a man who has just reminded us of Claudius.

One of the most celebrated recollections of *Hamlet* in *The Maid's Tragedy* comes when, on the second of the two nights, Evadne visits the king's bedchamber to murder him. The king is asleep, Evadne is armed, and the gentlemen of the bedchamber are absent. In a soliloquy she considers the awful burden imposed by revenge and then approaches the bed. Now might she do it pat:

> —'A sleeps. Oh, God,
> Why give you peace to this untemperate beast
> That has so long transgress'd you? I must kill him,
> And I will do't bravely: the mere joy
> Tells me I merit in it. Yet I must not
> Thus tamely do it as he sleeps: that were
> To rock him to another world; my vengeance
> Shall take him waking, and then lay before him
> The number of his wrongs and punishments.
> I'll shape his sins like furies till I waken
> His evil angel, his sick conscience,
> And then I'll strike him dead.
>
> [5. 1. 25–36]

She ties the sleeping man's arms to the bed (and, at The Other Place, his legs, too) before waking him. "In spite of its many echoes from his own plays, Shakespeare cannot have failed to appreciate the talent displayed in this drama," remarked Georg Brandes of *Philaster*.[8] Why not "because of" rather than "in spite of"? For the audience of *The Maid's Tragedy,* the parallel with the prayer scene in *Hamlet* comes appropriately to mind, and the disparity between precursor and derivative stimulates thought. Hamlet chooses to delay striking until Claudius is engaged in "some act / That has no relish of salvation in it," and we can compare his passive waiting upon events with Evadne's active revenge. She wakes the king so that he may fully experience his death, but the waking is not only from sleep. She is also concerned to rouse his sleeping conscience so that he may suffer the remorse that she herself now feels: he will not only be damned, but he will die knowing that he is damned. Where Hamlet declines to allow his uncle the sort of death that was denied his father "unhouseled, disappointed, unaneled," Evadne contrives to murder her seducer in the place where her virginity was lost. He is cut off even in the blossoms of his sin, in the rank sweat of his bed. The revenger is thus no reincarnation of the Prince of Denmark, rather her behavior as revenger can be measured against his. And perhaps his against hers.

Shakespeare curiously never names Claudius in the dialogue of his play. In *The Maid's Tragedy*, where the king is not even named in a stage direction, the dramatic possibilities of this small observation were extended. We notice with shock that Evadne has no name for the man whose bed she has been sharing:

> Ay, you shall bleed. Lie still, and if the devil,
> Your lust, will give you leave, repent. This steel
> Comes to redeem the honor that you stole,
> King, my fair name, which nothing but thy death
> Can answer to the world.
>
> [5. 1. 59–63]

The king has no name, but even more than that he is the instrument by which "the fair Evadne" who, we were told at the beginning of the play, "strikes dead / With flashes of her eye" (1. 1. 75–76), has come to lose her own "fair name."

In a previous scene (4.1), during the day that intervenes between the wedding night and the murder night, Evadne is confronted in her chamber by her brother Melantius. Behind locked doors he forces her to confess her guilt, and D. M. McKeithan in 1938 listed fifteen specific points of comparison with the closet scene in *Hamlet*.[9] In the same year, D. J. McGinn, without enumerating them, also assembled parallels.[10] More recently David L. Frost in his study of the influence of Shakespeare on Jacobean and Caroline drama has lighted upon this scene to demonstrate the dangers of raiding Shakespeare for "lively detail or touches of passion." He complains

> In *The Maid's Tragedy*, when the plot requires that Evadne should repent her unchastity, the dramatists fall back on Hamlet's interview with Gertrude: "h'as undone thine honour, poison'd thy virtue, and of a lovely rose left thee a canker." The cost of such borrowing is an unsettling disproportion or inappropriateness of sentiment to situation, for Evadne's brother Melantius talks as if their father's ghost had a husband's resentment of her sins: "consider . . . Whose honour thou has murdered, whose grave open'd / And so pull'd on the Gods that in their justice / They must restore him flesh again and life, / And raise his dry bones to revenge his scandal." Evadne's quick capitulation seems unmotivated without Gertrude's memory of her dead husband to undermine her.[11]

This is, in effect, Dr. Johnson's objection to the sort of mindless imitation that favors idleness and assists imbecility. But Shakespeare is not being used merely to supply "lively detail or touches of passion," and the Shakespeare echoes are not "casual," as Clifford Leech, no admirer of this particular scene, alleged.[12] The sheer pervasiveness of the *Hamlet* presence provokes a lively relationship, one that appeals to a sophisticated literary response, to develop between the two plays. Rather, as wedding-masque expectations conflict with what is revealed on the wedding night, and as the jilted Aspatia, in another famous scene (2.2), exploits the discrepancy between her experience and what is being depicted on a tapestry of Ariadne, so this scene counterpoints with a precursor in *Hamlet*. The dramatists do not idly "fall back" on Shakespeare's play—they rewrite it as Aspatia would the Ariadne story, since they are revisionists not plagiarists, and the new scene outrageously develops its original.[13] The mayhem of familial confusion that "husband's brother's wife" bespeaks, and the unfilial nature of Hamlet's reproaches of his mother, are here extended by introducing yet another kinship. The mother and son confrontation becomes in the troped version a brother and sister confrontation, the relationship associated in *Hamlet* with Laertes and Ophelia who at their last meeting enjoined chastity on one another. In the new closet scene, furthermore, cast in the role of Hamlet himself is not the revenger, but the Horatiolike friend and outsider, Melantius, while Gertrude's role is filled by Evadne, who by process of this scene, an early scene in the revenge rather than discovery phase of the play, is actually transformed into a female revenger. Boreas, as the masque warned us, has broken his chain indeed!

As befits a play more concerned with conflicting intellectual positions than with mental processes, the motivation for Evadne's capitulation at the turning point is the crude threat of physical violence, as in real life very persuasive, and more effective in performance than on the page.[14] But the apparition of Hamlet's father "in his habit as he lived" has not been forgotten, not quite. Whereas the ghost in the *Hamlet* closet scene is, in most productions, not perceived by Gertrude, in this play he becomes even less evident, reduced to a mere figure in Melantius's speech. Gertrude talks of "vacancy," but Evadne ridicules the very notion of a ghost having a physical presence at all—the bones that should lie sweet in the earth would stink. Such a facetious response not only counters Melantius by mocking his rhetoric, it also rejects the eschatology of Shakespeare's play, insolently employing *Hamlet*'s imagery to do so.

To say that *The Maid's Tragedy* or parts of *The Maid's Tragedy* imitate *Hamlet* is to say very little. Imitation may be of so many different kinds. One can think in terms of a whole gamut of imitation with the scale emerging at one end from the undistinguishable and disappearing at the other end into the unrecognizable. Barely distinguishable from its model is the close copy or single-source plagiarism, and from here the scale passes through the synthetic art of multiple plagiarism via various forms of counterfeiting to pastiche. Then on to slavish following of a model that, by degrees of transformation, leads to the literary form properly called Imitation. Beyond this lies emulation. Respect for the model is still a feature of the next stage, parody, where some distortion begins to appear, but resentment of the model encourages burlesque and, as the degree of distortion grows, we move to subversion, through increasing disavowal, and on to outright rejection, where eventually all features of the model are avoided and a relationship ceases to be recognizable. A single linear series is, of course, inadequate for anything more than a didactic game, but the exercise of assigning literary works to an appropriate point on the scale has a limited value as long as it is remembered that there are no correct answers, only cogent objections to any proposed answers.

In *The Maid's Tragedy* Calianax, the humorous, elderly court chamberlain, is, as others have pointed out, imitated from Polonius, though unlike his original he has a remarkable capacity for survival in spite of being "wronged / Almost to lunacy." Like Polonius he has a daughter, rejected by the man who has offered her marriage, the Hamlet figure of the play, and who reacts, like Ophelia, with behavior that embarrasses the court.[15] Like Ophelia she sings in her distress and is associated with the choosing of flowers and plants, but rather than madly uttering bawdry that cruelly conflicts with her innocence, she has to endure no less cruelly the bawdry of others. Our attitudes towards her are mixed, for although she rightly claims our sympathy her company becomes tiresome as she zealously explores artificial ways to grieve and stages her own death with the elaboration that Gertrude expends on describing Ophelia's drowning. It is as though *The Maid's Tragedy* were subversively inviting us to consider unsentimentally what it would really have been like at Elsinore to have had the jilted Ophelia continually making a show of herself. But to think of Aspatia in terms of *Hamlet* is to imagine an extraordinary version of Shakespeare's play in which the death of Ophelia is faked and the returning Laertes is none other than Ophelia in disguise, pretending to have come to avenge a sister's death, though in fact contriving to be killed in a duel by the man she might have married. On my scale of imitation, such drastic revision, whereby Ophelia becomes her own Laertes, would have to be registered as aggressive emulation at least.

The masque that precedes the wedding night is paralleled by a reception that precedes the murder night (4.2), and while the inserted masque corresponds to the inserted *Murder of Gonzago*, the following evening's entertainment turns into a version of the mousetrap. Calianax informs the king, correctly, that Melantius is planning treachery and has already

tried to suborn Calianax himself. The king finds this accusation difficult
to believe and tests it by the mousetrap device. Addressing Melantius in
public he speaks of treachery like that alleged by Calianax and closely
watches the suspect's reaction in the belief that he has "thrown out words
/ That would have fetch'd warm blood upon the cheeks / Of guilty men."
Melantius preserves his *sang froid*, Calianax is discredited, and the king's
destruction is thereby assured. The scene develops into high comedy as
Melantius repeatedly attempts to recruit Calianax to the conspiracy, is
denounced to the king each time, and responds by persuading the king
that Calianax is deluded. Once more *Hamlet* is being vigorously revised,
this time by having the mousetrap sprung by the Claudius figure (Hamlet's mouse), with the Polonius figure helping to observe the result, and
with the Horatio figure, the most unlikely of all, as the intended victim.
Not only by these displacements, however, is *Hamlet* revised. In *The
Maid's Tragedy* we discover what happens when a mousetrap fails to
work, and can enjoy all the sport of seeing the engineer hoist with his
own petard.

But when is an imitation not an imitation? At the end of *The Maid's
Tragedy* the Horatio-figure Melantius attempts suicide after the death of
Hamlet-Amintor, and is restrained. Before the new ruler speaks the
final words Melantius, now disarmed, offers no eulogy of the dead;
instead, still determined to die, he announces his resolve to go on hunger strike. Oh, that it should have come to this, and Shakespeare's play
scarce ten years on the boards.

Notes

1. E. K. Chambers, *The Elizabethan Stage*, 4 vols (Oxford, 1923), 1:180. *The Maid's
Tragedy* had been first acted at Blackfriars late in 1610 or early in 1611.

2. Francis Beaumont and John Fletcher, *The Maid's Tragedy*, ed. Howard B. Norland,
Regents Renaissance Drama Series (London: Edward Arnold, 1968), 2. 1. 205–8.

3. A. C. Sprague, *Beaumont and Fletcher on the Restoration Stage* (1926; reprint ed., New
York: Arno, 1965), pp. 59–63 and 182–83.

4. *The Letters of John Chamberlain*, ed. Norman Egbert McClure, 2 vols. (1939; reprint ed.,
Philadelphia: American Philosophical Society, 1962), 1:424.

5. Sir Anthony Weldon's description, reprinted in *James I By His Contemporaries: An
Account of His Career and Character as Seen by Some of His Contemporaries*, ed. Robert Ashton
(London: Hutchinson, 1969), p. 12.

6. " 'These Pretty Devices': A Study of Masques in Plays," in *A Book of Masques in Honour
of Allardyce Nicoll*, ed. T. J. B. Spencer and S. W. Wells (Cambridge: At the University Press,
1967), pp. 415–18, expanded by Michael Neill, " 'The Simetry, Which Gives a Poem
Grace': Masque, Imagery and the Fancy of *The Maid's Tragedy*," *Renaissance Drama*, N.S. 3
(1970): 111–35.

7. Philip J. Finkelpearl, "Beaumont, Fletcher, and 'Beaumont & Fletcher': Some Distinctions," *English Literary Renaissance* 1 (1971): 144–64.

8. Georg Brandes, *William Shakespeare: A Critical Study*, trans. William Archer, Mary Morison, and Diana White, 2 vols. (London, 1898), 2:303. See also Paul S. Conklin, *A History of* Hamlet *Criticism, 1601–1821* (1947; reprint ed., London: Routledge and Kegan Paul, 1957), p. 11.

9. Daniel M. McKeithan, *The Debt to Shakespeare in the Beaumont and Fletcher Plays* (1938; reprint ed., New York: AMS Press, 1970), pp. 44–48.

10. Donald J. McGinn, *Shakespeare's Influence on the Drama of His Age Studied in* Hamlet (1938; reprint ed., New York: Octagon, 1965), pp. 68–71.

11. David L. Frost, *The School of Shakespeare: The Influence of Shakespeare on English Drama, 1600–1642* (Cambridge: At the University Press, 1968), pp. 244–45.

12. Clifford Leech, *The John Fletcher Plays* (London: Chatto and Windus, 1962), pp. 123 and 126.

13. This scene (like 2. 2 and 5. 1–2) is usually attributed to Fletcher alone, but no matter who wrote particular scenes, the working relationship between the two dramatists was so close that *responsibility* is always joint.

14. See John F. Danby, *Poets on Fortune's Hill: Studies in Sidney, Shakespeare, Beaumont and Fletcher* (London: Faber and Faber, 1952), pp. 198–99, and Fredson Bowers, *Elizabethan Revenge Tragedy, 1587–1642* (1940; reprint ed., Princeton, N.J.: Princeton University Press, 1971), pp. 174–75.

15. In general, Amintor is the Hamlet figure of the play, but so utterly incapacitated is he by his unwavering allegiance to the crown that action is largely denied him. It is Melantius (the Horatio figure), therefore, who takes over the Hamlet role in the closet scene; it is Evadne, in the murder scene, who recalls the Hamlet of Shakespeare's prayer scene; and it is the king, as will be seen, who usurps Hamlet's function by setting the trap in the banquet scene.

Society and the Uses of Authority in Shakespeare

by ROBERT WEIMANN

1

Approaching Shakespeare from the point of view of the role of society in the Elizabethan theater and the role of the theater in society, I should like to take as my first text the words of a man of the theater who, confronting a complete lack of authority in affairs theatrical, attempts to explore the relationship of Elizabethan drama and society with a start- ling sense of historical self-consciousness. Here is John Lyly, addressing his audience:

> At our exercises, Souldiers call for Tragedies, their object is bloud: Courtiers for Commedies, their subject is love: Countriemen for Pas- toralles, Shepheards are their Saintes. Trafficke and travell hath wo- ven the nature of all Nations into ours, and made this land like Arras, full of devise, which was Broade-cloth, full of workemanshippe. Time hath confounded our mindes, our mindes the matter; but all commeth to this passe, that what heretofore hath been served in several dishes for a feaste, is now minced in a charger for a Gallimaufrey. If wee present a mingle-mangle, our fault is to be excused, because the whole worlde is become an Hodge-podge.[1]

The texture of Lyly's language is heavily metaphorical but the object is quite distinct. What Lyly is in fact concerned with is, ultimately, a new historical poetics of the theater in which the relationship between drama and society is viewed as dynamic and unpredictable, rather than static or normative in following any one given poetic precept or authority. In- stead of the neoclassical emphasis on the authority of rules, the point of departure is frankly empirical in that the stylized reference to different social identities within the audience, such as "Souldiers," "Courtiers,"

"Countriemen," is taken to sanction a multiple unity of dramatically rendered experience as against the demands of aesthetic dogma. What we have is, in very elementary and, even, reluctant terms, a reevaluation and affirmation of experience (and pleasure) as a legitimate point of departure for all endeavors theatrical. Unformulated in its assumptions, there is a new attitude toward experience as "something felt or perceived in an immediate or lively way, with the force of personal acquaintance and participation."[2] As far as the new poetics of the theater is based on this, it points not to an aesthetics of authority, but one of reception according to which various horizons of expectations are acknowledged as involving varying areas of dramatically usable social existence. The awareness of these expectations is used to apologize for a new (and unheard of) freedom in the dramatic assimilation and combination of hitherto exclusive levels of society and sensibility. In this connection, the culinary quality of Lyly's imagery ("what heretofore has been served in several dishes for a feaste, is now minced in a charger for a Gallimaufrey") serves more than a merely euphuistic conceit, because it points to that innovation through cultural synthesis by which the Elizabethan theater is just about to establish a more highly complex principle of national identity and dramatic unity.

For that, Lyly himself suggests some of the historical foundations: "Trafficke and travell hath woven the nature of all Nations into ours." If, as the fascinating etymology of the word suggests, "Trafficke" may, according to the Oxford Dictionary, here be read as "The transportation of merchandise for the purpose of trade; hence, trade between distant or distinct communities"; and if "travell" (in the sense of "travail") may, according to the same authority, be understood as "The outcome, product, or result of toil or labour," then the social correlatives of Lyly's language betray a historical imagination that is even more impressive for having been so neatly translated into the metaphorical texture of the imagery of "weaving." "Trafficke and travell," according to Lyly, "hath woven the nature of all Nations into ours, and made this land like Arras, ful of devise." The new pattern so "ful of devise," appears to the dramatist as richly tapestried with newly accessible forms of experience—social, national, and international. For Lyly, such "multimundity" (to use George Hunter's pregnant term) is literally overwhelming the dramatist's imagination whose response, at this stage, is almost apologetic and not too self-assured: "If we present a mingle-mangle, our fault is to be excused, because the whole worlde is become an Hodge-podge."

At this point, the verdict of modern historians seems to receive unsuspected confirmation, as when for instance A. L. Rowse writes about the "mobility of social classes" or when J. B. Black talks of a "babylonian confusion of classes."[3] The pre-Shakespearean stage can take such "confusion" for its platform, developing as it does at a time when traditional feudal and clerical hierarchies and institutions were economically, politically, and culturally uprooted without having as yet been superseded by the more modern forms of social organization associated with the rise to power of the commercial classes, the improving gentry, and the bourgeoisie. It was at this moment of transition and unprecedented social change that the cultural impact of "Trafficke" and "travell" and the resulting "Gallimaufrey" could be felt as spontaneously stimulating and, even, liberating in the sense that the Elizabethan theater was quite content not only to represent but, in its own dramatic function and structure, to exploit and bring to a head the mobility of classes, the confounding of consciousness, and the "mingle-mangle" of social and poetic standards.

What Lyly's statement seems to suggest is that the rise of a dramatically potent cultural synthesis in the theater was based on (and expressive of) an unprecedented freedom to juxtapose and assimilate hitherto exclusive levels of experience and, thereby, to use or reject any extant form of poetic authority or dramatic tradition—classical, humanist, courtly, and clerical. Amidst the "hodge-podge" and mobility of a transitional age, the various cultural traditions and dramatic genres were no longer "served in several dishes." Instead, they were so "minced" that in the country's metropolis the result was a drama neither farcical nor learned nor courtly. It was a drama unlike any of the continental burgess or neoclassical or pastoral genres, but one whose bewildering medley of kinds might for a moment be defined as "tragical-comical-historical-pastoral, scene individable, or poem unlimited." It was, indeed, in terms of its social foundations, a theater "individable" with a poetry almost "unlimited" in its social and aesthetic appeal; a theater that (in Lyly's words) acknowledged "the whole worlde" for its province.

2

If one distinctive achievement of the Elizabethan stage was based on an unprecedented freedom to use or reject any one given dramatic tradition or poetic authority, such unheard-of freedom was not equally available in the dramatic treatment of legal and political, let alone religious authority. On the contrary, the contemporary context in which the drama presented a "mingle-mangle" was still largely dominated by traditional forms of consciousness that emphasized the very idea of hierarchy and authority as something immutably fixed to every form of social existence, from the family to the state, from apprentice to prince. From our distance it may be exceedingly difficult to decide how much of the traditional element in the so-called Elizabethan world picture was widely accepted as a reality of feeling and thinking and how much of it was being proclaimed from above so as to help maintain a post-Reformation status quo. In any case, it seems safe to assume that the world picture that the Elizabethan homilies presented did not adequately comprehend a sizable proportion of the actually lived experience of the age. It seems more realistic to assume that the drama was confronted, not only with the conservative thought in the homilies and official pronouncements, but with more highly differentiated and transitional patterns of thinking and feeling. While (as I have suggested elsewhere) important standards of the older feudal idea of the great chain of hierarchical being could already be questioned, the social attitudes of the new era of capitalism (among them, individualism, "naturalism," acquisitiveness) were not as yet their necessary alternative. But if the theater, through the very exploitation of the hodge-podge character of the many standards and traditions, achieved a relative independence of either of the dominant ideologies, such independence could thrive on the peculiar balance of social forces that went into the making of the Elizabethan stage itself. To judge by the financing and the founding of the public theaters, they were all thoroughly commercial enterprises; but in spite of the post-feudal, postpatriarchal business ethics that made these playhouses materially viable, the bourgeois element was balanced by highly conspicuous (and eventually growing) connections with court and aristocracy. But again, apart from the necessary protection and occasional support that the common players received from the monarchy and aristocracy, they were largely left to pursue their own course. Under these conditions the theater was in fact free to respond to the needs and expectations of the popular and mixed audiences and, as a consequence, the stage was at liberty to take for its province large areas of experience unexpressed and unformulated in terms of the dominant ideologies.

Even more important, the transitional social balance provided the theater with a peculiarly rich and complex pattern of social function and communication. Combining the services to the community of both the recital of poetry and the precursor of the modern newspaper, this function can best be defined in terms of the complementarity of its traditional and modern aspects. On the one hand, the drama was deeply indebted to the traditional forms of a popular theatrical and oral culture and a conservative consciousness richly expressed in pictorial forms and poetic analogies; on the other hand, the theater was more immediately prepared than, say, either the pulpit or the lyrical and epic modes of poetry to assimilate a rapidly changing reality that could hardly be said to be adequately expressed by the dominant trends in social, political, and religious thought. There was an enormous gap between the traditional (and official) modes of consciousness and the actual state of society, and the drama, responding to both, was—as no other literary form in its day—confronted with the challenging need to face and, indeed, explore this gap.

The nature of this challenge was such that it involved the kind of difficulty that Lyly had anticipated when he wrote "Time hath confounded our mindes, our mindes the matter." For the Elizabethan drama—susceptible as it was to the most "confounding" of changes—there simply was not available, in the contemporary framework of formulated thought, any room for dramatically usable concepts and symbols of social change, let alone revolution. On the contrary, the dominant theoretical and metaphorical modes of consciousness all pointed in the direction of order, hierarchy, and organic wholeness. Because of "this crushing burden of belief in the need for social stability," as Lawrence Stone puts it, "all change had to be interpreted as the maintenance of tradition. In religion the reformation was defended as a return to the early church; in politics, parliamentary sovereignty was defended as the enforcement of fourteenth-century customs; in society, the rise of new men was disguised by forged genealogies and the grant of titles of honour."[4] Similarly, in science, astronomy, and philosophy, the inescapable breach with the past was not conceived in terms of radical change or innovation; in fact, "the actual innovator did not regard himself as such, or did not intend to substitute something fundamentally new for something old."[5]

Thus, while innovation was deprecated in favor of tradition and the lack of authority was concealed by appeals to authority, this type of traditional consciousness could not and did not adequately reflect or comprehend the actually prevailing conditions under which the majority of Englishmen, particularly the London theater audience, pursued the practical business of living and thinking in society. In order to suggest the extent to which the social foundations of the Tudor idea of authority were already threatened by crisis and decline, let me glance at some of the most pregnant sources of crisis, especially those that recent social historians have shown to be more deeply rooted than most of us may in the past have assumed. There were, first of all (although this is not a recent insight) the incalculable effects and immense consequences of the reformation crisis that involved so much more than religion since it was, as Joel Hurstfield notes, "in the profoundest sense a crisis of authority."[6] It is true, the consequences of the overthrow of the universal standards of the Church of Rome, with its profound implications for a radical critique of any outward form of authority, came to be felt only gradually, as the work of the Reformers began to sink into the consciousness of ever broader sections of the population. Even before that, the mid-Tudor crisis and the return to the throne of a catholic queen must—as so many

social historians have told us—have had a noticeable effect on contemporary attitudes to religious as well as political authority.[7] As has recently
been shown, the church was never again able to recover the "moral
authority lost during the Reformation and the Elizabethan years of neglect," especially since the ecclesiastical courts emerged from the Reformation "gravely weakened" and with the scope of their jurisdiction
reduced.[8]

But whereas the longterm effects of the Reformation and counter-
Reformation upheavals must have affected Shakespeare and his generation indirectly rather than directly, the remarkable series of political and
ideological changes occurring towards the end and at the turn of the
century was a different matter altogether. As historians like J. E. Neale
and Lawrence Stone have been telling us for some time, the greatest of
social changes took place not so much in the early seventeenth century
but in the 1590s when the Elizabethan compromise was increasingly
threatened by religious dissension, an early parliamentary opposition,
and the rise of political factions that, among other things, resulted in
repercussions such as the attempted coup and execution of Essex.

At the same time, the historical foundations of the Tudor idea of
authority must have been even more strongly affected by such farreach-
ing social divisions, as recent county historiography has revealed. As, for
instance, Peter Clark has shown in his study of politics and society in
Kent, there was, by the end of Elizabeth's reign, "a major expansion" of
local government culminating in "the growing of an all-powerful county
government centred on quarter sessions"; but "along with this horizontal
expansion of county government there was also . . . a vertical growth in
power: the Elizabethan regime sought to intervene increasingly in the
running of local communities, wherever possible absorbing functions
previously performed on an informal, seigneurial, or neighbourly
level."[9] In the case of Norfolk, where (with the execution, in 1572, of
Thomas Howard) the center of a great patronage network was irretriev-
ably uprooted, these developments led to sharply opposed views of
governmental authority and practice. There was a polarization on the
part of the gentry into two coherent and reasonably stable groups, one
willing to implement and profit from economic and administrative
policies formulated by the central government, the other concerned with
upholding the cause of county government, landowning interests, and
local privileges as against the authority of the Crown and Council. In
connection with the growth in function of the quarter sessions and increasing divisions over militia training and various forms of indirect
taxation, "this conflict between 'court' gentry and 'county' gentry
intensified during the 1590s,"[10] especially after the threat of a Spanish
invasion had ceased to induce unity. But even before that, this state of

affairs (which was not unlike developments in Wiltshire and Somerset-shire) involved "an intensely political situation" that " led to frequent debates about who did what and on whose authority."[11]

The significance of such conflicts was not of course that they already seriously threatened to upset the Elizabethan and early Jacobean polit-ical order. The rift among the gentry not only involved divisions on the nature and the sources of authority in some of the most rudimentary affairs of local government, from the justices of the peace down to the ordinary constables, involving such issues as the levying of militia rates or the collection of ship money. What is more important, such conflicts in loyalty and authority must have helped to constitute a new awareness of the particularity of social interests, and they must have pointed to what Joel Hurstfield has called "the enormous gap between the constitu-tion and the political reality, between those who wielded authority and those who merely legalized its use; between the language of law and the facts of life."[12]

Since, in recent years, a good many historians have become less at-tracted to the official records, the machinery of government, Parliament, and the constitution, they have tended to differentiate more stringently between Elizabethan government and the actual state and feeling of late sixteenth-century society. Here, the study of county records, mainly of quarter sessions and assizes, has at least in one case, in Essex, revealed a startling picture of disorder, with (in the words of F. G. Emmison) a "surprisingly large" number of persons indicted for seditious speech against the queen, the council, its leaders, or the established church, "some of it highly treasonable and two of the charges revealing plans for rebellion in Essex."[13] Similarly, Emmison's search of Essex Archidia-conal Records has revealed what he describes as an "extraordinary num-ber and variety of disturbances and quarrels which took place," together with the expression of "strong anticlerical feelings . . . both by religious-and irreligious-minded people," so that in truth "the Elizabethan clergy" can be said to have "received from the laity an abundant offering of slander and hostility."[14]

At the same time, new agencies of local government on a popular level were called into existence. During the sixteenth century, the parish with its town meetings began to absorb, or at least exist side by side with, the administrative activities of the court-leet. As Carl Bridenbaugh has shown, such meetings might consist of "the Chiefest" and "the most substantial," but they could also draw "a very large number of parishion-ers into the paramount business of running their community,"[15] from the church-wardens and inferior officers down to the parish clerk, the sexton, bell-ringer and town-crier. Thus, it may be claimed that in the sixteenth century, for the first time in their history, the ordinary men and women of Britain gained a considerable amount of political experience. It is true that the resulting "mass alertness" can easily be exaggerated even when in addition to their familiarity with the practical working of local government, the gradually increasing impact of literacy, together with the Reformation heritage of reading and much listening, is given its due.[16] But the question may be asked seriously whether the general drift of the evidence produced by recent research in social history does not tend to underline Carl Bridenbaugh's conclusion, according to which in the late sixteenth and early seventeenth centuries a growing number of ordinary men and women found themselves in a position where it was either possible or desirable for them to begin to form their own increasingly critical notions on the nature and quality of political authority.[17]

3

To emphasize the full extent of the crisis in the social foundations of the Tudor concept of authority is not, however, to claim that the concept itself had already become outdated or ineffectual in the language of contemporary political, religious, and poetic thought. On the contrary, as the work of Richard Hooker or, for that matter, the eloquence of Canterbury, Ulysses, Menenius, and some other Shakespearean characters witness, the language of authority, order, and degree assumed a great metaphorical cogency and was more stringently formulated at the very moment when the actual foundations of these concepts were becoming precarious. But unlike Hooker or the contemporary pulpit, the drama by virtue of its peculiar position in society was (as I have suggested) much more urgently exposed to an increasingly acute awareness of the rift between the dominant forms of consciousness and the ways of practical living and feeling in contemporary society. If Shakespeare was deeply committed to the "smooth-fac'd peace" and "smiling plenty" of the Tudor achievement and the concern for order, decorum, and tradition associated with the theory and practice of the Elizabethan settlement, he was also highly sensitive to the forces of decay, corruption, and abuse. It is "inconceivable," as a recent student of the dramatist's thought put it, "that Shakespeare should not have written with the same acute awareness of the issues of the day which his audience brought into the theatre with them. His living depended upon his proximity to their daily experience."[18]

Shakespeare, I suggest, was vitally confronted with a growing state of tension between ordinary experience and a traditional body of social and political thought, and as he moved from the two parts of *Henry IV* and *Henry V* to the problem plays and on to the tragedies, he began to use these tensions dramatically, as a mode of apprehending and comprehending the increasingly complex and conflict-ridden world around him. As a first illustration, the language of Menenius Agrippa may perhaps best serve as an example, since it reveals the organic and analogical vehicles of the imagery of authority at a supreme moment of crisis. Even more so than in the case of Canterbury and Ulysses this context of crisis seems significant, for it provides both a sense of junction and a foil against which the famous fable of the belly is offered to the mutinous citizens. What Menenius has to say may well be described as an orthodox expression of the traditional Elizabethan conception of the state as an ordered whole in which each class and occupation had its separate role and degree in the organic hierarchy of the body politic. But this officially sanctioned version of government here is offered as "a pretty tale" and Menenius "will venture / To stale't a little more" (1. 1. 88–90). The true irony of his fable, however, is revealed in the process of its reception. The citizens have rallied "in hunger for bread" (l. 22) only to be told that "the senators of Rome are this good belly" who "digest things rightly." If such a political pronouncement "essentially is absurd" and "sophistic," its paradoxical quality can be traced to Shakespeare deliberately changing his classical and medieval sources so as to reduce the partriarchical function of the senate as fathers of the commonwealth "to the lesser one of store keeper and manufacturer."[19] Therefore, what Menenius expounds is, to say the least, an irreverent version of a traditional political commonplace that does not respond to the dramatized experience of social disorder; it serves not as an answer to the citizens' grievances but as "a device to fob them off." In the words of G. R. Hibbard, Menenius "cynically uses the ideal of the interdependent community as a political weapon, without really believing in it, just as he cleverly gives the citizens the impression that he regards them as fellow-men by addressing them as 'my good friends, mine honest neighbours.' "[20]

At this point the language of the traditional Elizabethan conception of the common weal is found wanting as a source of value and it has ceased to be accepted as an unquestioned means of establishing a legitimate polity. What Shakespeare in fact attempts to convey is how the idea of the organic body politic deliberately can be used in what we would tend to call a function of false consciousness. As the direction of the whole play indicates, the Augustinian notion of divine power is superseded by an image of politics as an autonomous and entirely secular activity. In line with that, note the use of "authority" in the First Citizen's speech:

We are accounted poor citizens, the patricians good. What authority surfeits on would relieve us. If they would yield us but the superfluity while it were wholesome. . . (ll. 14–16).

Here, the concept is radically divorced from any sense of the divinity of power. In this context, "authority" is reduced to a hostile allegory of those who wield power: it is the language of the naked thing itself.

As E. C. Pettet, W. G. Zeeveld, Patricia Meszaros, and other students of *Coriolanus* have suggested, Shakespeare in writing the play was closely in touch with contemporary English politics that, if their overall direction may so be generalized, assumed an increasingly ideological cast. This is not the place to trace the connection between the growing prominence of more highly particularized social interests and the rise of a higher degree of articulateness in various sections of society. But there can be no doubt that, for a number of reasons, contemporary interests tended to be expressed in more highly generalized religious, constitutional, and political terms. As the impersonal texture of legal relationships rather than age-old ties and loyalties began to constitute the sources of authority, the definitions of rule and subordination were formulated accordingly. At the same time, it became easier for independent minds to assert themselves and to put forward coherent claims. As the new Protestant culture was spreading downwards and began to work its way into the texture of society, instead of remaining, as in the early days of the Reformation, the mark of a small, mainly clerical elite, this affected the capacities for generalizing hitherto unformulated forms of social existence. As Mervyn James has noted, "larger numbers of those who had been accustomed to articulate their world in terms of what tradition or their betters imparted," were either compelled to argue in generalized terms or were left alone somehow "to decide for themselves."[21] As a much broader section of the population was drawn into the process of bringing forth and communicating consciousness, the rift between the dominant concepts of the Elizabethan world picture and the realities in the practical experience of power and authority became a more widely felt contradiction, ripe for expression in a popular form.

It was against this background that Shakespeare must have sensed that the dramatic uses of some of the most widely accepted concepts and symbols of contemporary consciousness involved problems as well as challenges in that they were bound to stimulate both the originality and comprehensiveness of his own vision of society. Once the dramatist realized that the organic analogies and related similes of authority did not provide a helpful explanation of the thinking and acting of important groups of men in society, he must have tended to rely more firmly on his own intellectual assessment of what the sources of power and authority in society really were like. As far as this involved the need for a new perspective on the increasingly abstract quality of the links between thinking and living, consciousness and reality, Shakespeare found himself in a position to draw on the resources of a theater that, at least since

Kyd and Marlowe, had achieved a highly flexible interplay between language and action, word and gesture. Confronted in his own society with a problematic relationship between consciousness and reality, Shakespeare—as a man of the theater—must have been in a peculiarly fortunate position to be able to achieve a more complex view of the unity as well as the contradiction between language and action. In this respect, the ideological rhetoric of Menenius's fable corresponds to a series of comparable tensions, in speeches by other personages, "between their sound and their sense, or between their 'voices' and their 'heart'"—tensions that may well be said to constitute "one of the play's recurrent motifs."[22] In exploring and using the gaps between language and meaning as a positively structuring principle, Shakespeare—through characters such as Menenius and Ulysses, but also Angelo, Troilus, Julius Caesar, Brutus, Hamlet, and others—reveals the world of his plays as one in which action and thought do not constitute a rigidly fixed relationship.

If Shakespeare was, as Wilbur Sanders has said, "at the heart of historical change,"[23] he was also and at the same time in a position to be able to translate the experience of that change into a highly complex interplay between language, action, and images of consciousness—an interplay that, with all its tensions and areas of unity, was presented not as conclusion but as process. It was this readiness to apprehend and comprehend change in the very process of assimilating and confirming tradition that rendered his uses of "authority" so complex and so fundamentally different from those in the official language of the ruling class. If, for instance, we glance at the pronouncements of one of its most enlightened representatives, William Lambarde, indefatigable justice of the peace, author, and ever faithful servant of the Crown in Kent, addressing *his* "good neighbours and friends" at the Quarter Session at Maidstone, 1 April 1600, we come across the complaint that

> such is nowadays the bold sway of disobedience to law that it creepeth
> not in orders but marcheth in the open market. . . . yet how few are
> there found amongst us that will use the bridle of authority which they
> have in their own hand and cast it upon the head of this unruly
> monster![24]

"Authority," for the author of *Eirenarcha*, clearly serves as an unquestioned instrument of rule; it is, as Lambarde says elsewhere, "already given"[25] to the justices. It is a positive principle mainly insofar as it can be used like a "bridle" on the unruly and disobedient.

Obviously, such a concept is worlds apart from Shakespeare's uses of authority. The political diction of the law and the language of drama seem almost incompatible, each serving radically different functions of consciousness and communication. For the justice of the peace, the concept is—throughout his career—as unchanging as the need, expressed as early as 1586, "to take the bridle of the laws into our own hands."[26] But for the dramatist this is not so; for even while Shakespeare continues to use the familiar vehicles and symbols of the Elizabethan world picture, his dramatic vision expands as the theater—unlike the law or the language of politics—is in a position to relate to a much broader range of actually lived experience. Authority, for the dramatist, is not something "already given"; nor is it to be administered as a homiletic lesson, or just to be mirrored by way of theatrical representations. If the issue of authority does play a central part of Shakespeare's dramatic work, it is because he tends to treat such issues in terms of an experience more complex than that of even the most enlightened representatives of the ruling sections of society.

4

Shakespeare's treatment of the authority issue becomes apparent as the dramatist begins to give expression to ambivalent sentiments about "nobility and tranquillity, burgomasters and great oneyers," those who "pray continually to their saint, the commonwealth; or rather, not pray to her, but prey on her" (*1 Henry IV*, 2. 1. 75–77). Or when in *Henry V*, he takes into account the "heavy reckoning" the king will have to face "when all those legs and arms and heads, chopp'd off in a battle" (4. 1. 134–36) shall, as "a black matter," be presented to him. As Shakepeare uses the language of ordinary carriers, chamberlains, ostlers, thieves, and honest soldiers, he articulates their world not exclusively "in terms of what tradition or their betters imparted" but as part of a larger context out of which a few of them begin to be able "to decide for themselves" about the uses and abuses of authority.

In his early comedies and histories the Tudor premises of political authority (unlike those of sexual and parental authority) appear to be largely unquestioned. In *2 Henry VI*, for instance, the authority of rule is made to appear indivisible, and the strife of the nobles contradicts it just as much as, on a contrasting plane, Jack Cade's topsy-turvying assault upon civil order. Again, in *King John*, political authority is emphasized but in its very emphasis already reveals some of the precarious foundations upon which the whole idea of royal supremacy is being vindicated. Not only is it an upstart and bastard who turns out to be the most resolute spokesman of a national idea of royal supremacy, but the vindication of that authority itself is shown to be most effective in the breach of another, "usurp'd authority" (3. 1. 160), that of the supreme head of the Church of Rome. But the very same authority that is shown as usurped can, in a later scene, restore the crown to King John: "From this my hand, as holding of the Pope,/Your sovereign greatness and authority" (5. 1. 3–4). Authority, it seems, primarily is sanctioned by power and the idea of nationhood, rather than by any immutable cosmic or religious principle.

A strongly felt need for order and authority in civil government continues to be expressed in *Henry IV* where, in the closing scenes of part 2, the Lord Chief Justice so associates his "authority" with "the majesty and power of law and justice" (5. 2. 78–79) that their identity as well as their integrity can be assumed and emphatically confirmed in Prince Henry's generous response. The maintenance of civil peace seems all the more imperative when the Saturnalian suspension of order has throughout been celebrated in a vital form of misrule. As against that, authority is vindicated, but the resulting sacrifice weighs almost as heavily as the undoubted benefits of civil peace that the newly crowned head of state is called upon to safeguard. Authority, now that it is completely triumphant, assumes an austere air of harshness through exorcising the vitality in the spirit of its victims. As the angle of vision broadens, it includes not only those who do the praying for authority but those who are preyed upon in the name of authority.

After *Henry V*, the loss in the integrating function of the national experience makes the pragmatic clothing of the Tudor idea of authority appear rather seamy. There is, then, a kind of logic when Shakespeare, in *Julius Caesar, Hamlet,* and his problem plays, transposes the issue of authority onto a level where the political problem, once it is detached from English history, is more deeply absorbed in character and action and completely expressed by them.

In *Troilus and Cressida*, the nature of authority is shown as profoundly affected by a thoroughgoing discord between language and action, the expression of consciousness and the representation of reality. Most of the characters, as A. P. Rossiter has noted, "fancy or pretend they are being or doing one thing, whereas they are shown up as something quite different,"[27] something that egoism, power, will, and appetite prevent their recognizing. The rift between the consciousness and the doings of these characters has disastrous effects on the moral quality of their relationships. The resulting plight is articulated by Troilus, whose despairing voice is a true voice in crisis: "If beauty have a soul"—but it has none; "If there be rule in unity itself"—but there is no rule, and no authority, neither in the unity of lovers nor in that of the body politic. The show of honor and the lure of appetite are the two dividing forces that—each in an opposite direction—rent the common weal: once "a thing inseparate/Divides more wider than the sky and earth." Here, as C. F.

Tucker Brooke suggested many years ago, echoes of the state of early seventeenth-century society seem a possibility in the sense that Shakespeare somehow anticipated "the seriousness of the cleavage between Cavalier and Puritan" and that he sensed how the Elizabethan settlement "was threatened by the two great coarsening influences which in fact were then attacking the nation."[28] The hodge-podge world was ripe with crisis and division. Time has so confused the mind, the mind itself cannot control its madness and confusion:

> O madness of discourse,
> That cause sets up with and against itself!
> Bifold authority! where reason can revolt
> Without perdition, and loss assume all reason
> Without revolt: . . .
>
> [5. 2. 139–44]

But the crisis, which is most deeply one of consciousness, is quite absorbed in character and verbal action: Troilus, witnessing the falseness of Cressida, cannot reconcile his heart to the evidence of eyes and ears; his mind and reason, his whole consciousness would contradict the knowledge of his senses. The conflict—so central in Shakespeare's play—is one of experience versus ideology; for Troilus, it is the gap between the evidence of the senses and "the bonds of heaven" that so constitutes the "Bifold authority" of a divided consciousness that his refusal to trust his eyes and ears can claim to be exceedingly reasonable. But for all its great and passionate dignity this reason (much like the "reason" in some of the lofty apologies for the Elizabethan *via media*) is at loggerheads with the ordinary truth of common experience that Shakespeare does not care to ignore. Again, it is Thersites, that rude *vox populi* with his direct audience appeal, who has the comment, unheard by Troilus himself, "Will 'a swagger himself out on's own eyes?" (l. 134).

The dilemma is a central one in Elizabethan consciousness, but the imaginative depth with which Shakespeare explores it appears quite unique. As against Ulysses' oration on "degree," Troilus must be believed when he cries out, "The bonds of heaven are slipped, dissolved and loosed" (l. 154). If, in their place, there is so quickly to be had "another knot, five-finger-tied," then from now on heavenly absolutes give way to all the relativity that the hands of humans are stained with. If the great chain between sexual, political, and cosmic order can *reasonably* be contradicted, then the resulting consciousness is indeed one without bonds and without bounds, one without authority, one "that cause sets up with and against itself."

Once the "rule in unity itself" is revealed as an illusion, the issue of

authority resembles a broken cistern that can no longer supply a viable
stream of moral inspiration and guidance. It is true that, in a great
tragedy, "authority" can still be associated with royal dignity, which a
faithful servant like Kent "would fain call master" (1. 3. 28). But next to
such distinctly personalized usage, Shakespeare is intensely concerned
with the human dilemma resulting from the limitations and temptations
of "a little brief authority" (2. 2. 118). In *Measure for Measure,* this becomes a dominating theme but one where "the demigod Authority"
(1. 2. 114) is presented with the kind of ambivalence that corresponds, in
the structure of the play, to the bifold emphasis upon the forces of
discord and harmony, the severity of the law, and the surprising mercy
of those who finally wield it. If, as Ernest Schanzer suggested, the play
involves uncertainties in its moral bearings "so that uncertain and divided responses to it in the minds of the audience are possible and even
probable,"[29] then this reflects the uneasiness in the structural sequence
of two different versions of authority, one temporary and corrupt, the
other sovereign and merciful. The conflict is still between the justice of
heaven and the law of human beings, and although the corrupt knotting
of the latter contrasts with the merciful bondage of the former, the all-
consuming gap remains between law and justice, between those who
temporarily, in a brief little moment, wield it and those who are its
victims. In the face of this gap, authority cannot but "err like others,"
only its self-born remedies are the more delusive for it:

> authority, though it err like others,
> Hath yet a kind of medicine in itself
> That skins the vice o' th' top.
>
> [2. 2. 124–26]

This is close to the world of *King Lear,* where "Robes and furr'd gowns
hide all" (4. 6. 165) and where the "glass eyes" of the "scurvy politician"
provide the most deluding of perspectives on the antinomies of law and
justice. If a ruling ideology creates a need "to see the things thou dost
not," then, again, this antinomy is also one between seeing and saying,
between the ideology of the law and the reality of its execution. It is
because Shakespeare, in his theater, was able to draw on and vitalize an
area of experience, unheard of in the dominant philosophy and theology, that his tragic hero must suffer like a beggar in order to become
truly royal. This time, the ruler turns "a beggar in fact, not a mendicant
friar by way of disguise."[30] He must forfeit his sanity, not merely put an
antic disposition on. It is only when all the false consciousness is seen
through, when the "glass eyes" of the "politician" are plucked out, the
"boots" and "lendings" of privilege torn off that "a man may see how this
world goes with no eyes":

> Thou hast seen a farmer's dog bark at a beggar? . . . And the creature run from the cur? There thou mightst behold the great image of authority: a dog's obey'd in office. (4. 6. 150–58)

Lear's words, spoken as "reason in madness," point to an ultimate solution, one impossible without perdition, of closing the gap between the ideology of authority and the reality of its execution. This, indeed, is a radical response to the breach between the plains of ordinary experience and the towering edifice in the Elizabethan world picture. Behind it, there is a vision of society that is no longer that of kings and dukes and nobles but that, among other things, poetically formulates and communicates a consciousness that serves the experience of the victims rather than that of the spokesmen of authority. Lear's words are central to the play's meaning in that his own progress is one from authority to humanity. The tragedy of the play has a lot to do with how agonizing it is, in Lear's world, to reconcile authority to humanity.

This, no doubt, is the climax of Shakespeare's astonishing reevaluation of authority, but it is not his last word on it. There is, finally, in his late plays an image of a new kind of authority, exposed to a host of dangers when, as in *The Tempest*, it involves the deliberate surrender of all the false certainties in favor of something more deeply true to the human kind. But while law and justice, politics and morality move closer together, the feeling of security is strictly limited, and in each romance the serpent is only scotched; there is no certitude that a purely human design for authority cannot be abused or overthrown, that it cannot, together with all "the cloud-capp'd towers, the gorgeous palaces," go down in chaos. The promise of freedom is precarious, but it is strongest in young people's bondage to one another. And it is in relation to these that, finally, authority must stand or fall.

Shakespeare's vision of redeeming youth may or may not have been indebted to what Frances Yates has suggested was in connection with the Elizabethan revival (centered on James I's children), a strongly felt historical situation.[31] But "the legacy of authority tested against the aspirations of the young" may safely be said to be "one of the great Shakespearean themes." Nor is the youthful perspective on that legacy confined to the last plays; it may well be traced as central to Hamlet's and, in part, Brutus's tragic dilemma arising out of their ambivalent attitudes to the spirit of the fathers. As Shakespeare explores the ambivalence of authority and envisions its legacy as immersed in the destructive element, he sets out to create a tragic hero who can accept authority only as long as his own self is freely prepared to identify with it. Thus, the self-tormenting acceptance of the legacy leads to an attempt that, with all its delay and futility, aims at reintegrating the world of experience and the ways of consciousness and thereby points not to renewed authority but to self-knowledge.

Notes

1. Prologue to *Midas;* cf. *The Complete Works of John Lyly,* ed. R. W. Bond (Oxford: At the University Press, 1902), 3:115.

2. W. G. Moore, "Montaigne's Notion of Experience," *The French Mind. Studies in Honour of Gustave Rudler,* ed. W. Moore, R. Sutherland, and E. Starkie (Oxford: Clarendon Press, 1952), p. 40. Montaigne's idea of *expérience* exemplifies an advanced trend in Renaissance thought that, under the conditions of the Elizabethan theater, became a seminal element in theatrical theory and practice. Cf. *Realismus in der Renaissance,* ed. Robert Weimann (Berlin: Ausbau-Verlag, 1977), p. 737.

3. A. L. Rowse, *The England of Elizabeth: The Structure of Society* (London: Macmillan, 1950), p. 243; J. B. Black, *The Reign of Elizabeth: 1558–1603* (Oxford: Clarendon Press, 1949), p. 226.

4. Lawrence Stone, *The Crisis of the Aristocracy 1558–1641,* abr. ed. (Oxford: At the University Press, 1967), p. 16.

5. B. L. Joseph, *Shakespeare's Eden: The Commonwealth of England, 1558–1629* (London: Blanford Press, 1971), p. 18.

6. Joel Hurstfield, ed., *The Reformation Crisis* (London: E. Arnold, 1965), p. 1. In the north, the confusion of authority must have been especially marked. Cf. Christopher Haigh, *Reformation and Resistance in Tudor Lancashire* (Cambridge: At the University Press, 1975), p. 157: "The Edwardine Reformation was almost entirely destructive; the old church was damaged but Protestantism was not enforced."

7. "A child born in 1533, the year when Elizabeth was born, had, if his family was conformist, subscribed to five different versions of the Christian religion by the time he was twenty-six" (Joel Hurstfield, "The Elizabethan People in the Age of Shakespeare," in *Shakespeare's World,* ed. James Sutherland and Joel Hurstfield [London: Edward Arnold, 1964], p. 39).

8. Ralph Houlbrooke, *Church Courts and the People during the English Reformation, 1520–1570* (Oxford: At the University Press, 1979), pp. 221, 266, 269.

9. Peter Clark, *English Provincial Society from the Reformation to the Revolution: Religion, Politics, and Society in Kent 1500–1640* (Hassocks [Sussex]: County Council, 1977), pp. 111, 142, 144.

10. A. Hassell Smith, *Country and Court: Government and Politics in Norfolk, 1558–1603* (Oxford: At the University Press, 1974), p. 277.

11. Ibid., p. 334.

12. Joel Hurstfield, *Freedom, Corruption, and Government in Elizabethan England* (London: Cape, 1973), p. 25.

13. F. G. Emmison, *Elizabethan Life: Disorder. Mainly from Essex Sessions and Assize Records* (Chelmsford [Essex]: County Council, 1970), pp. viii, 39.

14. F. G. Emmison, *Elizabethan Life: Morals and the Church Courts. Mainly from Essex Archidiaconal Records* (Chelmsford [Essex]: County Council, 1973), pp. 112f., 215. While it is certainly true that "these cases must not be allowed to create an exaggerated impression of discontent or disorder" (*Elizabethan Life: Disorder,* p. 65), Emmison's assertion of the uniqueness, in Essex records, of "this persistent pestilence of treasonable talk" seems unwarranted as long as we accept Victorian editors' search of records as exhaustive. Cf., e.g., Emmison's reference to those "six Middlesex charges in the whole reign" (p. viii),

when John Cordy Jeaffreson (ed., *Middlesex County Records,* vol. 1 [London, 1886], p. 1) freely admits that "having given the abundant evidence, I have forborne to render it superabundant by needless example."

15. Carl Bridenbaugh, *Vexed and Troubled Englishmen: 1590–1642* (Oxford: At the University Press, 1968), p. 245.

16. But see David Cressy, *Literacy and the Social Order. Reading and Writing in Tudor and Stuart England* (Cambridge: At the University Press, 1980), p. 188: "The evidence indicates that the penetration of literacy in England was largely a response to need . . . rather than response to ideological pressures which might transcend narrow occupational requirements."

17. Bridenbaugh's assumption that "many Englishmen had begun silently to nourish, and occasionally to display openly, a genuine hostility against 'the demigod authority'" (p. 273) seems to anticipate a seventeenth-century political situation (which is not that in which Shakespeare's theater found itself) where critical sentiments gave way to hostile attitudes.

18. W. Gordon Zeeveld, *The Temper of Shakespeare's Thought* (New Haven, Conn.: Yale University Press, 1974), p. xiii.

19. Roy W. Battenhouse, *Shakespearean Tragedy: Its Art and Its Christian Premises* (Bloomington: Indiana University Press, 1969), p. 344.

20. William Shakespeare, *Coriolanus,* ed. G. R. Hibbard (Harmondsworth: Penguin, 1968), pp. 25f.

21. Mervyn James, *Family, Lineage, and Civil Society. A Study of Society, Politics, and Mentality in the Durham Region, 1500–1640* (Oxford: At the University Press, 1974), pp. 178f.

22. Battenhouse, *Shakespearean Tragedy,* p. 347.

23. Wilbur Sanders, *The Dramatist and the Received Idea* (Cambridge: At the University Press, 1968), p. 327.

24. Conyers Read, ed., *William Lambarde and Local Government. His "Ephemeris" and Twenty-nine Charges to Juries and Commissions* (Ithaca, N.Y.: Cornell University Press, 1962), p. 143.

25. Ibid., p. 80.

26. Ibid., p. 84.

27. A. P. Rossiter, *Angel with Horns* (London: Longmans, 1961), p. 133.

28. C. F. Tucker Brooke, "Shakespeare's Study in Culture and Anarchy," *Yale Review,* N.S. 17 (1928): 577f. I have cited the relevant passage from the New Variorum edition, ed. H. H. Hillebrand (Philadelphia: J. B. Lippencott, 1953), p. 381.

29. Ernest Schanzer, *The Problem Plays of Shakespeare* (London: Routledge & Kegan Paul, 1963), p. 6.

30. J. W. Lever, in his introduction to the Arden edition of *Measure for Measure* (London: Methuen, 1965), p. xcvii.

31. Frances A. Yates, *Shakespeare's Last Plays. A New Approach* (London: Routledge, 1975), pp. 13–19.

SEMINAR PAPERS

Romance in the Theater: The Stagecraft of the "Statue Scene" in The Winter's Tale

by JÖRG HASLER

In his introduction to the Arden edition of the play, J. H. P. Pafford has elaborated on the idea that there is "a strong web of realism running through the warp of romance."[1] While the web-and-warp image suggests that the two modes are inextricably interwoven, it yet seems possible to find places where one or the other of these styles clearly predominates. Two often-discussed episodes in the "Sicilia" plot appear to offer themselves for a comparative study of psychological realism versus ritualistic romance: the sudden attack of jealousy suffered by Leontes in 1. 2. 108ff., and the play's finale, the "statue scene" (5. 3).

What happens to Leontes from 1. 2. 108 up to the sudden death of Mamillius has in fact been accepted and praised by M. M. Mahood as the successful, accurate dramatization of a "libidinous invasion." She has described how the king's outburst is responsible for the compression, the "difficulty" of his highly metaphorical language: "Leontes's puns erupt like steam forcing up a saucepan lid, and by the end of some hundred lines he has fairly boiled over with 'foul imaginings'."[2] This explosion is paralleled on the gestic level by an equally striking agitation, contrasting with the yet undisturbed domestic harmony of 1. 2. 1–108.[3] The king's vehemence, his transformation into a dangerous, unpredictable "tyrant" is clearly reflected in the theatrical notation of Shakespeare's text—that is, his text read primarily as a script for performance.

His self-delusion causes Leontes to move swiftly towards increasing isolation, until he becomes a misanthrope, trusting no one among his most loyal and tested counselors. As I wish to concentrate on 5. 3, it is

203

perhaps sufficient here to indicate briefly that this development is visually driven home on stage by the king's repeated gesture of sending people away, ordering them to leave, having them thrown out if need be. The pattern is introduced by his willing, craftily ironic dismissal of Hermione and Polixenes, as they make off together for the garden:

> To your own bents dispose you: you'll be found,
> Be you beneath the sky . . .
>
> [1. 2. 179f.]

Moments later he sends away Mamillius ("Go play, boy, play . . ." l. 187) in a speech full of ironic double-entendres on the keywords *play, disgraced,* and *issue.* In 2. 1. 57 he asks Hermione to give him the boy, only to get rid of him again immediately afterwards: "Bear the boy hence . . ." (l. 59). From now on, the imperatives *hence, out, away* recur with increasing frequency in his speeches.[4] In l. 103 he has his wife removed from court: "Away with her to prison." In 2. 3 he is already on the defensive. Distraught, having lost his sleep, he desperately tries to fend off the undaunted intruder, Paulina (he knew she would come!), with her talk of the "good queen" and in her arms the "brat" he thinks a bastard. Already Leontes has become a pathetic figure, a helpless, unhappy little bully. Paulina has to be forcefully removed from his presence (l. 124: ". . . do not push me, I'll be gone"). The newborn child is cruelly expelled, to be exposed to the wilderness. All this may be a necessary part of the romance plot, but Leontes' passion and motivation are only too sadly plausible and familiar.

By the time the play moves to Bohemia, Leontes has broken with all who used to be dear to him. For the sacrifice of Mamillius there is no remedy. The estrangement from Polixenes and the denial of his daughter will be revoked and mended at the end of the play, as reported in 5. 2, when he "worries his daughter with clipping her" (5. 2. 52). For the reunion and reconciliation with the wronged Hermione, however, Shakespeare reserved an entire scene, 5. 3.

Style and atmosphere of this final scene differ entirely from the early scenes at the Sicilian court with their analysis of the effects of jealousy. Ernest Schanzer characterizes the finale as follows:

> The effect of Shakespeare's main departure from the plot of *Pandosto* in resurrecting Hermione was to bring the play closer to the world of Greek romance, not only in the happy ending it provides but also in the way in which the reunion is staged: the romance motif of a statue impersonated by a living woman believed dead, the sacrifice of psychological verisimilitude to theatrical effect (for looked at realistically the role Hermione is made to play in the statue scene must seem

intolerable), the subordination of everything else to the rousing of a feeling of wonder—all this is characteristic of Greek romance.[5]

As Schanzer points out, the enchantment of this famous episode had to be bought at the expense of any semblance of verisimilitude with regard to Hermione's behavior—not only in 5. 3 but during the sixteen years of Leontes' repentance. Theater-oriented critics tend to deal with implausibilities and inconsistencies by observing that in the theater there is no time to notice such things. No doubt that is quite true when we are dealing with phenomena such as the "impossible" time-scheme of *Othello*, for example; no doubt it is also pointless to make a fuss about the coast of Bohemia or the "Julio Romano" anachronism in *The Winter's Tale*. But the improbability of Hermione's willing cooperation in Paulina's brazen deception can only be forgotten if the statue scene is completely successful in casting its spell over an audience so rapt, so deeply moved that questions of character consistency cannot intrude into their emotional involvement. Let us therefore take a closer look at "the way in which the reunion is staged," or, more precisely, let us see what the dramatist's text tells about how it ought to be staged. Inga-Stina Ewbank has commented on the peculiarities of the dialogue in 5. 3:

> Speeches are short, the diction plain, the language almost bare of imagery: as if Shakespeare is anxious not to distract attention from the significance of action and movement. Characters' reactions to the statue are patterned in a fashion which approaches ritual. An unusual number of speeches are devoted just to underlining the emotions and postures of people on stage.[6]

This last sentence is another way of saying that the scene is particularly rich in explicit and implicit text directions. "Action and movement," as well as the emotional responses to the spectacle of the "resurrection" (it amounts to no less for Leontes and a "naive" audience), are reflected, mirrored in the dialogue to ensure the desired effect. Only in this way can Shakespeare be certain to get away with his daring *coup de théâtre*. Ewbank goes on to compare the scene to the central movement of a masque, with Hermione as the main "device" and Paulina as the pre-senter. The deception of Leontes (and the audience) concerning Hermione's death having all along been engineered by Paulina, that resolute lady now functions in fact not merely as presenter but as the virtual "director" of the statue scene (and through her, of course, the dramatist himself).[7]

Having witnessed Leontes's treatment of Paulina in 2. 3, we have now reached the stage where he eats out of her hand, as for example, in the matter of his ever marrying again in 5. 1. Still, it is a rather startling inversion, stressing Paulina's new status, that it is she who gives her sovereign leave to speak in line 22: "But yet speak: first you, my liege." Again it is Paulina who in line 95 demands the suitable solemnity (and freezes the other figures into a tableau) for the great moment: "Then all stand still. . . ," and Leontes who both indicates his willing obedience and reinforces her order ("No foot shall stir," l. 98). Paulina gives the signal for the music to "strike" and then directs—and by the same token describes—Hermione's descent in a series of precise imperatives:

> 'Tis time: descend; be stone no more; approach;
> Strike all that look upon with marvel. Come,
> I'll fill your grave up. Stir; nay, come away.
> Bequeath to death your numbness, for from him
> Dear life redeems you. You perceive she stirs.
>
> [Ll. 99–103]

She literally, concretely, reunites Leontes and his queen by joining their hands together ("Nay, present your hand," l. 107). She next intervenes by asking Perdita to kneel for her mother's blessing (l. 119). Her ensuing order—or request—to Hermione: "Turn, good lady: / Our Perdita is found,"[8] shows that it is necessary to disengage the queen from her husband, for she "embraces him" (Polixenes, l. 111) and "hangs about his neck" (Camillo, l. 112). Lost to the world, her attention has to be directed to her child. Earlier in the scene, under the first impact of the "statue," Perdita had once before sunk to her knees (l. 44), but then her gesture had been "superstition," as Perdita herself knew (cp. 43): however, now that Hermione has been "revived," Paulina herself calls for and thus sanctions this act of homage.

Such explicit directions, "orders" from the director/presenter, provide no more than a bare skeleton of essential elements. The actual shape of the stage event is registered in more detail in numerous mirror-passages, lines "underlining the emotions and postures of people on stage." The other figures all collaborate with Paulina in fixing the manner and acting style of the scene. Most important is of course the demeanor of Leontes, to whom the spectacle is mainly addressed. Our attention is constantly focused on him. His first reaction to the statue is stunned silence (Paulina: "I like your silence," l. 21). Leontes in his turn notes for us the effect on Perdita, who seems transfixed by the "magic" of the "royal piece," "standing like stone with thee" (l. 42). Paulina next ascribes intense emotion to the king in line 58: "If I had known the sight of my poor image / Would thus have wrought you. . . ." In line 68 he is "transported," in line 74 "so far stirred. . . ." This kind of mirroring is particularly useful to the dramatist here. In the study, it is difficult to decide on the way these lines function in performance. Of course

Paulina appears to be registering and interpreting some gestic or mimic play by Leontes betraying his inner feelings. On the other hand, the overall emphasis throughout lies on the complete lack of anything approaching lively expression or even commotion, keeping stage movements to a minimum and thus letting the significant, "ritualistic" gestures stand out. The restraint thus imposed on the actor encourages the view that far from serving as a mere reflector, Paulina is in fact projecting these emotions on Leontes, enhancing, making explicit what can at the most be hinted at by discrete and intimate expression. In a relatively large theater this view of the matter gains an additional, technical relevance: no matter how far the spectator may be from the stage, he is made to "see" things that he actually cannot perceive with his eyes.

When Hermione is descending from her raised position to become human again, Paulina's "Start not. . ." (l. 104) seems to be addressed to all present; then she turns to Leontes again, making it plain that, awed and overwhelmed, he appears to "shun" (l. 105) Hermione. He has to be *told* to present his hand (l. 108). His passivity, his misdoubting hesitation, is implicitly stressed further by the witnesses Polixenes and Camillo, who only see and report actions of Hermione—i.e., her embrace of tender forgiveness (cp. ll. 111, 112). In fact, from the moment of the descent to his conventional closing speech, Leontes speaks just once: "O, she's warm!" (l. 109). The childlike simplicity of his amazed exclamation not only expresses his "wonder" (cp. Paulina, l. 22), but technically speaking it is also an implied stage direction, confirming that he has now indeed obeyed Paulina in "presenting" his hand. Probably the only instance of wholly spontaneous impulsive action on the part of the king comes earlier in the scene, when Hermione is still a "statue": ". . . I will kiss her" (l. 80). His attempt to kiss a mere artefact bears a suggestion of unwholesome idolatry as in Perdita's first kneeling down (mirrored by herself in line 44); the parallel is underlined by the fact that both actions are preceded by expressions of apology and unease (Leontes: "Let no man mock me," Perdita: "And do not say 'tis superstition"). In both cases, too, the original impulse legitimately can be indulged when Hermione has given up her pretense.

Of course, the formidable Paulina is really staging a sham miracle and Hermione is playacting. The speechless amazement immediately evoked by the statue is quite plausible, since its much-praised "lifelikeness" is bound to be beyond art. In order to understand how Paulina contrives to inspire all with an almost religious sense of awe, we must examine her strategy in the opening phase of the scene. She is very careful to cushion the shock that awaits her royal guests. They have been invited to her gallery under false pretenses, and while they still think they are merely appreciating a supreme, miraculously mimetic work of art, she repeatedly refers to—and of course denies—the likely suspicion that the apparition might be the work of black magic. Her protestations that she is not assisted by "wicked powers" (l. 91) nor engaged in "unlawful business" (l. 96), however true, still prepare her audience—on and off the stage—for some miracle, some supernatural phenomenon. These suggestive references precede the "music," supporting it in creating the required, expectant atmosphere. At the supreme moment, when the "statue" stirs, Paulina's claim "my spell is lawful" still clings to the notion of a spell. Of course Leontes, Polixenes, Perdita, and the ever-silent Florizel are, as we say figuratively, "spellbound" at this moment, but in the context Paulina surely means the term to have its literal, technical sense. Just as important as this verbal coloring of the mood is the use Paulina makes of the curtain, drawn for the "discovery" at line 20 and first mentioned by Leontes in line 59. This stage property plays an important part in the phase leading up to Hermione's "rebirth." Leontes's repeated requests ("Do not draw the curtain," l. 59; "Let be, let be," l. 61, "Let't alone," l. 73) reflect the elaborate and ironic coquetry Paulina enacts concerning her statue. Four times does she make as if to draw the curtain because the sight could prove too much for the beholders (cp. ll. 60, 68, 73, 83). In line 83 she cleverly feigns to yield to the king's entreaties; her threat has become a mere question by now: "Shall I draw the curtain?" The climax of her coyly ironic playacting is reached in l. 69: "My lord's almost so far transported that / He'll think anon it lives." Only after much feigned hesitation, visually expressed by her recurrent handling of the curtain, does she proceed to the bold, formal announcement of her "miracle," and even this is preceded by a somewhat hypocritical "if":

> ... If you can behold it,
> I'll make the statue move indeed, descend
> And take you by the hand ...
>
> [Ll. 87ff.]

So it will shortly happen, point by point. Here Paulina is perhaps most reminiscent of a presenter who, "prologue-like," rehearses for the audience the action to follow. As it turns out, Paulina (still with the obedient, almost puppetlike cooperation of the queen) keeps to this gradual, solemn, step-by-step presentation to the last: Hermione is first made to "move" only (l. 103), her reconciliation with Leontes is allowed gestic expression only. Not before she is confronted with the kneeling Perdita, and only on her cue from the "director," does she speak. While she is still embracing Leontes (ll. 111–20), references to "life," "live," "living" multiply in the lines of the observing bystanders:

Camillo.	If she pertain to life, let her speak too.
Polixenes.	Ay, and make it manifest where she has lived,
	Or how stol'n from the dead.
Paulina.	That she is living,
	Were it but told you, should be hooted at
	Like an old tale: but it appears she lives,
	Though yet she speak not.

(Ll. 113–18]

The reiterative emphasis, from three speakers, on the idea of life and a return from death to life amounts to a choric comment on the event we have just witnessed.[9] Paulina's words about "an old tale" have often been noted, like similar references elsewhere in the play, as openly stressing the nonrealistic romance element in *The Winter's Tale*. With regard to the nature of the statue scene, however, the opposition she establishes between "telling" and "showing" is even more to the point: "Were it but *told* you . . . but it *appears* she lives."[10] Statues are designed to be looked at: Paulina begins by *exhibiting* a work of art and then *presents* the miracle of a resurrection: the miracle is literally a performance. This points to the important division of labor between the much-criticized "telling" in 5. 2 (the report by the Third Gentleman) and the "showing" in 5. 3. Because of this division of labor, the only embrace actually performed on stage is reserved for Hermione and Leontes. The impact of their reunion is bound to be greatly enhanced by this dramaturgical strategy. Blinded by his jealousy, Leontes had driven away his friend, spurned and shamed his wife, and expelled his daughter. The reunion with Polixenes and Perdita is reported in 5. 2, in florid terms suggesting an almost unbearable onrush of excessive joy, an ecstasy that beggars description:

> There might you have beheld one joy crown another, so and in such manner that it seemed sorrow wept to take leave of them: for their joy waded in tears. There was casting up of eyes, holding up of hands, with countenance of such distraction that they were to be known by garment, not by favour. Our king, being ready to leap out of himself for joy of his found daughter, as if that joy were now become a loss cries "O, thy mother, thy mother!"; then asks Bohemia forgiveness; then embraces his son-in-law; then again worries he his daughter with clipping her; now he thanks the old shepherd, which stands by like a weather-bitten conduit of many kings' reigns.

[Ll. 41–54]

In justification of this it has been argued that the dramatist wanted to avoid the repetition of similar joyful scenes on the stage. Yet, quite apart from the fact that 5. 2 reports and 5. 3 shows, the comparison between two scenes shows little similarity (except, as Fluellen would say, "there is

reunions in both"). On the contrary, one is struck by the contrast between the highly demonstrative self-abandonment described in 5. 2 and
the remarkable, controlled restraint shown in 5. 3. It seems that for very
good reasons Shakespeare entrusted the "wading in tears" to our imaginations rather than a concrete enactment by real actors. As a result,
Leontes, by the time he comes to the most important and most moving
reunion, has already shed all his tears and sighed his fill. He has had his
catharsis and comes to his supreme experience already purged, blessed
by the recovery of his lost child. He enters Paulina's house thanking her
for the "great comfort" he has had of her, but not suspecting what she
has in store for him. The emotions stirred up in 5. 3 are of the kind that
is beyond words, his silence therefore is the best and most adequate
response. Since the statue scene is concerned with "showing" a miracle
worthy of an old tale, the precise manner in which it is performed
becomes all-important. One false note and the whole thing would tum-
ble from the sublime to the ridiculous, the enchantment would turn into
low comedy. It is hardly surprising, then, that such a large proportion of
the dialogue is devoted, openly or indirectly, to the task of controlling
mood and pace, and directing the performance from moment to moment. While Paulina has the lion's share, every other figure assists her at
one time or another: even the silence of Florizel can enhance the general
effect. The statue scene thus illustrates the fact that Shakespeare, at
moments of great significance or particular delicacy, tends to assume
strict control of the scenic realization by means of an unusually dense
theatrical notation in his playtext.[11]

Notes

1. William Shakespeare, *The Winter's Tale*, ed. J. H. P. Pafford (London: Methuen & Co.,
1963; reprinted 1966), p. lxvi.

2. M. M. Mahood, "Wordplay in *The Winter's Tale*," in *Shakespeare's Later Comedies*, ed.
D. J. Palmer (Harmondsworth: Penguin, 1971), p. 348.

3. In the "Scandinavian" RSC production of 1976 (directed by John Barton and Trevor
Nunn, Leontes played by Ian McKellen) the shattering effect of this explosion was impressed on the audience by a truly inspired piece of stage business. At the climax of his
rage, Leontes stumbled over a large rug, tearing at it so vehemently that chairs and tables
collapsed into a confused heap. This brilliantly conveyed the instant destruction of the
king's home and family.

4. Most strikingly is this the case in scene 2.3:
   "*Away* with that audacious lady!" (l. 42)
   "Force her *hence*." (l. 61)
   "Out! / A mankind witch! *Hence* with her, out o' door . . ." (ll. 66f.)
   "Traitors! / Will you not push her *out*?" (l. 72f.)
   "This brat is none of mine; / It is the issue of Polixenes. / *Hence* with it . . ." (l. 92ff.)

"Once more, take her *hence*." (l. 111)

"*Out* of the chamber with her!" (l. 121)

5. William Shakespeare, *The Winter's Tale,* ed. Ernest Schanzer (Harmondsworth: Penguin, 1969), p. 16. Quotations are taken from this text.

6. Inga-Stina Ewbank, "The Triumph of Time in *The Winter's Tale*", in Palmer, ed., *Shakespeare's Later Comedies,* p. 327.

7. The functional importance of Paulina, the "Kent" to Leontes's "Lear" and arranger of the scheme that makes the eventual happy ending possible, is reflected in the length of her speaking part. After Leontes (681 lines) she has the second longest role with 331 lines.

8. Paulina here pointedly echoes the wording of the Oracle: "*and the king shall live without an heir, if that which is lost be not found.*" (3. 2. 134ff.)

9. The quoted passage forms the climax of this reiteration, which begins early in the scene. Birth and death are juxtaposed in Perdita's address to the "statue" in line 42: "Dear queen, that ended when I but began," which echoes the words of the old shepherd at the turning point of the play: ". . . thou met'st with things dying, I with things new-born" (3. 3. 112f.). The admiring comments on the statue's lifelikeness allow Shakespeare to keep the notion of life constantly in our minds. In the whole scene the relevant words— invariably referring to Hermione—recur with the following frequency: "life" three times, "lives"/"living" four, "breath"/"air" two, "warm" two, return from death three (including Paulina's "I'll fill your grave").

10. Cp. also line 103: "You *perceive* she stirs."

11. It goes without saying that Leontes's final lines (135–55) are not properly part of the statue scene. They constitute a thoroughly conventional comedy-closing speech: the business of the play has to be wound up, Paulina is offered a new "mate" in order to complete the trio of happy couples. In this mood we may be reminded of Antigonus, but Mamillius must not be mentioned. Yet in spite of its functional character, the speech brings one last touch of great subtlety. It returns to the mode of psychological realism when Leontes says to Hermione: "What! look upon my brother: both your pardons" (l. 147). This mirror passage completes the characterization of generous Hermione, stressing her delicacy in averting her gaze from Polixenes long after her innocence has been proclaimed by Apollo.

Shakespearean Comedy and Some Eighteenth-Century Actresses

by JEANNE ADDISON ROBERTS

In 1776, the year of David Garrick's retirement from the stage, Mrs. Thrale entered in her diary a vignette of the household of Bennet Langton, Sr., father of Dr. Johnson's friend. Dr. Johnson had visited the Langton family estate near Spilsby in Lincolnshire in 1764, and Thrale's description reports anecdotes of his visit. Langton had three daughters, wild, strong-minded, and eccentric "dowdies," to use Johnson's word, over whom their father was unable to exercise any authority. Thrale identifies the cause of this "disorder" in the household. The guilty party, as any modern analyst would guess, was Langton's wife. Not only had she spawned free-spirited daughters, she had also failed with the house-keeping—and all because of an addiction to the theater. She was, Thrale tells us,

> a *London Lady*, always teizing her husband to go to Town, and never regulating her Family for twenty Years, never buying a Cow, never putting up a Fowl to feed,—never repairing their Furniture or house in Lincolnshire where they always lived because they were to go to London next Year forsooth and see the Players, who made all the Subject of her Conversation, settling the Merits of M[rs.] Cibber and M[rs.] Pritchard in the midst of a Family ruined by Mismanagement, and running to speedy Decay; and in a Neighborhood of Country Gentlewomen who had never seen nor were like to see them.[1]

I confess to considerable sympathy for the slovenly Mrs. Langton in her protracted exile from the center of human felicity, but I also find her particularly interesting as a symptom of her time. It seems to me significant that she wants to go to London, not to see plays but players, and that at the very height of the Garrick years her theatrical interest is focused not on the brilliant Garrick or the romantic Spranger Barry, but on two leading female players, Susanna Maria Cibber and Hannah Pritchard. I should like to use Mrs. Langton's longing as a clue to the roles of women, both actresses and audiences, in the middle of the

212

eighteenth century and in particular, to suggest that female influences were crucial in one of the most striking developments on the stage of this period—the revival of Shakespeare's comedies.[2]

I will argue that the emergence of first-rate actresses who were neither dependent courtesans nor social pariahs but affluent and respected professionals was an unprecedented development in the social history of women; that these actresses, truly extraordinary individuals, would have found in the spirited, self-reliant heroines of Shakespearean comedy roles that expressed their characters much more fully than did the limp, tearful ladies of popular comedies. These actresses unquestionably had the power to influence repertory choices; and, in both private and stage roles, their influence on the theater public, male as well as female, was significant. I will examine in particular the careers of Hannah Pritchard, Kitty Clive, and Peg Woffington as they impinge on Shakespearean comedy, and I shall also glance briefly at Susanna Maria Cibber.

The contributions of these women have not been ignored, but they have suffered a partial eclipse as the result of an insistent male emphasis. This emphasis started, of course, with a theatrical structure that was in its origins entirely male. It was carried on by the male theatrical managers, actors, and reviewers of the period who strongly influenced public opinion, but it has been perpetuated by scholars. The tendency to ignore women is strongly apparent in G. C. D. Odell's pioneer work, *Shakespeare from Betterton to Irving* (2 vols., New York: Scribner's, 1920, repr. 1963), with its major divisions named for actors and its merely passing references to Cibber, Pritchard, Clive, and Woffington. Odell grants that *As You Like It* was "saved to the stage" by a succession of great Rosalinds, but he is less generous in claiming that *Much Ado About Nothing* and *Cymbeline* were constantly revived because of Garrick's "supreme success" in the leading roles (1:339). In fact, the praise accorded to Pritchard's Beatrice during the long run of *Much Ado* almost exactly matches (and sometimes surpasses—see below) that given to Garrick as Benedick; and since Garrick ceased playing Posthumus after two seasons, the remarkable success of *Cymbeline* can hardly be due solely to his performance. Much progress has been made since Odell, but a male bias persists.

James J. Lynch (*Box, Pit, and Gallery* [Berkeley: University of California Press, 1953]) lists the great Shakespearean roles of the Garrick period: in tragedy, Pritchard as Lady Macbeth, Garrick as Hamlet, Barry as Othello, Quin as Falstaff, Cibber as Juliet; in comedy, Pritchard as Beatrice, Clive as Portia, Theophilus Cibber as Pistol, Garrick as Benedick (p. 161). But in pointing out important factors in the Shakespeare revival he mentions only actors, specifically Garrick, Macklin, and Quin (p. 124). In another context, assigning credit for the Shakespearean revival of 1740–41, he mentions some of the revived plays—*As You Like*

It, Twelfth Night, The Winter's Tale, The Merchant of Venice, All's Well that Ends Well—and concludes that though these revivals cannot be attributed to Garrick, since they precede his career, some credit may be assigned to Charles Macklin (p. 95). Lynch's disregard of female contributions in dealing with these particular plays, with their strong female roles, seems especially striking. Lynch notes that midcentury audiences came to see stars rather than plays, but he specifies only Garrick and Barry (p. 139). He emphasizes the importance of Garrick in the 1744 revival of *Macbeth*, quoting Thomas Davies on the "indescribable excellence" of the actor in the banquet scene (p. 103). Lynch neglects to mention, however, that Davies specifically includes Pritchard, insisting "I will not separate these performers, for the merits of both were transcendent." In fact, his description of the banquet scene includes two lines on Garrick and seventeen lines on Pritchard.[3] Garrick himself felt Pritchard's importance so strongly that he retired from the part of Macbeth when she retired from the stage. All discussions of acting styles emphasize as innovative Garrick's great naturalness, but this observation is rarely linked in modern criticism with the praise of the great natural acting credited to Pritchard, Clive, and Woffington, all of whom preceded Garrick on the stage.[4] Finally, Arthur Scouten, in looking for influences other than Garrick's to account for new interest in Shakespeare in the early 1740s, lists the importance of editions of the plays, the reaction of licensing, the Shakespeare Ladies Club, and Theophilus Cibber—again without recognition of the possible impact of female stars.[5]

The lives and careers of the female stars demonstrate their personal and professional stature.[6] Spiritual descendants of Aphra Behn and the actresses of the Restoration and early eighteenth century, but no longer the first pioneers on the new frontiers of female professionalism, Clive, Cibber, Woffington, and Pritchard enjoyed security, affluence, and independence remarkable for their time. Each of them displayed in pursuit of her career a high degree of courage and determination but admirably combined these qualities with generosity and personal integrity.

Daughter of an impoverished Dublin lawyer, Kitty Clive was married at age twenty-two to a barrister, but within two years she had separated from him. She was already a successful actress, and with her earnings she supported herself and her aged father and provided a home for her brother. She was able to retire relatively early and comfortably, devoting time and energy to her friends—especially Horace Walpole and Jane Pope, a younger actress with whom she sustained a long and mutually supportive correspondence.

Susannah Cibber, daughter of a London upholsterer and sister of the musician Thomas Arne, was reluctantly propelled first into marriage with Theophilus Cibber and then, by her husband's avarice, into the arms of a lover. With the lover she took her stand, surviving two stormy lawsuits and bearing him two children. In spite of her adulterous situation, she established herself as a respected "wife" and mother; and in the midst of the strong pressures of a Protestant milieu she remained a devoted Catholic. Neither dubious social status nor religious discrimination prevented her from making and controlling her own fortune.

Peg Woffington grew up in Dublin in extreme poverty but early won attention as a professional actress. The most sexually adventurous of the four, she remained unmarried, preferring freedom to compromise. After a prolonged affair with Garrick, during which she shared quarters with him for perhaps five years and was visited by such notables as Dr. Johnson, she broke off the relationship before Garrick's marriage and steadfastly refused to return to Drury Lane while he was manager. Excluded from proper society herself, she nonetheless succeeded in educating her sister and marrying her advantageously to the second son of a lord. She gave up Roman Catholicism in order to qualify for an inheritance from an admirer, but most of the considerable fortune she left to her sister was the reward of a disciplined and dedicated dramatic career.

Hannah Pritchard was the child of a prosperous London staymaker. To all appearances her life was the most conventional of the four, but she added new dimensions to convention. Fortunate in having a supportive husband, she maintained a long marriage, successful motherhood, and an elevated social station without compromising her distinguished acting career. She must have been one of the first women in English history to perform such an impressive balancing act.

All four of these women made choices, made money, and made their way astonishingly well in a male-dominated society where they were often legally helpless. My particular interest in them here is that all four were also important in the revival of Shakespeare's comedies in the early 1740s. It is significant that the comedies revived were those with strong female leads, multiple female roles, and provocative examples of women moving, often helped by male disguise, with a freedom rare either in actual society or in the popular drama of the day. In the years of midcentury most often thought of as the Garrick years, female forces need to be reckoned with.

I have no wish whatever to denigrate Garrick. His importance in every aspect of theatrical production is beyond question. And indeed he deserves special credit for his recognition of female talent and his remarkable success in sustaining frequently difficult relationships with his leading ladies. However, his influence in the revival of Shakespearean comedy was actually negative. We know that he had, understandably, a strong interest in the plays in which he acted, and that only three of his established Shakespearean roles were in the comedies. Of these— Benedick, Leontes, and Posthumus—only Benedick can be considered major, since Leontes has only a small part in Garrick's adaptation of *The Winter's Tale*, and since Posthumus was played by others after two seasons. During the period of Garrick's management of Drury Lane, twenty-seven percent of all the tragedies produced there were Shakespearean, as opposed to only sixteen percent of the comedies.[7] Among the revivals of the comedies specifically initiated by Garrick, only that of *Cymbeline* in 1759 was a close approximation of Shakespeare's play, and even that suffered from a weakening and shortening of the role of Imogen. Managerial impetus for the numerous comic revivals of 1740– 46 was supplied by other entrepreneurs, and the three most frequently performed comedies of that period (see table) owed very little to Garrick.[8]

Performances of Shakespeare's Comedies, Seasons 1739–40 through 1760–61*

The Merchant of Venice	134
As You Like It	121
The Merry Wives of Windsor	94
The Tempest	87
Much Ado About Nothing	79
The Taming of the Shrew	58
A Midsummer Night's Dream	48
The Winter's Tale	44
Measure for Measure	39
All's Well that Ends Well	30
Twelfth Night	27
Cymbeline	10
The Comedy of Errors	5

*Includes adaptations, some musical.

Audiences at midcentury were more heterogeneous than they had been in the Restoration period, and tensions between classes and sexes were frequently projected onto the stage. The aristocrats in the boxes and the bourgeoisie in the pit often disagreed. A good example is the flap over *The Foundling* in 1748 (*The London Stage, Part 4*, vol. 1, pp. 30– 35), when Lord Hubbard formed a party to hiss the play off the stage in protest against its protracted run. When *As You Like It* was proposed as a successor, the pit rose and insisted on a continuation of *The Foundling*, a play in the sentimental tradition, which, though well acted, appealed more because of its middle-class values than its artistic standards. Judged by this incident, Shakespeare's comedy was regarded as a suitable pacifier for the upper class, but its appeal extended to the middle class and especially to women—both those in the audience and those on the stage.

The presence and power of women in the audience at midcentury is well attested. The existence of a club connected with Covent Garden, made up of some of the most intelligent and fashionable ladies of the time whose purpose was to foster Shakespeare on the stage, is regularly noted.[9] If it is a little disappointing to discover that the three revivals known to have been sponsored by the club in 1737–38 were of *King John, Richard II*, and *1 Henry VI* (none of them very memorable for their female characters), it is worth noting that the production of an adaptation of *Much Ado About Nothing* called *The Universal Passion* was mounted at Drury Lane in 1737, within a week of Covent Garden's *King John*, with a prologue specifically addressed to the "*noble Fair*" who now "*to* Shakespear's *Sense attend.*" It concludes with a plea to women as "*the ablest Judges of this Play*," entreating that they "*To* their *Protection* Shakespear's *Offspring take,/And save the* Orphan for the Father's *Sake.*"[10] The production was repeated for four nights (with Clive, as Liberia-Beatrice, and Pritchard, later to become the great Beatrice of the century, as Delia-Margaret) and seems to have stimulated a four-night revival of the original play at Covent Garden in the same year.

Women on the stage were also active in promoting Shakespeare. Pritchard and Clive, who maintained a close friendship during almost forty years, played together constantly until Clive followed Pritchard into retirement in 1768, even though she might have continued longer on the stage. Their partnership frequently extended into other Shakespearean comedies featuring two women. As early as 1735 they were playing in *A Cure for a Scold*, an adaptation of *The Taming of the Shrew*, with Clive as Peg-Katherine and Pritchard as Flora-Bianca. Later, in 1754, when Garrick's *Catherine and Petruchio* was mounted at Drury Lane, both actresses played the lead, though it was Clive who finally "owned" the part. In *As You Like It* Clive played Celia to Pritchard's Rosalind many times, beginning with the Drury Lane production of 1740–41, designed to challenge Woffington's success in two "breeches roles" at Covent Garden. In a reversal of role priority in *The Merchant of Venice*, Pritchard played Nerissa to Clive's Portia, and then, exchanging precedence again in *Twelfth Night*, Clive was Olivia to Pritchard's Viola. It is very difficult indeed to avoid the conclusion that these good friends discovered in the midthirties that they played well together, and, considerably before Garrick, fostered the production of the Shakespearean comedies with interesting dual roles.

The unflagging mutual support of Clive and Pritchard reflects on a

small scale a rather surprising system of female reinforcement in the
larger theatrical world. In spite of some notorious quarrels among actresses, we are repeatedly told of friendship and generosity within the
profession and of impressive support from female audiences, especially
the aristocracy. George Anne Bellamy says that she dates her theatrical
advancement from the notice given her by the duchess of Montague.
She also recounts how Mrs. Butler, a patroness in Dublin, supplied her
with diamonds for her elaborate costumes, and how the same lady kept
down the house for Garrick's *King John* when Bellamy was denied the
role of Constance. The duchess of Queensberry on one occasion took
250 tickets and all but one of the boxes for a Bellamy benefit.[11] Similar
benefits sponsored by women for women were apparently a regular
feature of the Dublin stage.[12] Davies repeatedly describes the esteem in
which actresses were held by members of their own sex of "the most
distinguished wealth and character."[13] Complaining publicly of her
difficulties with managers, Clive appealed to audiences, concluding "I
have in consideration of these hardships been promised the protection
of many ladies to whom I have the honour to be personally
known. . . ."[14] Theophilus Cibber speaks in his "Serio-Comic Apology"
of his efforts to comply with the "ladies who are desirous to see" his wife
act,[15] and we are reminded of the longings of Mrs. Bennet Langton.
Finally, in a footnote reference to a comment on the power of managers
in a letter from Mrs. Abington to Garrick, James Boaden, editor of
Garrick's correspondence, has added, "The power of a manager indeed!
what is it to an actress of powerful talent, backed by half the women of
fashion in the metropolis."[16] This kind of female solidarity certainly
suggests a strong identification between women in the audience and
actresses and helps to explain the appeal of Shakespeare's comedies.

Shakespeare's comedies were among the most popular of the period.
They were enacted with about the same frequency as the "humane comedies" of Farquhar, Vanbrugh, Colley Cibber, Congreve, and Steele.[17]
Shakespeare shared with these writers an underlying insistence on sexual morality and the sanctity of marriage, and, above all their pervasive
good humor, tolerance, and optimism about human nature. To some
critics his women seemed similar. Colley Cibber says that in writing
female roles for boys, Shakespeare knew that he could not expect much
and therefore emphasized simplicity, innocence, and virtue.[18] Even such
female characters as Celia, Portia, and the merry wives were, somewhat
incongruously, admired for being tender, modest, and delicate.[19] Davies
speaks more perceptively (*Dr. Misc.* 2: 237), however, when he praises
the "abundant and varied originality" of Shakespeare's women. In fact,
the most striking difference between Shakespeare and the writers of
"humane comedy" is their characterization of women. Whereas the later

writers, with a few exceptions, tended to create good women who were weak, humorless, and passive, Shakespeare's heroines combine goodness with aggressive intelligence and wit. For eighteenth-century as for Elizabethan audiences, they continued to bridge both class and sex barriers. They pleased the aristocrats with their wit and high spirits, but they also gratified the middle class with their lack of aristocratic pretension. John Upton observes that "Shakespeare seems . . . not to have known such a character as a fine lady; nor does he ever recognize their dignity. . . . Instead of the Lady Bettys, and Lady Fannys, who shine so much in modern comedies, he brings you on the stage plain Mrs Ford and Mrs Page, two honest good-humored wives of two plain country gentlemen."[20] In the comedies revived (in adaptations and in the original) in the late 30s and early 40s, Rosalind, Portia, Beatrice, Isabella, Viola, and Helena presented a stunning array of females uniquely qualified to satisfy both the middle-class demand for virtue and the interest of the discriminating of all classes in subtlety and spirited characterization.[21] Audiences could enjoy the beauty, charm, and occasional giddiness of these heroines and at the same time find horizons stretched by their display of female enterprise and determination. The stage characters must also have delighted the actresses, themselves risen from middle-class backgrounds through energy and talent to an artistic aristocracy. These powerful women surely did as much as actors to shift critical attention from dramatic structure to character and personality. Regrettably this fortunate conjunction of commanding actresses and roles that gave them scope was part of a rear-guard action. By the end of the century (with the help of the novel), the duller, more sentimental heroines of contemporary plays had triumphed; and a new generation of actresses either modified or played down the more unmaidenly aspects of the women in comedies.

At midcentury, however, the struggle to define the role of women and to analyze male-female relationships seemed to be at its height. Attitudes toward marriage in the popular comedies of the early part of the century have already been perceptively analyzed,[22] and these comedies continued to dominate the stage. The titles alone are eloquent: *The Provok'd Wife, The Careless Husband, The Modern Husband, The Provok'd Husband, The Distressed Wife, The Jealous Wife,* etc. Although the popular Shakespeare comedies are special in that they focus primarily on the brief heady period of courtship, where female freedom generates a particular excitement, heightened perhaps by its ephemeral nature, they still point up the perennial conflict between the sexes that was obviously of absorbing interest to midcentury audiences. From the exhilarating dominance of Rosalind, Portia, and the merry wives to the tenacious devotion of Viola and Helena, the comic heroines offered an intriguing spectrum

that male and female observers could use to test the varying shades of
their own feelings.

Restoration and eighteenth-century adaptations of *The Taming of the
Shrew* reflect the vicissitudes of fashion on this compelling subject. All of
them keep Petruchio's accurate but offensive announcement to his new
wife:

> I will be master of what is mine own;
> She is my goods, my chattels; she is my house,
> My household stuff, my field, my barn,
> My horse, my ox, my ass, my any thing. . . .
>
> [3. 2. 229–32]

But in other ways they temporize. *Sauny the Scot*, the 1667 version, in
general a vicious and sadistic play, still gives Margaret-Kate lines like "I'll
make Petruchio glad to wipe my shoes or walk my horse ere I have done
with him," although in the end she apologizes and utters a speech greatly
shortened from the original, conceding "They are our lords." Petruchio
is given a mollifying last word, however, with a prophecy:

> I've tamed the shrew, but will not be ashamed
> If next you see the very tamer tamed.[23]

In 1735 James Worsdale's *Cure for a Scold*, in which Peg-Kate was played
by Clive, duly prescribes for its heroine two final lines of wifely submission but then cancels them out with an epilogue where Clive reveals:

> Well, I must own, it wounds me to the Heart
> To act, unwomanly—so mean a Part.
> What—to submit, so tamely—so contented,
> Thank Heav'n I'm not the Thing I represented.

Her final word is to the women in the audience who know that in real life
they make the "Monsters tame." She pleads,

> Ye Fair, who form the radiant Circle here,
> Approve that Censure, which you cannot fear. . . .[24]

Garrick's version, *Catherine and Petruchio*, is closer to the original, but it
too offers some slight compromise. Though Catherine has six final lines
of total submission, Petruchio has already promised to "doff the lordly
husband" and live in "mutual love, compliance, and regard."[25] A great
attraction of Garrick's adaptation seems to have been that it was enjoyed
as a reflection of real-life antagonism between its principals, Clive and
Henry Woodward (one of Drury Lane's major comedians).[26] On this
level it was a contest between equals.

Kitty Clive was a comic genius. By 1756, the year of maximum popularity of *Catherine and Petruchio*, she had already been a favorite of the English stage for more than twenty years. Her range in comedy was extensive, including, says Davies (*Memoirs*, 2:192), "country girls, romps, hoydens, and dowdies, superannuated beauties, viragoes, and humourists." Her special forte was "sprightliness of humour." Boswell quotes Johnson as saying, "she was a better romp than any I ever saw in nature." Offstage, Clive was famous for direct speech and a no-nonsense temperament. It was she who, after a notorious battle with Mrs. Cibber in 1736 (during which she was dubbed in a popular ballad, "a Green-Room Scold"), won back the role of Polly in *The Beggar's Opera* from Cibber who had been briefly slated to play the part. Samuel Foote said that Clive's forcible manner was assumed in order "to procure a more decent Entertainment," and obviously she was a force not to be ignored (*Biographical Dictionary*, 3:344–59).

Garrick valued Clive enough to beg her to postpone her retirement, and a mutual respect seems to have tempered their frequently stormy relationship. Davies says that Garrick dreaded altercations with her and was happy to get a draw because she was so "true game" that she "would have died upon the spot rather than have yielded the field of battle to any body" (*Memoirs*, 2:190–98). Clive's most famous comic role was Portia in *The Merchant of Venice*, and yet ironically it was also the role that drew the most critical attack, since she apparently played the courtroom scene in a style recognizable as a parody of a local judge.

Obviously an influential figure, Clive was also delightfully capable of self-parody. She wrote a farce in imitation of *The Rehearsal* called *Bays in Petticoats*,[27] which, though not a dramatic triumph, is full of revealing personal references. Her female lead, Mrs. Hazard, is an actress who has written a play. Mrs. Hazard's male "friend," appropriately named Witling, warns her that "there is not ten Women in the Creation that have sense enough to write a consistent *N. B.*" (i.e., compose a sensible footnote). This satirically drawn male chauvinist is balanced by a laughing denigration of the "conceited, and insolent" Mrs. Clive who has been scheduled to act in the play-within-the-play but sends word that she cannot come because she is busy with "Ladies about her Benefit." The author is careful to note that the actress makes £ 800 a year, but still she refers to her alter ego as a "poor Lady . . . ignorant as Dirt." Clive's self-portrait comes close to some of the criticisms made of her, and she clearly enjoys the joke of her own caricature.

In the same vein Clive could enjoy the role of Kate in *Catherine and Petruchio*. During her struggle with Cibber, Woodward, now her Petruchio, had called her in a rhyme a "Fierce Amazonian Dame" and an anonymous pamphlet had described her as a "little Gypsy" whose "natural Temper is inclined to be Shrewish" (*Biographical Dictionary*, 3:346, 349). Even though she is finally tamed in the drama, personality and role merged in a way to give actors maximum opportunity and audiences maximum pleasure. Witnessing Clive and Woodward in action must have been as fascinating as watching Elizabeth Taylor and Richard Burton in the parts on the modern screen. Clive seems to have reinstituted an epilogue,[28] and it is interesting to speculate whether Garrick's own feelings or his accurate gauging of the temper of his audience was responsible for his tipping the sexual equilibrium in his text slightly to the male side. In any case *Catherine and Petruchio* was extremely popular, and Clive's early experience of the play and her special suitability for the role made it a logical choice for adaptation.

Clive deserves major credit for the success of *The Shrew* in two versions and some notice for her Portia, whether or not it conformed to Shakespeare's intention. She also should be credited with long and successful support of Pritchard in her roles in *As You Like It* and *Twelfth Night*. Her virtue was well rewarded. She lived to enjoy long and prosperous golden years in a cottage on Horace Walpole's Strawberry Hill estate. She carried on a lively correspondence and moved frequently in the highest circles. Dr. Johnson said to Boswell, "Clive, sir, is a good thing to sit by: she always understands what you say" (*Biographical Dictionary*, 3:360). And Davies praised her power to "raise admiration" and "excite mirth," thus uniting, he announces (without any sense of hyperbole), the qualities of Milton and Samuel Butler (*Memoirs*, 2:195).

Katherine in *The Shrew* is only one example of the female freedom and female aggressiveness, sometimes to the point of dominance, that characterize all the popular Shakespearean comedies played repeatedly without adaptation in the middle of the century. This freedom is pointed up emblematically in *As You Like It, The Merchant of Venice, Twelfth Night,* and *Cymbeline* by the presence of women who assume male disguises that free them from the conventional confines of feminine activity and enable them to experience social relationships from new perspectives.

Although the importance of the ascension of female players after the Restoration to the roles of Shakespeare's women characters is regularly noted, the impact of the change has never been sufficiently appreciated. There is a vast difference between watching "women" behave as men when the watcher is secure in the knowledge that they really are male, and in seeing women in these roles—the effect must have been all the more powerful when the audience knew that the women on the stage were also confidently and competently assuming "male" roles in real life. The popularity of breeches roles has been explained in terms of the delectable opportunities they provided for male appraisal of the usually discreetly shrouded female leg. Certainly I would not deny this attraction, but I suggest that a different fascination must have exerted itself far more strongly, not only especially for the female audience, but indeed for all—the revolutionary prospect of actually witnessing a sort of female emancipation acted out with applause in a public place.

As we have seen, the female emancipation in life that was played off against male-female characters on the stage is a strong characteristic of all the great Shakespearean actresses of the period. There is no precedent in English culture for a class of self-made women of such stature, and their impact must have been electrifying, inspiring, and perhaps frightening.

The greatest contrast between stage roles and private life is in the case of Susanna Cibber. I mention her chiefly as an example of a woman who created for herself a central role in the theater, perhaps in spite of her natural inclinations. After leaving her husband, she kept control of her very considerable funds (her husband, who complained that in losing her he had been deprived of income, said she was making a salary of £1200 a year at Drury Lane in 1744–45, for less than six months' work; *Biographical Dictionary*, 3:267–72). Mrs. Cibber was widely respected and admired by both sexes—especially for her great tragic roles—Juliet, Desdemona, Cordelia, Ophelia, and Constance in *King John*. In comedy she regularly played Isabella in *Measure for Measure* and Perdita in adaptations of *The Winter's Tale*. Arthur Murphy wrote that on seeing her as Isabella he was moved to make excuses for Angelo because, "when I saw Mrs. Cibber before him on her knees: the elegance of her figure, the musical plaintiveness of her voice, and the gentleness of her manners [were] sufficient to make any one fall in love with her."[29] But her tenderness, sweetness, and pathos on stage were complemented offstage by the tenacity and strongmindedness of a real-life Isabella. Although she and Garrick were said to be "formed by nature for the illustration of each other's talents" (Davies, *Memoirs*, 1:116), they were not perfectly harmonious in daily life. In 1745 the idea of buying the patent for Drury Lane seems to have been Susanna Cibber's, but in the end Garrick consummated the deal without her.[30] She reputedly had a contract that gave her the privilege of choosing new roles,[31] and "illness" more than once prevented her appearance in a role she did not fancy. After Cibber's death in 1766 Garrick lamented that tragedy had expired with her. But he also added,

> she was the greatest female plague belonging to my house. I could easily parry the artless thrusts and despise the coarse language of some of my other heroines. . . . but she was always sure to carry her point by the acuteness of her invective and the steadiness of her perseverance. (*Biographical Dictionary*, 3:281, 279.)

Breeches roles were not for Cibber (she was slight in stature and girlish in figure until the end of her career), but the aura of power that singled her out from other females was fundamental to her image.

Much more closely related to the revival of Shakespearean comedy is the career of Peg Woffington. All accounts agree that she was breathtakingly beautiful. John Rich's initial reaction to her is typical. He described her as "an amalgamated Calypso, Circe, and Armida . . . as majestic as Juno, as lovely as Venus, and as fresh and charming as Hebe."[32] This ravishing feminine beauty was uniquely combined with a lack of affectation and an extraordinary dedication to freedom and independence. In her *Apology*, George Anne Bellamy plaintively describes the outrage of her elegant patroness, the duchess of Queensberry, when Bellamy, hoping to demonstrate the wit and polish of actors, took the duchess on a long-anticipated visit to the Green Room after a benefit performance of *All For Love*, and they were greeted by Woffington in Cleopatra costume drinking porter and crying "Confusion to all order! Let Liberty thrive" (Bellamy, *An Apology*, 2:51–53). Woffington was, in fact, famous for her wit, frequently displayed in interchanges with the militantly chaste Clive, who once complained that "a pretty face . . . excuses a multiplication of sweethearts," only to be answered by Woffington, "And a plain one insures a vast overflow of unmarketable virtue" (Daly, *Woffington*, p. 46). Woffington liked men (she was elected president of the all-male Beef Steak Club in Dublin [Davies, *Memoirs*, 1:341]) and her unconventional sexual morality was notorious (a popular ballad praising her pointedly conceded "one fault" [Daly, *Woffington*, p. 107]), yet this did not prevent her carrying off such virginal roles as Isabella, Cordelia, and Ophelia with great success. Indeed she was particularly praised by a Dublin newspaper that marveled, "You each character so close pursue/We think the author copied it from you" (ibid., p. 122).

And yet actor and role were finally inseparable. Woffington seems to have found a way, particularly in comedy, of joining her own personal freedom of spirit with projections of stage character so intriguing and irresistible to her audiences that her name virtually guaranteed financial success. Her greatest gift was for comedy, but she was more versatile than Clive or Cibber and also more wideranging in her career, which included professional residence in Dublin and Paris as well as at Drury Lane and Covent Garden. Her contribution to the revival of Shakespearean comedy was both direct and indirect. During her London career she played Rosalind, Adriana (in *The Comedy of Errors*), Helena (in *All's Well that Ends Well*), Portia, Nerissa, Isabella, Beatrice, Viola, and Mistress Ford. Her indirect influence is linked with the particular kind of versatility that made possible her astounding success in breeches roles, both in those, such as Sylvia in *The Recruiting Officer*, that featured women in male disguise and in the actual male role of Sir Harry Wildair in *The Constant Couple.*

Woffington prided herself on avoiding female company (because women spoke only of silks and scandal), and she seems never to have enlisted the female patronage that benefited other actresses (perhaps because of her great success with males), but women as well as men admired her (Davies, *Memoirs,* 1:341). When she first played Wildair in Dublin, the Green Room was packed afterwards with both sexes, and several popular ballads record her "universal conquest" as the result of roles in *The Beggar's Opera* and *The Constant Couple.* All agree that

> Her charm resistless, conquers all—
> Both sexes vanquished lie,
> And who to Polly scorned to fall,
> By Wildair, ravaged, die.
>
> [Daly, *Woffington,* p. 18]

Charles Macklin described Woffington's male-female performances as showing "an ease and elegance of deportment that seemed almost out of the reach of female accomplishments."[33] She was acclaimed widely as "a creature uncommon,/ Who's both man and woman/ And the chief of the belles and the beaux!"[34]

The usual account of Woffington's sensational arrival on the London stage as Sylvia in *The Recruiting Officer* in 1740 attributes the idea of the role to Rich and to the Prince of Wales who "commanded" the perform-ance (at Rich's instigation), but there is little doubt that the moving spirit behind this and other breeches roles was Woffington herself. At the Aungier Street Theatre Royal in Dublin she had in 1734 played the part of Rose in *The Recruiting Officer* to the Sylvia of Mrs. Bellamy (Sr.), and from that time she was ambitious to try the leading role. It was she who suggested the production there of *The Female Officer,* in which she made her transvestite debut, and it was she who urged the revival of *The Recruiting Officer* in 1738, in which she was Sylvia. In 1739, when Quin was playing to packed houses at Smock Alley, Woffington conceived the idea of launching her career as Sir Harry Wildair in competition.[35] Predictably, her huge success in Dublin prepared the path for her trium-phant conquest of London as Sylvia and Wildair at Covent Garden in the fall of 1740. It was these Woffington triumphs that led to the Drury Lane counterattack in the form of the revival of those Shakespeare's comedies that had breeches roles and women in male disguise (*Twelfth Night, As You Like It,* and in *The Merchant of Venice*), providing new scope for the team of Clive and Pritchard and elevating Pritchard as Rosalind to a stardom that she maintained during her long and distinguished Shakespearean career. Woffington herself went on to later success as

Rosalind, and Clive was alternately Celia to the one or the other of the two leads. The winning androgyny of Rosalind suited Woffington well. It seems especially appropriate that her last lines on the stage were from the epilogue of *As You Like It*. Following an "unapproachable performance" as Rosalind, she collapsed after the words, "If I were among you [note the necessary change from "If I were a woman"], I would kiss as many of you as had beards that pleased me." John Hoole, in a monody on her death, describes Shakespeare as the first of many grateful poets bending "o'er his favorite's tomb" (Daly, *Woffington*, pp. 146, 172).

Whatever Shakespeare's ghost may have felt for Woffington, however, the poet's greatest debt to a Shakespearean actress at midcentury was to Hannah Pritchard. Her most famous role was Lady Macbeth, and we need only look at a contemporary illustration to see how the commanding figure of Pritchard, towering over the diminutive Garrick, must have helped to shape their interpretation of the play. Similarly, her dignity and presence and her distinctively "articulate harmonious voice,"[36] combined with striking command of stage business, gave a rare importance to her Gertrude (Davies, *Dram. Misc.*, 3:116–17). Pritchard lacked the beauty of Woffington. In fact, Mrs. Thrale, though admiring her *Mind*, concedes the "supreme Ugliness" of her person (Vaughan, *Born to Please*, pp. 112, 130). Endowed with a figure that made her an impressive and convincing male in her earlier years, Pritchard grew heavy at the end of her career, a disability that she managed to offset by sheer force of dramatic skill. *The Theatrical Examiner* of 1757 records that "though [she was] not the girl Beatrice," her performance was such that she compensated for all the advantages of 18" (Vaughan, *Born to Please*, p. 126). She seems to have had a genius for body language, and even in Garrick's truncated version of *The Winter's Tale*, where she spoke "hardly 10 words" as Hermione, the *Universal Museum*, 1762 (Vickers, *Shakespeare*, 4:462) describes her rendering of the statue as "truly great," elaborating, "While she descends from the temple her face is a perfect picture, and her countenance so serene and composed, so expressive of that part that perhaps the whole theatre cannot produce so remarkable an instance."

In other Shakespearean comedies Pritchard was Imogen, Mistress Ford, both Portia and Nerissa, Helena and the Countess of Roussillon (abdicating the lead in favor of her daughter), and most successfully Viola, Rosalind, and Beatrice. These three roles, with their dramatic force and their scope for female versatility, provided her and her audience with opportunities, all too rare in the theater of the period, to realize on the stage the fulfillment of female potentialities that Pritchard had regularly demonstrated in her own life. A devoted mother of three daughters and a successful wife, she was obviously the chief support of her family. Her husband's will disposes of "my worldly affairs received through the bounty of God and the greater part being through the industry of my dear and loving wife . . . whom I do hereby constitute my whole and sole executrix." Her social importance is documented by the fact that she was appointed dresser to Princess Charlotte of Mecklenberg on the occasion of her wedding and coronation as queen (Vaughan, *Born to Please*, pp. 92, 84). Pritchard's theatrical success considerably predates Garrick's. John Hill recollects her debut as Rosalind, noting that at first her modesty inhibited her, and that she did not put forth all her talent until she received great applause for her rendering of the "Take the cork out of thy mouth" speech. Then, he adds, "She was applauded throughout and for ever after" as "the best actress of the British Stage" (ibid. p. 19). Davies admired her independence in playing Constance in Colley Cibber's *Papal Tyranny* (an adaptation of *King John*) when only she ignored Cibber's directorial advice and gained approval and applause (*Dram. Misc.*, 1:23). Samuel Foote in 1747 awarded her his ultimate accolade: "I would, were I a Pattentee, rather have her in my service than any Woman in England" (Vaughan, *Born to Please*, p. 123).

Pritchard's partnership with Garrick was legendary, and her crowning achievement as Beatrice was perfectly complemented by his Benedick. Arthur Murphy and Davies conferred credit on the two equally, suggesting that every scene was a struggle in which the audience could determine no victor. Mrs. Thrale and Horace Walpole gave the edge to Pritchard on the basis of "spirit and originality" (ibid., pp. 54, 130). Certainly these qualities, embodied in Shakespeare's comic heroines, made Pritchard, like Cibber, Clive, and Woffington, mind-stretching models of female possibility for the audiences of midcentury. Their achievements were neatly celebrated in verse in *A Letter of Compliment* (with lines on Cibber, Woffington, Clive, and Pritchard, respectively):

> Four ladies in one happy Era born,
> Did once the English Stage adorn;
> THE FIRST assumed the moving tragick part,
> And drove successful Pity to the Heart;
> THE NEXT, beside the Magick of her Face,
> Had softness, Air, Gentility and Grace;
> THE THIRD in Comick Pleasantry surpass'd;
> In ev'ry Character, in all THE LAST:
> The Force of Nature cou'd no further flee,
> To make a Fourth, she join'd the former THREE.
> [Vaughan, *Born to Please*, p. 129]

After her death admirers erected a white marble slab in honor of Pritchard next to Shakespeare's monument in Westminster Abbey (ibid., pp. 1, 104), but it was later removed to a less prominent spot. The demotion is symbolic. As the century waned, women like Pritchard were pushed from center stage in the public imagination. In the last quarter of the century the feminine ideal was narrowed and diminished. By the end of 1768, Woffington, Cibber, and Pritchard were dead and Clive was in retirement. A new vision of womanhood, epitomized in the passive romantic victims of the novels, began to dominate popular literature. Something of the spirit of their revivers lived on in the Portias, Violas, Rosalinds, and Beatrices of younger actresses (none as distinguished as those of midcentury),[37] but increasingly Shakespearean comic heroines were either divorced from life or modified to conform with new standards. Their virtue but not their versatility was to be imitated. In doubtful cases, texts were altered, and as a result Imogen, Hermione, Paulina, and Helena survived only in Garrick's amputated versions. Victor advised actresses against male roles because they required something beyond the propriety of their sex (3:5), and toward the end of the century the decorous Sarah Siddons covered the breeches of her Rosalind with an abbreviated skirt.[38] Meekness and modesty were celebrated in sermons on female character, and a learned doctor said to his daughters, "I am sorry to say there are few English comedies a lady can see without a shock to delicacy."[39]

With the passing of the principal players in the drama of female self-discovery and the changing of social and literary values, the briefly glorious convergence of Shakespeare's comic heroines with the superwomen of the mid-eighteenth-century stage faded from the memory of a new era. A generation of giants had vanished from the land.

Notes

1. Hester Lynch Thrale, *Thraliana: The Diary of Mrs. Hester Lynch Thrale* (later Mrs. Piozzi), ed. Katharine C. Balderston, 2 vols. (Oxford: Clarendon, 1942), 1:105.

2. I have focused on comedy in this paper because the women of Shakespeare's comedies are strikingly more dominant, active, and interesting than those of most of the tragedies, whose important female characters tend to be villains or victims.

3. Thomas Davies, *Dramatic Miscellanies*, 3 vols. (1784; reprint ed., New York: Blom, 1971), 2:93, 105–6.

4. There is some evidence in early stage accounts: see, e.g., Thomas Davies, in *Memoirs of the Life of David Garrick*, ed. Stephen Jones, 2 vols. (1808; reprint ed., New York: Blom, 1969), 1: 341. But modern discussions of acting usually say little about the women.

5. Arthur H. Scouten, "The Increase in Popularity of Shakespeare's Plays in the Eighteenth Century: A *Caveat* for Interpretors," *Shakespeare Quarterly* 7 (Spring 1956): 189–202.

6. I am indebted throughout this paper to Philip H. Highfill, Jr., Kalman A. Burnim, and Edward A. Langhans, *A Biographical Dictionary of Actors, Actresses, Musicians, Dancers, Managers & Other Stage Personnel in London, 1660–1800* (Carbondale, Ill.: Southern Illinois University Press, 1973–.) Specific acknowledgement is given for extensive or distinctive borrowing. (I am also indebted to Professor Highfill personally for his generous and invaluable aid and advice.)

7. George W. Stone and George M. Kahrl, *Garrick: A Critical Biography* (Carbondale, Ill.: Southern Illinois University Press, 1979), p. 505. Lynch records (p. 57) that Shakespearean plays constituted about one-fourth of the entire London repertory for these years.

8. I have used both Charles Beecher Hogan's *Shakespeare in the Theatre 1701–1800* (Oxford: Clarendon, 1952) and *The London Stage, Part 3*, ed. Arthur H. Scouten, and *Part 4*, ed. George W. Stone (Carbondale, Ill.: Southern Illinois University Press, 1961–) in assembling information. Figures are based on *The London Stage*.

9. See unsigned essay from *Daily Journal*, 1737, in *Shakespeare: The Critical Heritage*, ed. Brian Vickers (London: Routledge & Kegan Paul, 1975), 3:72. Also Lynch, *Thraliana*, pp. 89–94, and Emmett L. Avery, "The Shakespeare Ladies Club," *Shakespeare Quarterly* 7 (Spring 1956): 153–58.

10. James Miller, *The Universal Passion* (1737; reprint ed., London: Cornmarket, 1969), p. A4.

11. *An Apology for the Life of George Anne Bellamy*, 5 vols. (London: J. Bell, 1786), 1:vii, 144, 129, 71.

12. Benjamin Victor, *The History of the Theatres of London & Dublin*, 6 vols. (1761; reprint ed., New York: Blom, 1969), 1:260. Influential women apparently often bespoke performances of special plays in the provinces. Price notes four examples in Bath. In one of these cases the countess of Northumberland asked for *The Merry Wives of Windsor*, a Shakespearean comedy of strong female interest. See Cecil Price, *Theatre in the Age of Garrick* (Oxford: Blackwell, 1973), p. 182.

13. Said of Mrs. Abington, *Memoirs* (see note 3), 2:175. Davies notes that Woffington, unlike Cibber and Mrs. Oldfield, did not visit with ladies of quality (1:347); Cibber's favor with her own sex is again noted 2:110. A similar statement about Clive occurs in 2:198–99.

14. "The Case of Mrs. Clive," quoted by Percy H. Fitzgerald, *The Life of Mrs. Catherine Clive* (1888; reprint. ed., New York: Blom, 1969), p. 37.

15. In *Romeo and Juliet: A Tragedy Revis'd and Alter'd from Shakespear, By Mr. Theophilus Cibber. To which is added "A Serio-Comic Apology . . ."* (1748; reprint ed., London: Cornmarket, 1969), p. 95.

16. Quoted in *The Life of Mrs. Abington* (London: Reader, 1888), p. 77.

17. See Shirley Strum Kenny, "Humane Comedy," *Modern Philology* 75 (August 1977): 29–43 for a discussion of the term. See also her "Perennial Favorites: Congreve, Vanbrugh, Cibber, Farquhar, and Steele," *Modern Philology* 73 (May 1976): S4–S11, where she shows that in the 1744–45 season, of the 523 performances of plays, 245 were of comedies and 196 of tragedies. Of the comedies 40 were Farquhar's, 40 Vanbrugh's, 30 Colley Cibber's, 22 Congreve's, 14 Steele's. In the same season there were 31 performances of Shakespeare's comedies.

18. "An Apology for the Life of Colley Cibber," in Vickers, 3:105.

19. N. S., "Remarks on the Tragedy of the Orphan," *Gentleman's Magazine*, 1748. In Vickers, *Shakespeare*, 3:332.

20. John Upton, *Critical Observations on Shakespeare*, 1748. In Vickers, *Shakespeare*, 3:297.

21. Even the negative evidence of plays *not* revived in the original version is suggestive because they are plays with relatively uninteresting female roles. *The Comedy of Errors* was performed only four nights. *A Midsummer Night's Dream* and *The Tempest* were turned into musicals, and *The Winter's Tale* was reduced to a three-act pastoral. Among the tragedies, *Romeo and Juliet* was the most popular at midcentury—again suggesting the importance of a strong female part.

22. See especially Robert D. Hume, "Marital Discord in English Comedy from Dryden to Fielding," *Modern Philology* 74 (1974–77): 248–72, and Shirley Strum Kenny, "Elopments, Divorce, and the Devil Knows What: Love and Marriage in English Comedy, 1690–1720," *The South Atlantic Quarterly* 78 (1979): 84–106.

23. John Lacy, "Sauny the Scot," *Dramatic Works* (1874; reprint ed., New York: Blom, 1967), pp. 384, 388.

24. James Worsdale, *A Cure for A Scold* (1735; reprint ed., London: Cornmarket, 1969), pp. 59–60.

25. David Garrick, in *A Collection. Farces and Other Afterpieces, Selected by Mrs. Inchbald*, 7 vols. (London: Longman, Hurst, Rees, Orme, and Brown, 1815), 4:171.

26. Lynch, *Thraliana*, p. 105; Davies, *Memoirs*, 1:312.

27. "The Rehearsal or Bays in Petticoats" (London: Dodsley, 1753) in F. Long collection, Library of Congress, passim.

28. For 6 April 1756, *The London Stage*, 4, 2, p. 537 lists "a New *Epilogue* by Mrs. Clive, in the Character of Catherine, containing a hint to the Ladies for the taming of a Husband." On 18 April 1757 there is the announcement of "a New *Dialogue Epilogue* spoken by Mrs. and Miss Pritchard," 4, 2, p. 592. I have not found copies of either of these epilogues.

29. *London Chronicle*, 1758. In Vickers, *Shakespeare*, 4:347.

30. Letters from Garrick to Somerset Draper in George W. Stone and George M. Karhl, *Garrick: A Critical Biography* (Carbondale, Ill.: Southern Illinois University Press, 1979), pp. 59, 66–68.

31. Kalman A. Burnim, *David Garrick, Director* (Pittsburgh, Pa.: University of Pittsburgh Press, 1961), p. 34.

32. *Dublin Review*, quoted by Augustin Daly, in *Woffington: A Tribute to the Actress and the Woman* (1891; reprint ed., New York: Blom, 1972), p. 24.

33. Charles Macklin, "Mackliniana," *European Magazine*, May, 1800. Quoted by Daly, *Woffington*, p. 29.

34. *Theatrical Magazine* 1:129. Quoted by Daly, *Woffington*, p. 19.

35. Janet Dunbar, *Peg Woffington and Her World* (London: Heinemann, 1968), pp. 29–38.

36. See Anthony Vaughan, *Born to Please: Hannah Pritchard, A Critical Biography* (London: Society for Theatre Research, 1979), p. 117, for descriptions of her voice.

37. Frances Abington, a distinguished actress, was not notable for Shakespearean roles. Dorothea Jordan, a capable humorous actress, could not stop the sentimental tide, and Sarah Siddons, perhaps the greatest Shakespearean actress of the century, never distinguished herself in comedy.

38. St. Vincent Troubridge, *The Benefit System in the British Theatre* (London: Society for Theatre Research, 1967), p. 122.

39. Quoted by Janet Camden Lucey, *Lovely Peggy* (Watford, Herts.: Hurst & Blackett, 1952), p. 237.

Charles Kean's King Lear and the Pageant of History

by ADELE SEEFF

Charles Kean's revival of *King Lear* at the Royal Princess's Theatre in 1858 exemplified the culmination of a production style that combined historical realism, lavish spectacle and illusionism. Kean's proximate sources, as we know, were Planché and Macready; Kean, in turn, strongly influenced the productions of Irving and Tree. In his day, Charles Kean was hailed by *The Times* as "the great magician" whose revivals of Shakespeare's plays dazzled audiences with a display of scholarship, spectacle, and ensemble acting that lured Queen Victoria to the Princess's Theatre no fewer than four times in as many weeks.[1] Kean's staging set a standard of splendor for Shakespeare production that lasted to the end of the nineteenth century and into the second decade of the twentieth, until modernism and the cinema swept away the flamboyant productions of the nineteenth-century actor-managers.

Whatever the nature of the controversies Kean stirred in his age over his acting ability or his attitude to scenic adjuncts, he was a great favorite with London audiences from his introduction to London in 1838 to his own farewell production of *Much Ado About Nothing* in November, 1859. Indeed, Kean is credited with bringing the educated middle class back into the theaters where they could admire Shakespeare, and today, he is regarded by a twentieth-century theater historian as "having outdistanced every rival in his age."[2]

This paper, then, focuses on Charles Kean's 1858 production of *King Lear* at the Royal Princess Theatre as a characteristic example of mid-nineteenth-century actor-manager attitude toward text, production aesthetic, and nineteenth-century audience expectations. A reconstruction of the text and production suggests that, through his "pageant of historical realism," Kean transformed myth into history.

231

How did Kean arrive at his performance text? An examination of his promptbook for the production, later published as his "edition" of *King Lear*, indicates that it descended in a direct line from Nahum Tate's adaptation, passing through the cautious hands of William Charles Macready to Kean himself. Contrary to prevailing scholarly opinion, as we shall discover, neither Macready nor Charles Kean merits the title, bestowed on them from their age to ours, of "restorer of the true text." Rather, Kean was an adapter who precisely judged the tastes and interests of his audiences, creating for them a filtered theatrical experience of *King Lear.*

Lear survives in Nahum Tate's 1681 "newmodelling" of Shakespeare to see Edgar, the hero, share the throne with Cordelia. Of greater significance, however, for the purposes of this study, were the structural changes Tate wrought by transposing key speeches, conflating particular scenes, and radically cutting speeches, often for the purpose of heightening a climax or permitting a "discovery scene." Tate closed his first act on Lear's curse, his second on Lear's departure into the storm. His third act opened with Lear on the heath (Shakespeare's second scene of act 3), and the hovel scene was telescoped with a mangled version of the scene in the farmhouse (scenes 4 and 6 of act 3 of the original). Every reference to the mock trial of Goneril and Regan was excised. Act 4, scene 5 (4. 7 in the original) opened on Lear "discovered" asleep on a couch and act 5, scene 4 (5. 1 and 5. 3 in the original) opened with the entrance of Albany, Goneril, Regan, and Edmund with Lear, Kent, and Cordelia as prisoners. Tate allowed a version of Gloucester's blinding and the leap from Dover Cliff, but at the play's close, Gloucester, alive, is reunited with his "pious Son," and Kent retires to a monastic cell. Most of these structural changes Kean chose to preserve since his sense of dramatic structure coincided with Tate's.

It was Tate's version that held the stage until, and in some cases, while, the process of restoring the text began.

Kean's received text was Macready's 1838 promptbook, the text Macready had prepared for his production of *King Lear* at Covent Garden. Macready, of course, had been hailed as the restorer of the original text. A careful examination of Macready's 1838 promptbook is at odds with this view.

Far from preparing for the stage a "true text," Macready, as adapters had done before him, restored Shakespeare's language and the "sublime, but terrible catastrophe of the original," eliminating forever the romance between Edgar and Cordelia.[3] However, he preserved those structural Tate conventions that permitted an act to close on a high dramatic moment; he preserved Tate's treatment of the heath and farmhouse scenes; he allowed an extremely truncated version of Gloucester's torture by Regan and Cornwall that merely suggested the imminent blinding, and like Colman, he deleted Gloucester's leap, leaving Gloucester alive at play's end. His text was an adaptation, and from it, Charles Kean created yet another adaptation.[4]

What version of *King Lear* are we presented with when we read Kean's edition?[5] Except for major cuts and the radical reduction of the Fool's role (restoration of the Fool's role is minimal—Kean cut approximately sixty percent of the Fool's lines), the language of the play through the first two acts is largely Shakespeare's. Kean preserved the by-then two-centuries-old conclusion of act 1 on Lear's curse and act 2 on "O reason not the need!" (2. 4. 259). The Tate legacy is responsible for changing the essential structure of act 3. The first three scenes appear in their original sequence, but the conflation of the hovel and farmhouse scenes remains.

Indeed, to look closely at Kean's conflation of these scenes is to dispel for all time the idea that Kean, or Macready, for that matter, was an authenticator. This arrangement of 3. 4 and 3. 6 represents the most significant debt to Tate. Furthermore, it is a treatment that begins with Garrick and follows in an unbroken tradition through Colman, Kemble, Edmund Kean, and Macready.

What is most striking about Tate's arrangement of the heath scenes in 3. 3 of his version, is his preservation, with minor exceptions, of Shakespeare's language. Using Shakespeare's dialogue, Tate has woven back and forth between the two scenes, cutting, transposing, and reordering. The result is a scene 164 lines long in which Lear prays and is then persuaded to enter the hovel just as Edgar emerges. Lear and Edgar conduct a brief dialogue whose theme is filial ingratitude with choric comments from Kent. Lear acts the role of "a poor, infirm, weak, and despised old man" (3. 2. 20). Towards the scene's close, Gloucester enters with injunctions to carry Lear "where he shall meet both Welcome, / And Protection" (Tate, 3. 3. 157–58). The scene (and act 3) concludes neatly with Lear falling asleep. The Fool, of course, has disappeared completely, and except for a single brief reference at lines 160–61, so has the mock trial. The excruciating interplay between mad king, mad beggar, and the Fool has been diminished.

Kean merely duplicated this treatment precisely, restoring an additional eleven or twelve lines of Shakespeare's dialogue that include two very brief references to the mock trial and the minimal role of the Fool. (The Fool speaks or sings three and a half lines!)[6]

Kean did not adopt Macready's arrangement of a telescoped 3. 5 and 7 to suggest the blinding, but cut it completely. He closed the fourth act with a scene in which Lear's entrance as "mad, fantastically dressed with flowers" (Kean, 4. 4) interrupts Gloucester in his leap. Act 5 consists of two scenes—an abbreviated reconciliation scene (a "discovery" scene after Tate) and a final scene, a conflation of 5. 1 and 5. 3 (5. 2 is deleted). 5. 3 is drastically reduced since the triangle between Goneril, Edmund, and Regan has been deemphasized and Edgar has been deprived of most of his lines. This cut includes the account of Gloucester's death. We understand, therefore, that Gloucester is alive at the play's close as is Kent, and presumably, the Fool.

Undoubtedly, Kean's goals coincided with Tate's. Tate wished for a tight structure with fast-moving scenes. Kean shared some of these interests, simplifying the action, shortening the play, and reducing the number of scene changes.[7] Clarifying the structure, however, radically altered the meaning of the play. As Kean simplified the plot, he also reduced the scale, scope, and resonance of the tragedy and the tragic hero.

Lear, as tragic hero, is drained of all complexity and recast in a one-dimensional mold as the old, fond, doting father, wronged by his daughters. There is nothing in Kean to suggest a departure from Garrick's sentimentalized portrayal of a "*Weak* man, . . . violent old and *weakly* fond of his daughters."[8]

Shakespeare's play gives both Titan and father, as Maynard Mack has observed. The eighteenth and the nineteenth centuries chose the father, omitting what Mack has described as the "brooding, mythic, almost apocalyptic hints and intimations that for most of us today lie just beyond the story of domestic pathos."[9]

Reshaping Lear's character in this way renders him less culpable, and, in harmony with this change, his suffering seems less. His stature as a tragic hero is reduced by the heavy cutting in act 3.

This process of sentimentalizing is begun with Kean's deletions in acts 1 and 2. Lear's "rashness" and "unruly waywardness" is toned down. He banishes Cordelia and Kent, of course, but in harmony with this softer characterization, his malign speeches, cursing and vilifying his daughters, and denying his own relatedness to them are deleted. In the original, Lear's interaction with his daughters through the first two acts of the play is stained by the allusive power of the poetry with elements of disease and putrefaction. These images are all eliminated.[10]

Definable criteria shaped Kean's text, the most striking of which was decorum. The result is a paring away of Lear's dialogue of sexual revulsion. While Warburton may have glossed the lines "Behold yond simp'-ring dame, / Whose face between her forks presages snow" (4. 6. 118–19) as "That is, her hand held before her face in sign of modesty, with the fingers spread out, forky," neither Macready nor Kean allowed that fourteen-line evocation of the "sulphurous pit" of "luxury."[11] Lear rages at a world of "handy-dandy" justice, but it is a world purged of sexual excesses. His resonating line of pardon for that world, "None does offend, none—I say none!" (4. 6. 165) is deleted. The world of "the superfluous lust-dieted man" disappears. The loss of complex, allusive poetry shrinks the Lear universe, rendering it less cosmic, more domestic.

To reflect for a moment on the preceding discussion is to acknowledge the extent to which Kean's text, in terms of language, was a function of his age. Victorian ideas about purity, about the idealization of love and women, rooted in a strong protective movement in morals were in conflict with the theme of a play that depicts a breakdown in the bonds of love, family, and community. With regard to that pattern of the play, and it is, of course, oversimplified here, Kean responded as a man of his time. For the continuously complex mutations of emotional acquisitiveness, compassion, lust, and humility in Shakespeare, he substituted fondness, folly, and terror.

Shorn of the power of its characteristic language, of images of violence, of bodies twisted on a rack, the play focuses instead on what a contemporary called an "imbecile, passionate, fond, degraded old man, exciting alternately terror and compassion" (*The Daily Telegraph,* April 19, 1858). The result is a far simpler play with a clearer structure. It is also, according to the tastes of the nineteenth century, less violent, less sadistic, less universal. While Kean may have failed to grasp the true nature of Shakespearean tragedy, being all too willing to follow Tate, Colman, and Macready, he understood clearly the tastes and expectations of his audiences. His reduction of *King Lear* to a domestic tragedy met those expectations.

In contrast to the eighteenth-century flavor of Tate's text, Kean's production style belonged to the nineteenth century. Kean's production of *King Lear* at the Royal Princess's Theatre was a curious blend of spectacle and detailed archaeological realism. Kean's style was an inevitable outcome of developments in sets, costumes, the playhouse, audiences, royal patronage, and the intellectual climate of the age.

In addition to the love of spectacle, Kean's production style reflected several interests, new in the nineteenth century. Among these were the growing antiquarianism, the beginnings of history as a scientific discipline, and an archaeological interest in the past. All of these helped to foster the already lively interest in earlier cultures and promoted historically faithful representations of that past on stage.

Thus, typically, scenery was spectacular but also authentic with regard to actual found or researched models. In this respect, sets reflected an interest in the particularities of nature rather than its universal laws. The picture the nineteenth century most wanted to see was one that was faithful to the period being portrayed, but clothed in gorgeous splendor.

The age was fascinated with the representation of exotic past ages, particularly the Middle Ages.

The rise of history as an objective "scientific" discipline during the nineteenth century made it possible for men to catalogue the specifics separating one age from another. Not only were finer discriminations drawn between the already known ages, but new ages were introduced as archaeologists gradually pushed the limits of time further and further back. The nineteenth century, with a developed sense of the idea of movement and change in history, a strong sense of the characteristics of each age, and its own differentiation from those ages, stressed the distinctions.

The nineteenth-century historian was to assemble the evidence for these distinctions, empirically, without preconceived theory or metaphysical assumption. An examination of primary sources in a scientific way would eventually lead the facts to speak for themselves. In this regard, nineteenth-century history emulated nineteenth-century science. The best history contained the least speculation and the most eloquent facts. Ideally, according to Froude, history should be written like drama: "Wherever possible, let us not be told *about* this man or that. Let us hear the man himself speak; let us see him act, and let us be left to form our own opinions about him."[12]

If history were to become like drama, drama or the arts would imitate the historical method; instruction about the past would fall within the province of art. One might even draw a parallel between the empiricism of nineteenth-century historical method, divorced from judgment and assumption, and the meticulously accurate detail massed on the nineteenth-century stage; both placed a higher premium on fact than feeling. Both the historical method and the application of that method laid emphasis on verifiable concrete detail in support of an evocation of a period of the distant past.

This "archaeological impulse of the nineteenth-century stage to convert poetry and myth into history" can be seen as a shaping force molding tragedy into the form of history.[13]

It is no surprise that Kean chose to set *Lear* in a precise time and location, eighth-century Anglo-Saxon England. He resisted the opportunity to turn the production into a display of pageantry and pomp, focusing instead on conveying, through the play, "a living and pictorial embodiment of the past," transforming his theater into a "valuable school of antiquarian illustration, and a living lecture on the past."[14]

The idea of a living lecture was one of the meanings that Kean, as the well-read scholar and devoted antiquarian, found in the play—an illustration of an exotic, distant but verifiable period in British history. "In historical plays, especially," wrote one reviewer, "this mode of illustration is most desirable, for it materially helps us to the poet's meaning, and by reproducing, as far as practicable, the very scenes and person- ages of the drama, impresses them more vividly and indelibly on our minds. . . . *Lear* may thus be regarded as the play in this historical series which presents to us the external forms and habits of our early Saxon ancestors."[15]

Indeed, Kean treated certain scenes of the play as if Shakespeare had intended to portray the "external forms and habits" of the Saxons. To this end, Kean demonstrated both ingenuity and the results of laborious research. The best example (although there are many) is the second scene of the play, the much-vaunted "Room of State in *King Lear's* Palace."

An extended flourish of trumpets and the sounds of a march playing in the orchestra introduced the tableau on a brightly lit stage (Prompt 23, p. 8; Prompt 21, facing p. 8).

A vast raftered hall set at a diagonal extended the full depth of the stage. Paralleling the oblique angle of the hall, on a platform raised on two steps, stood Lear's throne, midway against the right wall. Goneril and Regan reclined on either side of his throne on the top step while Cordelia sat at his knee on the lowest step.[16] Lear's entire court thronged the hall.

Fifty-seven actors were grouped most carefully on a stage vivid with scarlet, gold, white, and blue.[17] Gigantic crimson banners, decorated with animal iconography and held aloft by gold spears, flanked Lear's throne. Albany, Cornwall, Gloucester, and Kent were ranged in a diagonal complementary to the throne, left of the fire, set apart from the knights and ladies of Lear's court who crowded the entrances at stage left. At center stage, smoke from the fire, set on a raised slab of stone, curled upwards. It was a brilliant tableau vivant; and one can imagine the actors frozen in this tapestry from history, waiting for Lear to speak his opening lines, while applause filled the theater.

Every reviewer mentions this scene, praising it as "one of the most striking scenes of all, this primitive room of state in King Lear's palace ornamented with heads of game and hunting implements in a manner that would do honour to a fine old Saxon gentleman."[18] It was seen as "lifelike," "picturesque," "a real glimpse into Saxon times." For a specta- cle, one could not desire anything more animated, varied, and imposing. Everything was "pictorial and historical." The *Illustrated News of the World* was delighted with the "rude, raftered hall, with its walls covered with the skins of beasts, hung over with weapons of war and with the trophies of the chase. The eye is pleased with the wild groups with their gleaming spears, double-headed axes and bossed bull's-hide shields, and we have reproduced for us with picturesque effect the Anglo-Saxon castle primitive in interior, as in exterior—gone many an age ago into ivy-clad ruins."[19]

Against this massive wood-beamed room of state, the scene was a spectacular study in color. Lear was resplendent in floor-length scarlet, gold, blue, and purple. This pageant of color was extended by the costuming of the whole cast, and each item of costume had been painstakingly researched. Indeed, page after page in Art Volume d49 testifies to the care lavished on this research.

Later in the scene, when France and Burgundy entered, followed by a retinue of six lords each, the visual brilliance was further intensified. France's costume, repeating the blue robe and red cloak motif of Lear's dress, was the most ornate dress in the entire cast. Primarily blue and gold with a red cape, it conveyed the impression of dignity, splendor, and wealth. France was royal! Gold fleur-de-lys covered the three-tiered robe. Every detail of this costume was lavish: red and green jewels adorned the large, three-spired crown, red and gold emblems covered his scabbard, and gold scrolling was embroidered on his cloak. Visually, the two suitors were in sharp contrast to one another, Burgundy's dress of white, blue, and gold trim recalling Roman dress.

If we may trust the costume book as a faithful record of what appeared on stage, the supernumeraries were all clothed in varying designs of red and blue, ornamented with gold. All wore deep pointed vizors, carried convex buckle shields, axes, and swords sheathed in scabbards.

It should be noted, however, that faithful as the costumes and scenery just described were to historical originals, these originals were not all of the same period. The research was painstaking; the search for verifiable models was exhaustive, but sources from a range of several centuries were used to document a period of approximately eighth-century Anglo-Saxon England.[20] Each item that appeared on stage, was, no doubt, a duplication of its original. What is overlooked by most modern historians of the theater, and by Cole, is that very few items could be precisely dated as belonging to the eighth-century. Fidelity to the original, whatever its date, took precedence over conformity to a specific period, and on the pages of any of the volumes so compulsively cherished by Kean, we may find artifacts whose origins range from the fifth or sixth century to the eleventh or twelfth. Absolute conformity to time was not important. The production looked "historical" and that was paramount. Said one delighted reviewer:

With admirable judgment, he [Kean] has, for the sake of securing uniformity in the accessories of this great drama, selected the Anglo-Saxon era of eighth-century for the regulation of the scenery and the dresses as affording a date sufficiently remote and at the same time as being one intimately associated with British soil. A degree of *approximate correctness* in these respects is thus attained, all important for the dramatic purposes, but which would have been found absolutely impossible had the scene been laid in the mythical age to which "Lear" belongs [italics mine]. In a brief but cogent preface to his version of "Lear," Mr. Kean announces it to be his firm belief, "that accuracy of detail is on all occasions, not only necessary, but advantageous to the stage." In this belief we entirely concur, and Mr. Kean may rest assured that his hope will be fulfilled, that this last attempt of his to realise a picture of early English history will be "in truth accepted as a pleasing and instructive appendage to the intellectual lessons of the author." (*The Morning Star,* April 19, 1858.)

Men of the theater like Planché, Macready, and Charles Kean were preoccupied with the idea of the theater as an instrument of instruction. Wrote Planché, in the 1834 edition of his *History of British Costume,* "The true spirit of the time is in nothing more perceptible than in the tone given to our most trifling amusement. Information of some description must be blended with every recreation to render it truly acceptable to the public" (p. xv).

In this, Planché and his colleagues were simply following the Victorian trend of the middle classes for combining recreation with instruction.[21] Add to this penchant the equally Victorian belief that instruction would naturally consist of a collection of more or less uninterpreted facts, and the mind behind the Princess's *King Lear* emerges.

In securing accuracy of detail (in scenic terms), Kean achieved particularity of time and place rather than the timeless, universal quality of the original. He sacrificed the myth so that history could be illustrated instructively for the audience. In Shakespeare's *King Lear,* the visual forms are of characters in motion rather than of scenic forms. Stress on a specific environment took emphasis off the impact of the tragedy. The production style, then, reinforced the reduction in scope and impact of the tragedy we have already perceived in a close reading of the text of Kean's edition.

We can tell from the promptbooks that Kean concluded his production much as he had begun it. Against a flourish of trumpets, clashing of swords, shouts and "Alarums of Distant Battle," the scene proceeded as a colorful and somewhat noisy pageant (Promptbook 23, p. 81). Every entrance of a major character was accompanied by officers, soldiers, and attendants, and, we recall, their costuming was brilliant in color. In all, there were thirty-six soldiers on the small stage, vizored, dressed in purple, brown or blue tunics, bare-legged, all carrying glittering spears and shields. Ranked by color, they crossed the stage on a trumpet cue, assuming positions upstage center and filling the entrances (Prompt 11,

p. 81). Banner carriers strode on to occupy a position at center stage, followed by lords in colorful dress. Once again, the members of a lavish court dressed in red, blue, purple, gold, and white splashes of color crowded the stage. Soldiers hurried on and off, escorting the prisoners Lear and Cordelia, returning to observe the combat between Edgar and Edmund, and marching off again, this time very slowly, to a dead march, as they carried Edmund aloft on their shields. The visual effect of the scene was rich and splendid, full of movement, and very different from the effect of the original on a platform stage.

"We that are young/Shall never see so much, nor live so long" are the final words of the play, whether they are spoken by Edgar or Albany. Kean chose to cut those lines from his version, preferring instead to end the play twelve lines earlier, omitting all references to the "gored state."

The promptbooks do not tell us how Lear carried Cordelia's body on stage, nor how he uttered his lament for her. We do know that many of the soldiers and attendants remained on stage, together with Kent, Edgar, and Albany, as a muted dead march was sounded for the death of Lear and his daughter (Prompt 11, p. 86). We can assume that as the curtain fell to the persistent throb of the dead march, members of the audience felt that they had just witnessed, against the rich tapestry of his times, the death of an historic monarch who had suffered greatly.

For two and three-quarter hours, audiences had been spellbound by this simple, touching drama. They were spared the metaphysical speculation, the references to excess of appetite. They were delighted by the vivid recreation of a splendid but very distant period of their own past. It satisfied both their antiquarian tastes and their concept of Shakespeare. "May it not be worth consideration whether Shakespeare himself, were he now living, would not be the very man of all men to approve of introduction of these illustrative adjuncts in the performance of his plays," speculated one very pleased member of the audience.[22]

It remains to spell out more specifically what it was that the production meant to the Victorians who so admired it. The world of Kean's *Lear* was rich and elaborated, filled with material objects. The production was a vividly illustrated description of a past age. Neither the particularities of time and place nor the tasteful archaeological embellishments distanced the audiences of that day from the tragic events they witnessed on stage. They responded to the drama of a kindly old father heartbrokenly abused by the base ingratitude of his daughters. His saddest misfortune was the loss of his reason, but, in the world of this Lear, misfortune was clearly ascribable to specific causes. As the colorful, historic pageant unfolded, audiences identified with the passions, crimes, and treachery enacted onstage. For them, all the elements of tragedy were present, powerfully communicated by their favorite tragedian.

Notes

1. *The Times,* August 30, 1859.

2. W. Moelwyn Merchant, *Shakespeare and the Artist* (London: Oxford University Press, 1959), p. 100.

3. Ralph W. Elliston, "Advertisement," *King Lear* (London, 1820), p. v.

4. I have not considered the problem of how Kean received Macready's promptbooks. Apparently Ellis, originally assistant prompt to Macready's prompt, Willmott, became Kean's stage manager at the Princess's in 1850. From 1845 onward, he had funneled Macready's texts to Kean. See Charles H. Shattuck, *Mr. Macready Produces "As You Like It"* (Ipswich: W. S. Cowell, Ltd., 1962), no. 3, pp. 4–5; Charles H. Shattuck, "A Victorian Stage Manager: George Cressall Ellis," *Theatre Notebook* 22 (Spring 1968): 102–12.

5. My analysis of Kean's text is based on Promptbook 11 (Folger Shakespeare Library).

6. Kean was commended for his "dramatic taste and tact which cast the accomplished songstress, Miss Poole, for the part of the court jester, instead of entrusting it to the low comedian." Miss Poole, according to *The Daily News,* Monday, April 19, 1858, "sang the quaint old snatches of songs with much unaffected pathos . . . [in] the 'little' part of the Fool."

7. Considerations of staging must have motivated some of Kean's deletions. Excisions such as those of 1. 5; 4. 3; 4. 5; 5. 2 and the transposition of 4. 1 and 2 probably all fall into this category. Possibly the omission of Gloucester's leap belongs in this class, although once again, Kean followed an earlier adapter, Colman.

8. The words are Garrick's in a letter to Dr. Stone, reprinted in Arthur C. Sprague, *Shakespearian Players and Performances* (1953; reprint ed., New York: Greenwood Press, 1969), p. 34.

9. Maynard Mack, *King Lear in Our Time* (Berkeley: University of California Press, 1965), p. 20.

10. Deletions include Harbage, 2. 4. 160–63, 206–12, 216–20, all references to the mock trial, and Lear's speeches at 1. 1. 108ff., 2. 4. 160–63, and 216–20. The cumulative effect of "infect," "blister," "burn," "plague-sore," and "corrupted blood" is lost.

11. Horace H. Furness, ed., *King Lear.* New Variorium. (1880; reprint ed., New York: Dover Publications, 1963), p. 279.

12. J. A. Froude, "The Science of History," in *Short Studies on Great Subjects* (New York, 1868), pp. 12, 34, reprinted in Jerome H. Buckley, *The Triumph of Time: A Study of the Victorian Concepts of Time, History, Progress, and Decadence* (Cambridge, Mass.: Harvard University Press, 1966), p. 30.

13. Mack, *King Lear in Our Time,* p. 23.

14. John William Cole, *The Life and Theatrical Times of Charles Kean* (London: Richard Bentley, 1860) 2: 102, 104.

15. *The Daily Telegraph,* April 19, 1858; *The Morning Star,* April 19, 1858.

16. A smooth transition to this second spectacular scene was carefully prepared. Everybody had been gathered onstage behind the flat before the curtain was rung up for the opening two-minute scene between Gloucester, Edmund, and Kent. The three-walled built set was already in position. Drum and trumpet were ready and only the five harpists and the guards entered left and right as the scene changed and the flats for the first scene were drawn off. See directions in Prompt 11, facing p. 7; Prompt 23, p. 8; Prompt 21, facing p. 8.

17. In addition to the main characters, the stage held twenty knights, ten lords, three banner carriers, six ladies, the royal sword bearer, six pages, a falconer, first gentleman, Curan, and the boy, "discovered replenishing the fire" (Prompt 11, facing p. 8).

18. *The Sun,* April 19, 1858. *The Morning Post,* Monday, April 19, 1858, wrote: "The

huge wood fire blazing on the stone hearth, in the midst of the hall, and casting its light upon the arms and dresses of the assembled nobles, soldiers, and retainers, who fill the spacious hall, produce one of the strangest and most striking effects ever seen on the stage."

19. Exhaustive research into these shields and the sources for the different varieties that appeared on stage can be seen in Art Vol. d4. An engraving pasted into Prompt 21, probably from *The Illustrated London News,* captures the second scene. It shows a roiling fire, smoke rising to the ceiling, and long-robed knights and noblemen focused intently on the throne.

20. A more sceptical reviewer said hesitantly that everything seemed correct, although some costumes verged on Roman and some on Norman dress. Another mentioned the fact that the interior and the exterior of Gloucester's castle varied by about two centuries. In fact, a careful scrutiny of the research conducted by Colonel Smith and his daughter reveals intense concern for authenticity. Saxon coins, Roman ensigns bearing icons of eagles, dragons, and dolphins, and sketches from "The British Bronze Collection of Goodrich Court" are all cited as models in the Art Volumes.

21. See Peter Bailey, *Leisure and Class in Victorian Society* (Toronto: University of Toronto Press, 1979).

22. *The Leader,* undated.

APPENDIXES

Appendix A: Complete List of Lectures and Papers from the Program of the Congress

Shakespeare, Man of the Theater
The International Shakespeare Association Congress
1–7 August 1981, Hilton Hotel, Stratford-upon-Avon, England

Sunday, 2 August
"Shakespeare and a Playwright of Today," John Mortimer

Monday, 3 August
"The Many-headed Audience," Andrew Gurr
"Historic and Iconic Time in Later Tudor Drama," Bernard Beckerman
"Shakespeare Imagines a Theater," Stephen Orgel
"Shakespeare and the Uses of Authority," Robert Weimann
" 'To the judgement of your eye': Emblems and the Theatrical Art of *Pericles*,"
    Mary Judith Dunbar
"Shakespeare and a Cry of Players," John Russell Brown

Tuesday, 4 August
"Shakespeare and Jonson," Anne Barton
" 'The Players . . . will tell all': The Actor's Role in Renaissance Drama," M. T.
    Jones-Davies
"Shakespeare and Two Jesters," Guy Butler
"Characterization through Language in the Early Plays of Shakespeare and
    His Contemporaries," A. R. Braunmuller
"Shakespeare and Kyd," Philip Edwards
"Beaumont and Fletcher's *Hamlet*," H. Neville Davies

Wednesday, 5 August
"Time and Motion in *Julius Caesar*," Roma Gill

245

"*King Lear* and the Magic of the Wheel," Rolf Soellner
"Suiting the Word to Action? Scholarship and Stage Direction," Charles Frey
"'Conjectures and Refutations': The Positive uses of Negative Feedback in Criticism and Performance," Harriet Hawkins
"Reading, Watching, and Listening to *King Lear*," Dieter Mehl
"Some Approaches to *All's Well That Ends Well* in Performance," Roger Warren
"A Sense of Occasion: Some Dramatic Sequences," Emrys Jones
"The Ghost of Hamlet's Father," Benedict Nightingale

Thursday, 6 August
"The Word in the Theater," Inga-Stina Ewbank
"Staging Shakespeare's Sub-texts," Marvin Rosenberg
"Between a Sob and a Giggle," George Hibbard

Forum: "Shakespeare in the Theater (I)"
A forum with directors, including Maurice Daniels and Ronald Eyre
"Shakespeare in the Theater (II)"
A forum with directors, including Ron Daniels and Leon Rubin

Friday, 7 August
The Annual Lecture of the Shakespeare Association of America
Lecture: "Shakespeare: Man of the Theater," G. E. Bentley

Appendix B: Seminars and Their Chairmen

1. "Bad Quartos" as Documents of the Theatre (Paul Werstine)
2. The Court Theatre (Glynne Wickham)
3. The Playwright in his World: Patterns in Shakespeare's Transformation of Sources (Meredith Anne Skura)
4. Gender and Genre: Feminist Approaches to Shakespearean Roles (Coppélia Kahn)
5. Elements of Liturgy and Ritual in Shakespearean Performance (R. Chris Hassel, Jr.)
6. Pageantry in the Shakespearean Theatre (David M. Bergeron)
7. Shakespeare's Contemporaries: From the Original Staging to the Critical Reading (G. B. Shand)
8. The Character of Verse and Prose in the Early Plays, 1590–1595 (Gail Kern Paster)
9. Continental Influence on Shakespearean Theatre (Louise George Clubb)
10. Shakespeare on the Eighteenth-Century Stage (Philip H. Highfill, Jr.)
11. Shakespeare on the Nineteenth-Century Stage: A Representative and Comparative Study (Carol J. Carlisle)
12. The Use of Theatre History and Practice for the Scholar and Critic (Bernard Harris)
13. Shakespeare on the Socialist Stage (Nico Kiasashvili)
14. The Double Translation: To Language, To Stage (Kristian Smidt)
15. Shakespeare's Eye: The Art of the Emblem in Shakespeare's Theatre (Alan R. Young)
16. Shakespeare and Film: The Director and the Scholar (Kenneth S. Rothwell)
17. The Psychology of Theatrical Experience (Janet Adelman)
18. Shakespeare's Art of Manipulating the Audience (J. L. Styan)
19. *A Midsummer Night's Dream* (Gareth Lloyd Evans)
20. *A Midsummer Night's Dream* (D. J. Palmer)
21. *The Winter's Tale* (Stanley Wells)
22. Teaching Shakespeare with Actors: A Critical Assessment (Alan C. Dessen)
23. Televised Versions of Shakespeare's Plays (Herbert S. Weil, Jr.)
24. Current Trends in Non-English Shakespearean Performances (Werner Habicht)

Appendix C: Delegates and Participants

ABEL, Richard — Drake University, Des Moines, Iowa
ADELMAN, Janet — University of California, Berkeley
ALI, Florence — Newcastle-upon-Tyne Polytechnic
ALLEN, Michael J. B. — University of California, Los Angeles
ALLEN, Shirley S. — San Diego State University, California
ALMANSI, Guido — University of East Anglia
ALTER, Iska — Bard College, New York
ANDERSON, Mark A. — Loughborough University
ANDERSON, R. F. — Edmonton, Alberta
ANDRESEN-THOM, Martha — Pomona College, Claremont, Calif.
ANDREWS, Joan Kastick — Virginia
ANDREWS, John F. — Folger Shakespeare Library
ANDREWS, Peter C. — McLean, Va.
ANIKST, Alexander — Institute of Art Studies, Moscow
ANNABLE, J. S. — Kenilworth, Warwickshire
ANTOINE, Rainer — Berlin Free University
AQUINO, Deborah T. Curren — Catholic University of America, Washington, D.C.
AQUINO, John — Silver Spring, Md.
ARMSTRONG, Jane — Methuen and Company Ltd.
ARNOLD, Margaret J. — University of Kansas, Lawrence
ARNOTT, James Fullarton — University of Glasgow
ARPS, Horst — Ratingen
ARPS, Mrs. Horst — Ratingen
ASTINGTON, John H. — University of Toronto
ATKINSON, Renate — Stratford-upon-Avon
AUSTIN, Warren B. — Stephen F. Austin State University, Texas
AVEN, Richard C. — Michigan State University, East Lansing

Note: Not all participants in the lecture and seminar program were registered delegates.

BALE, John C. — Luther College, Decorah, Iowa
BALL, Fred — Biggleswade, Bedfordshire
BALL, Mrs. Fred — Biggleswade, Bedfordshire
BAMBER, Linda — Tufts University, Medford, Mass.
BAN, Eileen — New York, N.Y.
BANKS, Jenifer — Michigan State University, East Lansing

BANKS, John — Manchester University Press
BARBER, Deirdre — Lansdowne, Penn.
BARKER, Clive — University of Warwick
BARKER, Kathleen M. D. — Society for Theatre Research
BARTHOLOMEUSZ, Dennis — Monash University
BARTON, Anne — New College, Oxford
BARTON, John — Royal Shakespeare Company
BARTOSHEVICH, Alexei Vadimovich — State Art Research Institute, Moscow
BATES, Paul A. — American Studies Center, University of Warsaw

BATES, Mrs. Paul A. — Warsaw
BATTENHOUSE, Roy W. — Indiana University, Bloomington
BATTENHOUSE, Mrs. Roy W. — Bloomington, Ind.
BECKERMAN, Bernard — Columbia University, New York, N.Y.
BECKERMAN, Gloria — Adelphi University, Garden City, N.Y.
BEDARD, Beatrice W. — University of Dayton, Ohio
BEDARD, Bernard J. — University of Dayton, Ohio
BELL, Lisa K. — Pomona College, Claremont, Calif.
BELLIZIA, Frank — Phillips Academy, Andover, Mass.
BELSEY, Catherine — University College, Cardiff
BENBOW, R. Mark — Colby College, Waterville, Me.
BENNETT, William E. — University of Tennessee, Martin
BENTLEY, Gerald Eades — Princeton University, Princeton, N.J.
BEREK, Peter — Williams College, Mass.
BERNAUER, Reinhard — Deutsche Shakespeare-Gesellschaft West

BERRY, Herbert — University of Saskatchewan
BERRY, Ralph — University of Ottawa
BIES, Werner — University of Trier
BIRNEY, Alice L. — Library of Congress, Washington, D.C.
BLACK, James — University of Calgary
BLACKSTONE, Mary — University of Toronto
BOLTZ, Ingeborg — University of Munich Shakespeare Library

BOOTH, Michael — University of Warwick
BOOTH, Stephen — University of California, Berkeley
BOURGY, Victor — University of Rennes
BOWEN, Hoyt E. — Western Kentucky University, Bowling Green

BOWERS, A. Robin	University of Nebraska, Lincoln
BOWERS, Mrs. A. Robin	Lincoln, Neb.
BRADBROOK, Muriel C.	University of Cambridge
BRADLEY, David	Monash University
BRASHEAR, Lucy	Appalachian State University, Boone, N.C.
BRAUNMULLER, Albert R.	University of California, Los Angeles
BRAUNMULLER, Lee Bliss	Los Angeles, Calif.
BREITENSTEIN, Rolf	Bonn University
BREITENSTEIN, Mrs. Rolf	Bonn
BRILLIANDE, Robert	First Hawaii Shakespearean Society
BRILLIANDE, Mrs. Robert	Honolulu, Hawaii
BRISTOL, Michael D.	McGill University
BRITTIN, Geoffrey M.	University of California, San Francisco
BRITTIN, Mrs. Geoffrey M.	Fresno, Calif.
BRITTIN, Norman A.	Auburn University, Alabama
BRITTIN, Mrs. Norman A.	Auburn, Ala.
BROCKBANK, Philip	Shakespeare Institute, University of Birmingham
BROOK, Stephen	London
BROOKS, Harold F.	University of London
BROOKS, Jean Rylatt	Christchurch College, Canterbury
BROOKS, Thomas R.	Wheaton College, Norton, Mass.
BROWN, Evelyn	Reston, Va.
BROWN, John Russell	University of Sussex
BROWN, Keith	University of Oslo
BROWN, Laura	Cornell University, Ithaca, N.Y.
BRYDEN, Ronald	University of Toronto
BUCH, Susanne	Münster
BUCHHOLZ, Eva Maria	University of East Anglia
BUCKLEY, E. J.	Oxford
BURKE, Robert R.	Rockhurst College, Missouri
BURKHARDT, Erika	Buchholz
BURNIM, Kalman A.	Tufts University, Medford, Mass.
BURTON, Ian	University of Bristol
BUTLER, Guy	Rhodes University
BYLES, Joan M.	Syracuse University, New York
CALLIES, Valerie Wayne	University of Hawaii
CARLISLE, Carol J.	University of South Carolina, Columbia
CARTELLI, Thomas P.	Muhlenberg College, Pennsylvania
CARTWRIGHT, Kent	Kansas State University, Lawrence
CAVALLONE ANZI, Anna	Universitá Degli Studi, Milan
CAVANO, Arthur J.	Fayetteville, N.C.
CAVANO, Janet M. Jeffrey	Methodist College, Fayetteville, N.C.
CEROVSKI, John	North Central College, Naperville, Ill.

CHALFONT, Don	West Georgia College, Carrollton, Ga.
CHALFONT, Fran	West Georgia College, Carrollton, Ga.
CHARNEY, Maurice	Rutgers University, New Brunswick, N.J.
CHATTEN, Beth	Rose Bruford College of Drama
CHERMSIDE, Caroline P.	Virginia Polytechnic Institute and State University, Blacksburg
CHIAPPA, Rita Manuela	University of Milan
CHRISTOPHER, Georgia B.	Emory University, Atlanta, Ga.
CHURCH, Tony	Royal Shakespeare Company
CLARK, Earl John	Northeastern Illinois State University, Chicago
CLATANOFF, Doris A.	Concordia College, Seward, Neb.
CLUBB, Louise George	University of California, Berkeley
CLUBB, William	Padua
COHEN, Walter	Cornell University, Ithaca, N.Y.
COLLEY, John Scott	Vanderbilt University, Nashville, Tenn.
COLLINS, David C.	Westminster College, Fulton, Mo.
CONEJERO, M. A.	Shakespeare Institute, University of Valencia
COOK, Ann Jennalie	Shakespeare Association of America
COTHARY, Jean	Tenino, Washington
COX, Gerard H., III	University of Washington, Seattle
COX, Molly Hite	Seattle, Wash.
CRAIK, T. W.	University of Durham
CRANDALL, Catherine M.	San Jose, California
CRANDALL, Jerry R.	West Valley College, Campbell, Calif.
CRAWLEY, Derek F.	Queen's University, Ontario
CROWL, Samuel	Ohio University, Athens
CUNNINGHAM, Dolora G.	San Francisco State University, Calif.
DACHSLAGER, Earl L.	University of Houston, Texas
DALY, Peter M.	McGill University
DANIELS, Maurice	Royal Shakespeare Company
DANIELS, Ron	Royal Shakespeare Company
DASH, Irene	Hunter College, City University of New York
DATE, TOSHIHIRO	Shakespeare Society of Japan
DAVID, Lady	Cambridge
DAVID, R. W.	Clare Hall, Cambridge
DAVIES, Eva	Lewes, Sussex
DAVIES, H. Neville	Shakespeare Institute, University of Birmingham
DAVIS, Allen R.	Blacksburg, Virginia
DAVIS, Charles	Kansas State University, Lawrence
DAY, Roger	Open University

DeCatur, Louis A.	Ursinus College, Collegeville, Penn.
Deese, Helen	California State Polytechnic University, San Luis obispo
De Grazia, Margreta	Georgetown University, Washington, D.C.
Delvecchio, Doreen A.	McMaster University
Deprats, Jean Michel	University of Nanterre
Desai, R. W.	University of Delhi
De Sousa, Geraldo Udex	University of Kansas, Lawrence
Dessen, Alan	University of North Carolina, Chapel Hill
De Stasio, Clotilde	State University of Milan
Devereux, E. J.	University of Western Ontario
Dhesi, Nirmal-Singh	California State College, Sonoma
Dickerson, David C.	Seattle Pacific University, Washington
Doebler, John	Arizona State University, Tempe
Doye, Michael	Cologne
Drakakis, John	University of Stirling
Drake, Fabia	London
Draudt, Manfred	University of Vienna
Drew-Bear, Annette	University of California, Santa Barbara
Dunbar, Mary Judith	University of Santa Clara, California
Dundas, Judith	University of Illinois, Urbana
Dusinberre, Juliet	Girton College, Cambridge
Edmond, Mary	London
Edwards, Philip	University of Liverpool
Eggers, Walter	University of Wyoming, Laramie
Eisenbart, Constanze	F.E.S.T., Protestant Institute for Interdisciplinary Research, Heidelberg
Ellrodt, Robert	University of Paris, Sorbonne Nouvelle
England, Eugene	Brigham Young University, Provo, Utah
Erickson, Peter	Williams College, Massachusetts
Evans, Gareth Lloyd	University of Birmingham
Evans, William R.	Kean College of New Jersey
Ewbank, Inga-Stina	University of London
Eyre, Ronald	Royal Shakespeare Company
Ezawa, Tetsuya	English Literature Society of Japan
Felperin, Howard	University of Melbourne
Fitz, Linda T.	University of Alberta

FLECK, Sister Agnes — Scholastica College, Minnesota
FLINT, Kate — Shakespeare Club, Stratford-upon-Avon

FLINT, Lorna — Shakespeare Club, Stratford-upon-Avon

FOWLER, James — Theatre Museum, London
FOX, Levi — Shakespeare Birthplace Trust
FREUND, Elizabeth — Hebrew University of Jerusalem
FREY, Charles — University of Washington, Seattle
FRIDEN, Ann — University of Gothenburg
FULTON, Robert C. — University of Tennessee, Chattanooga
FULTON, Mrs. Robert C. — Chattanooga, Tenn.
FULTON, Sheila — University of Bristol
FUZIER, Jean — University of Montpellier

GALLOWAY, David — University of New Brunswick
GARDINER, Judith Kegan — University of Illinois, Chicago
GARIN, Inmaculada — Barcelona
GARNER, Shirley Nelson — University of Minnesota, Twin Cities
GAUDET, Minnette Grunmann — University of Western Ontario
GAUDET, Paul — University of Western Ontario
GERRITSEN, Johan — University of Groningen
GIACOBELLI, Francesco — University of Padua
GIBBONS, Brian — University of Leeds
GIELGUD, John — International Shakespeare Association
GILBERT, Miriam — University of Iowa, Iowa City
GILL, Roma — Sheffield
GINGRAS, Robert — Bainbridge Junior College, Georgia
GOCKE, Rainer — University of Münster
GOHLKE, Madelon S. — University of Minnesota, Minneapolis
GORFAIN, Phyllis — Oberlin College, Ohio
GRANDJEAN, Christine — University of Zurich
GRAUE, Martin — Beckum
GREENBLATT, Stephen J. — University of California, Berkeley
GREENE, Gayle — Scripps College, Claremont, Calif.
GREENE, John C. — Maryland
GRIEF, Karen — Harvard University, Cambridge, Mass.

GREIG, Donald — University of Kent
GRISE, Martha S. — Eastern Kentucky University, Richmond

GRISE, Robert — Richmond, Ky.
GROIS, Lyuben — "Salza i Smiath" Theatre, Sofia
GRÖKEL, Ursula — Cologne
GROSS, Sheryl W. — Oakland Gardens, N.Y.

Gunther, J. Lawrence   Technische Universitat Braunschweig
Gurr, Andrew   University of Reading

Habicht, Werner   University of Würzburg
Hakam, Wendy   University of California, Los Angeles
Halio, Jay L.   University of Delaware, Newark
Hallett, Charles A.   Fordham University, Bronx, N.Y.
Hamburger, Maik   Deutsches Theater, Berlin
Hammond, Antony Derek   McMaster University
Hankins, Jerome   Nice
Hapgood, Robert   University of New Hampshire,
                                          Durham
Harder, Ingrid   Munich
Hardman, Christopher Barrie   University of Reading
Harris, Bernard   University of York
Harris, Duncan   University of Wyoming, Laramie
Hartwig, Joan   University of Kentucky, Lexington
Hashimoto, Teiko   Shakespeare Society of Japan
Hasler, Jörg   University of Trier
Hassel, Chris   Vanderbilt University, Nashville,
                                          Tenn.
Havely, Cecily Palser   Open University
Hawkes, Terence   University College, Cardiff
Hawkins, Anne   Middletown, Conn.
Hawkins, Harriett   Linacre College, Oxford
Hawkins, Sherman H.   Wesleyan University, Middletown,
                                          Conn.
Haywood, Charles   Queen's College, City University of
                                          New York
Hedrick, Donald K.   Kansas State University, Manhattan
Hennedy, Hugh L.   Saint Francis College, University of
                                          New England
Hibbard, George R.   University of Waterloo, Ontario
Highfill, Philip H.   George Washington University,
                                          Washington, D.C.
Highfill, Mrs. Philip H.   Bethesda, Md.
Hilali, Maqsudur Rahman   Ummul-Qura University, Mecca
Hinely, Jan Lawson   University of Illinois, Urbana
Hinman, Myra   University of Kansas, Lawrence
Hirai, Masako   Shakespeare Society of Japan
Hirata, Yasushi   Kobe
Hisae, Niki   St. Luke's College of Nursing, Tokyo
Histrop, Lesley J.   Scarborough Board of Education,
                                          Ontario
Hobhouse, Janet   University of Oxford
Hodgdon, Barbara   Drake University, Des Moines, Iowa

HODGE, Nancy Elizabeth	Vanderbilt University, Nashville, Tenn.
HOENIGER, F. D.	University of Toronto
HOLBEIN, Woodrow L.	Military College of South Carolina
HOLLAND, James	Palos Verdes, Calif.
HOLMER, Joan	Georgetown University, Washington, D.C.
HONIGMANN, E. A. J.	University of Newcastle-upon-Tyne
HONIGMANN, Mrs. E. A. J.	Newcastle-upon-Tyne
HOOD, Gervase	London
HORTMANN, Wilhelm	University of Duisberg
HOWARD, Jean Elizabeth	Syracuse University, New York
HOWARD-HILL, T. H.	University of South Carolina, Columbia
HOWLAND, Mary C.	Golden West College, Huntington Beach, Calif.
HOYLE, David Charles	Open University
HUNTER, Dianne	Trinity College, Hartford, Conn.
HUNTER, G. K.	Yale University, New Haven, Conn.
IKAWA, Fuku	Doshisha University
IMAI, Sachiko	Tokyo
INGRAM, William	University of Michigan, Ann Arbor
IONESCU, A. Medeea	Institute of Art History, Bucharest
IOPPOLO, Grace	University of California, Los Angeles
ISENBERG, Seymour	Norwood, N.J.
ISENBERG, Mrs. Seymour	Norwood, N.J.
ISONO, Morihiko	Aichi Prefectural University
IVANOVA, Anna	Sofia
JACKSON, Russell	The Shakespeare Institute, University of Birmingham
JARRETT, Hobart	Brooklyn College, City University of New York
JARRETT, Mrs. Hobart	New York
JASPERSON, Michael	U.S. Naval Academy, Annapolis, Md.
JAUSLIN, Christian	Swiss Broadcasting Corporation
JENKINS, Anthony W.	University of Victoria, British Columbia
JENKINS, Harold	University of Edinburgh
JOHNSON, Barbara J.	Northfield, Minn.
JOHNSON, Gerald D.	University of Alabama, Birmingham
JOHNSON, Gloria E.	University of Oregon, Eugene

JOHNSON, Lowell E.	St. Olaf College, Northfield, Minn.
JOHNSON, Mr.	Eugene, Ore.
JONES, Eldred D.	Foura Bay College, Sierra Leone
JONES, Mrs. Eldred D.	Freetown, Sierra Leone
JONES, Emrys	University of Oxford
JONES-DAVIES, M. T.	University of Paris, Sorbonne
JORGENS, Jack	The American University, Washington, D.C.
KAANG, Jung-Ki	Waseda University
KACHUCK, Rhoda S.	University of La Verne
KAHN, Coppélia	Wesleyan University, Middletown, Conn.
KALMAR, Elaine B.	University of Northern Iowa, Cedar Falls
KAPPLER, Beatrice	Hersbruck
KATTERFELD, Karin	Pomona College, Claremont, Calif.
KATZ, Wendy R.	Wolfville, Nova Scotia
KAUL, A. N.	University of Delhi
KAWACHI, Yoshiko	Kyoritsu Women's University
KAWATE, Hirokazu	Shakespeare Society of Japan
KAWATE, Koichi	Shakespeare Society of Japan
KEMP, Else	Borken
KENNEDY, Eileen	Kean College of New Jersey
KENNY, Shirley Strum	University of Maryland, College Park
KHALAF, Lamis	Beirut University College
KIASASHVILI, Nico	Tbilisi State University
KIM, Joo Hyon	Soong-Jun University
KIM, Tae Jin	Chonnam National University
KIM, Yong-Duck	Dong-A University
KINCAID, A. N.	Lansdowne, Penn.
KING, Arthur Henry	Brigham Young University, Provo, Utah
KING, Joan H.	New City, N.Y.
KING, T. J.	City College of New York
KIRITANI, Shiro	Shakespeare Society of Japan
KISHI, Tetsuo	Kyoto University
KLEIN, Joan Larsen	University of Illinois, Urbana
KLIMAN, Bernice W.	Nassau Community College, Garden City, N.Y.
KLINGSPON, Ronald P.	Nipissing College, Laurentian University
KNIERIM, Ulla	Duisburg
KNIGHT, Nicholas	University of Missouri, Rolla
KNIGHTS, L. C.	University of Cambridge
KNIGHTS, Mrs. L. C.	Cambridge
KNOWLES, Richard Paul	Mount Allison University
KNUTSON, Roslyn L.	University of Arkansas, Little Rock

KOHLER, Richard C. — San Diego State University, Calif.
KORNINGER, Siegried — University of Vienna
KOSZYN, Jayne Nan — Princeton University, Princeton, N.J.
KRANZ, David L. — Dickinson College, Carlisle, Penn.
KRKICH, Lorna — University of California, Santa Cruz
KUCKHOFF, Armin-Gard — Theaterhochschule "Hans Otto," Leipzig

KURAHASHI, Ken — Theatre Museum, Waseda University
KUSANAGI, Taro — Toyama University
KUSUNOKI, Akiko — University of London

LAMB, Mary — Southern Illinois University, Carbondale

LANCASHIRE, Anne — University of Toronto
LANDON, Antony — University of Turku
LANDON, Elisabeth — Turku
LANGHANS, Edward A. — University of Hawaii
LAROQUE, François — University of Montpellier
LASCOMBES, André — University of Tours
LEA, Marjorie — Shakespeare Birthplace Trust
LECH, G. I. — Brussels
LEDEBUR, Ruth Freifrau von — Bonn University
LEIGH-HUNT, Barbara — Royal Shakespeare Company
LELL, Gordon — Concordia College, Moorhead, Minn.
LEVENSON, Jill L. — Trinity College, University of Toronto

LEVIN, Richard — State University of New York, Stony Brook

LEWIS, Cynthia — Davidson College, N.C.
LIEBLEIN, Leonore — McGill University
LINDBLAD, B. S. — Stockholm
LINDBLAD, Ishrat — University of Stockholm
LIPPINCOTT, H. F. — Montgomery, Ala.
LITTLEFIELD, Thomson — State University of New York, Albany
LOMBARDI, Michael — Success Motivation Institute, Tokyo
LOMBARDI, Mrs. Michael — Tokyo
LONG, William B. — AMS Press, New York
LORDI, Robert J. — University of Notre Dame, Indiana
LOWER, Charles B. — University of Georgia, Athens
LUCK, Larry — Bay Village, Ohio
LUCK, Susan G. — Lorain County Community College, Elyria, Ohio

LUSARDI, James P. — Lafayette College, Easton, Penn.
LYLE, Emily B. — Edinburgh University
McCALLUM, Ruth — Buckland St. Mary, Somerset
McDONALD, Gail — Rochester, N.Y.
McDONALD, Marcia — Belmont College, Nashville, Tenn.

McDONALD, Russ   University of Rochester, N.Y.
McGLINCHEE, Claire   City University of New York
McGLINCHEE, Constance   New York, N.Y.
McGUIRE, Philip C.   Michigan State University, East
                                             Lansing

MACK, Florence   New Haven, Conn.
MACK, John A.   Dearborn Heights, Mich.
MACK, Maynard   Yale University, New Haven, Conn.
MACK, Nancy A.   Livonia Public Schools, Michigan
McLEAN, Andrew M.   University of Wisconsin, Parkside
McLEOD, Randall   University of Toronto
McMILLIN, Scott   Cornell University, Ithaca, N.Y.
McNAIR, Carol   Southern Oregon State College,
                                             Ashland

McNAIR, Mr.   Ashland, Ore.
McNAMEE, Lawrence Francis   East Texas State University,
                                             Commerce

MAHER, Mary Z.   University of Arizona, Tucson
MAHON, John William   Iona Collge, New Rochelle, N.Y.
MAHON, Ellen MacLeod   Stamford, Conn.
MAHOOD, Molly   University of Kent
MALE, David A.   Homerton College, Cambridge
MALLAT, Chibbi   Beirut University College
MANHEIM, Michael   University of Toledo, Ohio
MARDER, Louis   University of Illinois, Chicago
MARGOLF, Diane Claire   Pomona College, Claremont, Calif.
MARTINET, Marie-Madeleine   University of Paris, Sorbonne
MARUTA, Kei   Fukuoka Women's University
MARX, Joan C.   Stanford University, Calif.
MASON, MICHAEL A.   Royal Military College of Canada
MASON, Mrs. Michael A.   Kingston, Ontario
MATHESON, T. P.   Shakespeare Institute, University of
                                             Birmingham

MATHIESON, Cecilia   Stratford-upon-Avon
MATSUMOTO, Mami   Shakespeare Society of Japan
MATSUMOTO, Shinko   Tokyo
MAY, Gerda   Munich
MEHL, Dieter   University of Bonn
MELCHIORI, Barbara   University of Rome
MELCHIORI, Giorgio   University of Rome
MELLO MOSER, Fernando de   University of Lisbon
MENAGE, Sarah Jane   Stratford-upon-Avon
MENDONÇA, Barbara Heliodora   University of Rio de Janeiro and
     Carneiro de   University of Sao Paulo
MERRIX, Robert P.   University of Akron, Ohio
MICHELI, Linda McJ.   Harvard University, Cambridge,
                                             Mass.

MIDDLETON, Margaret	University of Warwick
MILLARD, Barbara C.	La Salle College, Philadelphia, Penn.
MILLS, Catherine	City Literature Institute and City University, London
MIRENDA, Angela M.	Virginia Polytechnic Institute and State University, Blacksburg
MIRFIN, Derick	Macmillan Press
MIYAJIMA, Sumiko	Shakespeare Society of Japan
MONTROSE, Louis Adrian	University of California, San Diego
MOORE, Heidi	University of California, Santa Cruz
MORGAN, Shirley Dandridge	Chadron State College, Nebraska
MORIOKA, Shin	Sapporo Medical College
MORRIS, Christopher	King's College, Cambridge
MORRIS, Helen	Homerton College, Cambridge
MORRIS, Marcia	Montreal, Canada
MORTIMER, John	Henley-on-Thames, Oxfordshire
MOURA MATOS, Marco Aurelio de	Rio de Janeiro
MOURA MATOS, Mrs. Marco Aurelio de	Rio de Janeiro
MUIR, Kenneth	University of Liverpool
MULLIN, Michael	University of Illinois, Urbana
MULRYNE, J. R.	University of Warwick
MUNKELT, Marga	University of Münster
MURAMATSU, Nao	Shakespeare Society of Japan
MURRAY, Timothy	Cornell University, Ithaca, N.Y.
NAH, Yong-Gyun	EWHA University, Seoul
NAITO, Kanshu	Tokyo
NAKANORI, Koshi	University of Tokyo
NAMERI, Dorothy E.	Technion-Israel Institute of Technology
NARBETT, Cliff	Stratford-upon-Avon
NEELY, Carol Thomas	Illinois State University, Normal
NEELY, Wright	Champaign, Ill.
NEILL, Michael	University of Auckland
NEVILLE, Oliver	University of Bristol
NEVO, Ruth	Hebrew University of Jerusalem
NEWMAN, Karen	Brown University, Providence, R.I.
NIEHOFF, Rita	
NIGHTINGALE, Benedict	"The New Statesman," London
NOVY, Marianne	University of Pittsburgh, Penn.
NUNN, Trevor	Royal Shakespeare Company
OCCHIOGROSSO, Frank	Drew University, Madison, N.J.
OCCHIOGROSSO, Jane	Madison, N.J.
ODLE, Selma	Abilene Christian University, Texas
OKADA, Mineo	Shakespeare Society of Japan

OKADA, Seiko	Shakespeare Society of Japan
OKAMOTO, Yasumasa	Shakespeare Society of Japan
OKUMURA, Haruko	Kyoto
OKUMURA, Nobuyoshi	English Literary Society of Japan
ORGEL, Stephen	Johns Hopkins University, Baltimore, Md.
ORRELL, John	University of Alberta
OSHIO, Toshiko	Ferris College for Women, Tokyo
OTTE, Verner	Syke
OZ, Avraham	Tel-Aviv University
OZU, Jiro	Tsuda College, Tokyo
PALMER, Barbara D.	Chatham College, Pittsburgh, Penn.
PALMER, David	University of Manchester
PALMERTON, Ann Ruth	Pomona College, Claremont, Calif.
PAPETTI, Maria Viola	University of Rome
PARTRIDGE, A. C.	University of the Witwatersrand
PARTRIDGE, I. M.	Johannesburg
PASCO, Richard	Royal Shakespeare Company
PASTER, Gail Kern	George Washington University, Washington, D.C.
PEARLMAN, E. H.	University of Colorado, Boulder
PEDICORD, Harry William	Thiel College
PEPPER, Robert D.	San Jose State University, Calif.
PFEIFFER, B. Pichon	Siegen
PFEIFFER, K. Ludwig	University of Siegen
PHELEN, M. J.	Shakespeare Institute, University of Birmingham
POLAINE, Albert	Dagenham, Essex
POPE, Deborah Judith	City University of New York, N.Y.
PRICE, Janice	Methuen and Company Ltd.
PRINGLE, Marian J.	Shakespeare Birthplace Trust
PRINGLE, Roger	Shakespeare Birthplace Trust
QIU, Ke'an	Chinese Shakespeare Society
QUEALLY, Chris	Thornton Academy, Maine
RABINOWITZ, Trudi	New York, N.Y.
RAMAMOORTHI NAIDU, Parasuraman	M. K. University, Madurai
REES, Mandy	Pomona College, Claremont, Calif.
REID, S. W.	Kent State University, Ohio
REISING, Waltraud	Buchholz
REPLOGLE, Carol	Loyola University, Chicago
RHOME, Frances Dodson	Indiana University, Bloomington
RICHMOND, Hugh M.	University of California, Berkeley
RICHTER, Hans Michael	Leipzig
RIEHLE, Wolfgang	University of Graz

RIEMER, Andrew Peter	University of Sydney
RIPLEY, John	McGill University
ROBERTS, Jeanne A.	American University, Washington, D.C.
ROBERTS, Patrick	University of London
RODES, David Stuart	University of California, Los Angeles
RONAN, Clifford J.	Southwest Texas State University, San Marcos
RONAN, Mrs. Clifford J.	San Marcos, Texas
ROSENBERG, Marvin	University of California, Berkeley
ROSENBERG, Mary	University of California, Berkeley
ROTHSCHILD, Lady	Cambridge
ROTHSCHILD, Victoria	Queen Mary College, London
ROTHWELL, Kenneth S.	University of Vermont, Burlington
ROTHWELL, Marilyn G.	Burlington, Vt.
ROWAN, Donald F.	University of New Brunswick
RUBIN, Leon	Royal Shakespeare Company
RUDNICK, A. H.	Sunrise Medical Center, Las Vegas, Nev.
RUTTER, Carol C.	University of Warwick
SABOL, Andrew J.	Brown University, Providence, R.I.
SACCIO, Peter	Dartmouth College, Hanover, N.H.
SALINGAR, Leo	Trinity College, Cambridge
SALLES, A. M.	Montpellier
SALOMON, Brownell	Bowling Green State University, Ohio
SAMPLE, Carol	Southwestern Adventist College, Texas
SANDERS, Norman	University of Tennessee, Nashville
SASAYAMA, Takashi	Kwansei-Gakuin University, Japan
SCHALK, Izabel	Deutsche Shakespeare-Gesellschaft West
SCHANFIELD, Lilian	Barry College, Miami, Fla.
SCHANFIELD, Mr.	Miami Lakes, Fla.
SCHLAFER, Ute	University of Munich
SCHLEINER, Winfried	University of California, Davis
SCHLUETER, Kurt	University of Freiburg
SCHLUETER, Mrs. Kurt	Merzhausen
SCHMIDT, Axel	Vaterstetten
SCHMIDT, Helga	Vaterstetten
SCHOENBAUM, S.	Shakespeare Association of America
SCHRICKX, Willem	University of Ghent
SCHULZ, Volker	University of Osnabrück
SCHUMAN, Samuel	University of Maine, Orono
SCHUSTER, Louis A.	St. Mary's University, San Antonio, Tex.

Schwartz, Murray M.	State University of New York, Buffalo
Scott, Michael	Sunderland Polytechnic
Seeberger, Michèle	University of Paris, Sorbonne
Seeff, Adèle	University of Maryland, College Park
Shalvi, Alice	Hebrew University of Jerusalem
Shalvi, Moshe	Hebrew University of Jerusalem
Shalvi, Puina	Jerusalem
Shamgochian, Marie	Boston University School for the Arts, Mass.
Shand, G. B.	York University, Ontario
Shapiro, Michael	University of Illinois, Urbana-Champaign
Sharrock, Geoff	University of Melbourne
Shattuck, Charles H.	University of Illinois, Urbana
Shattuck, Mrs. Charles H.	Urbana, Ill.
Shelley, Paula	University of California, Los Angeles
Shewring, Margaret	University of Warwick
Shibata, Fumiko	Niimi Women's College
Shibata, Toshihiko	University of Tokyo
Shirley, Frances A.	Wheaton College, Norton, Mass.
Simon, Irene J. J.	University of Liège
Simpson, Harold B.	Adrian College, Michigan
Singer, Julianne D.	Pomona College, Claremont, Calif.
Skura, Meredith Anne	Rice University, Houston, Tex.
Slade, Tony	University of Adelaide
Sledd, Hassell B.	Slippery Rock State College, Pennsylvania
Sledd, Mrs. Hassell B.	Slippery Rock, Penn.
Sliwinski, Ilse	Luisengymnasium, Dusseldorf
Slover, George W.	University of Massachusetts, Boston
Smallwood, Robert	Shakespeare Institute, University of Birmingham
Smidt, Kristian	University of Oslo
Smidt, Mrs. Kristian	Oslo
Smith, Bruce R.	Georgetown University, Washington, D.C.
Smith, Hallett	Huntington Library, Pasadena, Calif.
Smith, Mary Elizabeth	University of New Brunswick
Söderwall, Margreta	Stockholm
Soellner, Rolf	Ohio State University, Columbus
Somerset, J. A. B.	University of Western Ontario
Speed, H. C.	Dunstable, Bedfordshire
Spencer, Robert	Woodford Green, Essex
Spevack, Marvin	Westfaelische Wilhelms-Universität, Münster
Sprague, Arthur Colby	Bryn Mawr College, Penn.

SPROAT, Kezia Vanmeter	Ohio State University, Columbus
SQUARZINA, Luigi	University of Bologna
STAMM, Rudolf	University of Basle
STAMM, Mrs. Rudolf	Basle
STANLEY, Audrey E.	University of California, Santa Cruz
STANTON, Sarah	Cambridge University Press
STEPPAT, Michael P.	University of Müster
STERN, Beverley	Open University
STERNLICHT, Sanford	State University of New York, Oswego
STETTLER, Stephen F.	St. Alban's School, Washington, D.C.
STEVEN, Percy	Rose Bruford College of Drama, London
STEWART, Patrick	Royal Shakespeare Company
STEWART, William D.	University of Tampa, Fla.
STOLL, K. H.	University of Mainz
STONE, George Winchester, Jr.	New York University, N.Y.
STRATHMANN, Margaret	University of Cologne
STRAULI, Barbara	University of Zurich
STŘÍBRNÝ, Zdeněk	Prague
STURUA, Robert	Rustaveli Theatre, Tbilisi
STYAN, J. L.	Northwestern University, Evanston, Ill.
STYAN, Mrs. J. L.	Evanston, Illinois
SUZUKI, Hiroshi	Shakespeare Society of Japan
SWANDER, Homer	University of California, Santa Barbara
SWIFT, Carolyn Ruth	Rhode Island College, Providence.
TAKAHASHI, Michi	Tokyo
TAKAHASHI, Yasunari	University of Tokyo
TANAKA, Yasuo	Shakespeare Society of Japan
TARSITANO, Marie	Moorhead State University, Minn.
TATSPAUGH, Patricia E.	Prince George's Community College, Washington, D.C.
TATUM, Nancy R.	Washington College, Chestertown, Md.
TAYLOR, Gary	Oxford University Press
TAYLOR, R. Thad	Shakespeare Society of America
TEAGUE, Frances	University of Georgia, Athens
TEICHMANN, Eike	Krefeld
TELLER, Stephen J.	Pittsburg State University, Kansas
TELLER, Mrs. Stephen J.	Pittsburg, Kansas
TENNENHOUSE, Leonard	Wayne State University, Detroit, Mich.
TENNENHOUSE, Mrs. Leonard	Birmingham, Mich.

Thaler, Brigitte — Seminar für Erziehung und Didaktik, Stuttgart
Thomas, Mary Olive — Georgia State University, Atlanta
Thomas, Sidney — Syracuse University, N.Y.
Thompson, Ann — University of Liverpool
Thompson, Edward — Heinemann Educational Books
Thorne, W. B. — Queen's University, Ontario
Timm, Norbert — Deutsche Shakespeare-Gesellschaft West

Tobin, John J. M. — Boston State College, Mass.
Tobin, Mrs. John J. M. — Cambridge, Massachusetts
Torii, Tadanobu — Mie University
Trinsey, Anna M. — Stratford-upon-Avon
Truax, Elizabeth — Chapman College, Orange, Calif.
Tsuruta, Takiko — Jiyu Gakuen, Tokyo
Turell, M. T. — Barcelona University
Tyson, J. Patrick — Whitman College, Walla Walla, Wash.

Uéno, Yoshiko — Tokyo Metropolitan University
Unverferth, Gabriele — Deutsche Shakespeare-Gesellschaft West
Urkowitz, Steven — State University of New York, Bronx

Velz, John W. — University of Texas, Austin
Verch, Maria — Free University of Berlin
Verdurmen, Hertha Lamm — Shuwaikh, Kuwait
Verdurmen, J. Peter — Riyadh University
Vishwanadha, Hari Hara Nath — Texas Tech University, Lubbock

Wagner, Joseph B. — Kent State University, Ohio
Wahrenholz, Hanna Ruth — Deutsche Shakespeare-Gesellschaft West
Wainscott, Ann E. — Frankfort, Ky.
Walch, Gunther — Humboldt University, Berlin
Waller, Gary F. — Wilfred Laurier University
Wanamaker, S. — World Centre for Shakespeare Studies, London

Warren, Michael J. — University of California, Santa Cruz
Warren, Roger — University of Leicester
Wasson, John — Washington State University, Pullman
Watanabe, Yoshiyuki — Hosei University
Weber, Robert W. — University of Hanover
Weigt, Hans-Georg — University of Duisburg
Weil, Herbert S., Jr. — University of Manitoba
Weil, Judith — University of Manitoba
Weimann, Robert — Akademie der Wissenschaften, Berlin

WEINIG, Edelbert	Alexander-von-Humboldt-Gymnasium, Schweinfürt
WELCH, Margaret M.	Folger Shakespeare Library
WELLS, Stanley	Oxford University Press
WERSTINE, Paul	King's College, University of Western Ontario
WESTLAKE, John H. J.	Brooklyn Technical College, Birmingham
WHEELER, Richard	University of Illinois, Urbana
WHITE, Dorothy	Longview, Tex.
WHITE, M. Deane	LeTourneau College, Longview, Tex.
WICKHAM, Glynne	University of Bristol
WIENER, Norman	Unified School District, Downey, Calif.
WILDERS, John	Worcester College, Oxford
WILDS, Lilian	California State University, Pomona
WILLBERN, David	State University of New York, Buffalo
WILLIAMS, Gary Jay	Catholic University of America, Washington, D.C.
WILLIAMS, Josephine S.	Washington, D.C.
WILLIAMS, Simon	Cornell University, Ithaca, N.Y.
WILLIAMS, Susan M.	McGill University
WILLIAMSON, Jane	University of Missouri, St. Louis
WILLIAMSON, Marilyn L.	Wayne State University, Detroit, Mich.
WILLSON, Barbara	Kansas City, Mo.
WILLSON, Robert F., Jr.	University of Missouri, Kansas City
WILSON, Richard	Open University
WILSONIA, Emma D. Cherry	University of North Carolina, Asheville
WINSTON, Alecia R.	Denton, Texas
WINSTON, Florence	Texas Woman's University, Denton
WINTON, Calhoun	University of Maryland, College Park
WOLFENSPERGER, Peter	University of Zurich
WOLFF, I. R.	London
WOOTTON, Suzanne D.	Lincoln College, Oxford
YAGHTIAN, Lucretia B.	Loretto Heights College, Denver, Col.
YAJIMA, Naoko	Tokyo Metropolitan University
YAMADA, Reiko	Shakespeare Society of Japan
YAMANAKA, Takeshi	Saga University, Japan
YI, Duck-Soo	Yeungnam University, Korea
YOCH, James J., Jr.	University of Oklahoma, Norman
YOH, Suk-Kee	Korea University, Seoul
YOUNG, Alan R.	Acadia University, Nova Scotia
ZIEGLER, Georgianna	Wofford College, Spartanburg, S.C.
ZITNER, Sheldon P.	University of Toronto